REPRESENTING AFRICAN AMERICANS in TRANSATLANTIC ABOLITIONISM and BLACKFACE MINSTRELSY

REPRESENTING AFRICAN AMERICANS in TRANSATLANTIC ABOLITIONISM and BLACKFACE MINSTRELSY

Robert Nowatzki

LOUISIANA STATE UNIVERSITY PRESS)((BATON ROUGE

Published by Louisiana State University Press
Manufactured in the United States of America
FIRST PRINTING

DESIGNER: *Amanda McDonald Scallan*
TYPEFACE: *Whitman*
PRINTER AND BINDER: *Thomson-Shore, Inc.*

Library of Congress Cataloging-in-Publication Data
Nowatzki, Robert, 1965–
  Representing African Americans in transatlantic abolitionism and blackface minstrelsy / Robert Nowatzki.
      p. cm.
  Includes bibliographical references and index.
  ISBN 978-0-8071-3640-9 (cloth : alk. paper) 1. Antislav-
ery movements—United States—History—19th century.
2. Antislavery movements—Great Britain—History—
19th century. 3. Minstrel shows—Social aspects—United
States—History—19th century. 4. Minstrel shows—Social
aspects—Great Britain—History—19th century. 5. African
Americans in popular culture—United States—History—
19th century. 6. African Americans in popular culture—
Great Britain—History—19th century. I. Title.
  E449.N92 2010
  305.896'073—dc22

                                    2009049517

Portions of chapter 4 appeared previously, in slightly different form, in "'Our Only Truly National Poets': Blackface
Minstrelsy and Cultural Nationalism," *ATQ* 20.1 (March
2006). Reprinted by permission of The University of Rhode
Island.

Chapter 5 makes use of material previously pulished as
"Blurring the Color Line: Black Freedom, Passing, Abolitionism, and Irish Ethnicity in Frank J. Webb's *The Garies
and their Friends*," *Studies in American Fiction* 33.1 (Spring
2005). Used by permission.

To the memory of my father, Joseph Nowatzki

CONTENTS

Acknowledgments   ix

Abbreviations   xi

Introduction   1

1. Strange Bedfellows: Blackface Minstrelsy and Abolitionism in America   10

2. Abolitionism, Nationalism, Blackface Minstrelsy, and Racial Attitudes in Victorian Britain   42

3. Race, Abolitionism, and Blackface Imagery in Victorian Literature   80

4. "Our Only Truly National Poets": Blackface Minstrelsy, Slave Narratives, Cultural Nationalism, and the American Renaissance   100

5. Blackface Tropes in Nineteenth-Century American Literature   140

Afterword   166

Notes   169

Bibliography   187

Index   207

ACKNOWLEDGMENTS

Writing a book can often seem to be a solitary activity, but in looking back over the past few years, I realize how collaborative such a task really is. I wish to thank Ball State University, my academic home for the past ten years, for supporting me financially with a one-semester paid leave as well as a number of internal grants that enabled me to travel and conduct archival research at a number of libraries in the United States and at the University of Oxford. Several archival librarians and curators merit special mention for their assistance: Julie Anne Lambert of the John Johnson Collection of Printed Ephemera at the Bodleian Library, University of Oxford; Annette Fern of the Harvard Theatre Collection; R. Eugene Zepp of the Rare Books and Manuscripts Division of the Boston Public Library; John Atteberry of the Burns Library at Boston College; and John Straw of the Bracken Library Archives and Special Collections of Ball State University. I would also like to thank Alisa Plant, acquisitions editor at Louisiana State University Press, for her invaluable assistance in answering my questions and working with me in revising my manuscript, as well as the members of the editorial and production staff who helped to produce this book.

On a more personal note, I want to express my gratitude toward several of my colleagues and friends in Ball State's English Department for reading and critiquing drafts of parts of this book; for offering emotional support, collegiality, and friendship; and for patiently listening to me talk at length about the ideological complexities of blackface minstrelsy: Adam Beach, Patrick Collier, Joyce Huff, Kecia McBride, and Deborah Mix. I am also indebted to my longtime friend and fellow Americanist Pat Okker of the University of Missouri for reading my manuscript and giving excellent advice for improving its organization. Both she and my Ball State colleague Bob Habich have kindly and selflessly helped me many times in applying for funding to support my research on this book. Another Ball State colleague, Frank Felsenstein, repeatedly encouraged me by expressing interest in my work, and his suggestion that I read the English magazine *Punch* helped me strengthen my analysis of British attitudes toward minstrelsy, slavery, abolitionism, and African Americans. My research assistant Chris Manus worked tirelessly by my side as we pored over anti-slavery pamphlets in the archives of Ball State University's Bracken Library, and my research assistant Lydia Storie far exceeded her duty in helping me sift through issues of *Punch* and in finding relevant material in *Dwight's Journal of Music* and nineteenth-century anti-slavery literature. I am also grateful to Alasdair Pettinger for offering helpful advice on seeking an academic publisher for this book.

Others who helped me in less direct but still important ways include my friends Elizabeth Price and Gerald Weber, with whom my wife and I bought a cabin in northern Wisconsin that provided a quiet and beautiful space to write for three summers. In addition, many colleagues and friends at Ball State offered encouragement while I was working on this book for the past decade: Tim Berg, Jill Christman, Cindy Collier, Dave Concepción, Michael Doyle, Carolyn MacKay, Jackie Grutsch McKinney, Todd McKinney, Mark Neely, Klaus Neumann, and Frank Trechsel.

Most of all, I wish to thank Lauren Onkey, my wife, colleague, and friend, who carefully read my manuscript and offered thoughtful suggestions about it, supported my efforts over the past decade, and never stopped believing in my ability to finish this book and see it into print.

ABBREVIATIONS for ARCHIVAL COLLECTIONS

BPL   Rare Books and Manuscripts Division, Boston Public Library

HTC   Harvard Theatre Collection

JJC   John Johnson Collection of Printed Ephemera, Bodleian Library, University of Oxford

RH   Bodleian Library of Commonwealth and African Studies at Rhodes House, University of Oxford

SSMC   Starr Sheet Music Collection, Lilly Library, Indiana University

REPRESENTING

AFRICAN

AMERICANS in

TRANSATLANTIC

ABOLITIONISM

and BLACKFACE

MINSTRELSY

Introduction

When Thomas Dartmouth Rice performed his song and dance "Jim Crow" at New York City's Bowery Theatre in late 1832 and launched a nationwide obsession with burnt-cork entertainment, the American antislavery movement was just getting underway. William Lloyd Garrison had founded *The Liberator* at the beginning of the previous year, and the American Anti-Slavery Society would form during the following year. By then, the second wave of the British antislavery movement had already been active for nearly a decade. As a result of its efforts, Britain abolished chattel slavery in its West Indian colonies in 1834 and ended the subsequent apprenticeship system there four years later. In the meantime, Rice took his Jim Crow act across the Atlantic to London in 1836, an event that laid the foundation for a minstrelsy craze there. Rice returned to the Bowery in 1854 as Uncle Tom in H. E. Stevens's stage adaptation of Harriet Beecher Stowe's abolitionist juggernaut *Uncle Tom's Cabin* (Lott 214). His performance of Jim Crow in New York City and London and his later role as Uncle Tom symbolize two major concerns of this book: the transatlantic nature of blackface minstrelsy and abolitionism and the overlap between them, particularly in minstrelsy's early years. The transatlantic antislavery movement scored two major victories during the mid-nineteenth century—the Emancipation Act in 1833 and the Thirteenth Amendment to the U.S. Constitution in 1865. Not coincidentally, the three decades bracketed by these events witnessed the triumph of minstrelsy on American and British stages. The concurrent rise of abolitionism and minstrelsy produced innumerable representations of black people, and these images proved to be serviceable in discussing other issues, such as nationalism, labor, and class.[1] This book examines how abolitionism and blackface minstrelsy emerged together in both nations and analyzes their parallels, alliances, differences, conflicts, and influences on each other in their representations of enslaved and free black people. It also investigates how white Americans and Britons used these depictions of blacks in discussing the nature of work and socioeconomic class and in defining themselves and each other in national terms. Yet these images also formed part of a transatlantic culture that transcended American and British nationalist discourses. Because abolitionism and minstrelsy were transatlantic movements, this study examines how both movements and their depictions of black people were shaped by their transatlantic crossings and by Anglo-American relations.

The fact that Rice played both Uncle Tom and Jim Crow might surprise anyone who sees minstrelsy and abolitionism simply as opponents in a cultural tug-of-war over representations of African Americans and slavery. Indeed, minstrelsy and abolitionism were often at loggerheads over these issues. In many cases, however, they borrowed characters, images, songs, rhetoric, conventions, and sentiments from each other. This book charts not only the conflicts between abolitionism and minstrelsy from the 1830s to the abolition of slavery in the United States, but also the ideological overlap symbolized by Rice's performances of Jim Crow and Uncle Tom. In this book I argue that the tensions, parallels, and borrowings between minstrelsy and abolitionism in their depictions of African Americans and slavery were significantly shaped by their transatlantic crossings and by ideologies of class, race, and nation in the United States and the United Kingdom during the mid-nineteenth century. I support this argument by analyzing these representations in a wide range of literary and non-literary texts, including fiction, poetry, slave narratives, travelogues, minstrel song lyrics and stump speeches, and antislavery pamphlets and speeches. My analyses of these texts recognize the ideological shifts during this period, both within and beyond minstrelsy and abolitionism, such as the intensification of racism in Britain during the 1850s and 1860s and minstrelsy's shift from vulgar, working-class rebellion and fun to respectable sentimentality to outright racist ridicule and the nostalgic glorification of plantation life. By examining how abolitionists and minstrel performers in both nations represented black people and slavery in these varied texts, I hope to provide a more complete understanding of the relationship between abolitionism and minstrelsy as transatlantic phenomena than can be found in previous scholarship, which usually focuses mostly or exclusively on one phenomenon or on one nation.

While several recent studies of minstrelsy have emphasized the subversive nature of its early phase, its reputation in the popular imagination, at least in the United States, is often based on the proslavery sentiments and unambiguous racism of later minstrelsy. If one neglects the complexity and dynamic nature of minstrelsy, its conflicts with abolitionism are self-evident. Although this oversimplified notion of antagonism rests upon an incomplete understanding of both minstrelsy and the racial attitudes of many white abolitionists, it is undeniable that minstrelsy and abolitionism often battled each other for the hearts and minds of white Americans and Britons regarding their attitudes toward black people and slavery. For instance, abolitionists rarely ridiculed African Americans (though their descriptions of them were often condescending and unconsciously racist), and minstrel shows never seriously portrayed an intelligent or courageous black person. Additionally, as Robert Toll points out, one of the favorite targets of minstrel humor was abolitionism (113), even though early minstrelsy often depicted slavery negatively or elicited sympathy toward or identification with slaves. As minstrelsy later became more consistently proslavery and racist, it both reflected and encouraged such attitudes in its audience and drifted further away from abolitionism. It is not difficult to understand why an entertainment genre that often denigrated African Americans and portrayed them as happy slaves would run afoul of a reform movement that worked to emancipate them.

While these ideological clashes are important, an exclusive focus on the mutual hostility between minstrelsy and abolitionism does not explain why they emerged in the United States and Britain at the same time. Therefore it is crucial that we examine the common ground they shared, such as their fascination with black people and especially black bodies. Such an examination reveals that the racial attitudes of many white abolitionists and minstrelsy's depictions of black people often paralleled and informed each other. Our understanding of both phenomena also benefits from recognizing how they borrowed rhetoric, sentiments, and imagery from each other. For instance, while abolitionism was not as mainstream in the United States as in the United Kingdom and faced virulent opposition in northern cities like New York and Philadelphia as well as in the South, it enhanced its appeal by taking a cue from the entertainment world and putting black people on stage to lecture, sing, recount their nightmarish experiences under slavery, or display their mutilated bodies for white audiences. Abolitionism's attempt to make itself more entertaining also made it more visible, which in turn made it an available target for minstrel satire. This visibility also made it easier for minstrelsy to tap into antislavery feeling by appropriating abolitionism's melodramatic depiction of the separation of slave families and other sorrows caused by slavery. Abolitionism's complex relationship with minstrelsy reminds us that both were multivocal rather than monolithic, and that they both included a range of attitudes and tropes. White abolitionists were not united in their racial thinking. For example, the New York abolitionist Gerrit Smith gave land to Frederick Douglass and contributed generously to Douglass's newspaper *The North Star,* much to the chagrin of Garrison, who resented his former protégé's increasingly independent spirit (McFeely 151). The variety of racial thinking among white abolitionists in the United States and the United Kingdom may be linked to other ideological differences, such as the conflicts among Garrisonians of both countries, the more political American and Foreign Anti-Slavery Society, and the increasingly anti-Garrisonian British and Foreign Anti-Slavery Society. Given the rifts that formed between these groups, both within each nation and between nations, it is little surprise that they did not all share the same racial attitudes. Likewise, not all minstrelsy was equally racist or subversive, particularly in its first three decades (roughly, from the early 1830s until the mid-1860s), the period that I study here. The representations of black people and slavery in minstrel songs like "Dearest Lilla," "Blue-Tail'd Fly," "Lubly Fan," and "Old Folks at Home" were not interchangeable; white minstrels' appropriation of black dance styles was not as derogatory as their travesty of black dialect; and the working-class consciousness that inflected early minstrelsy faded out in its later years, when it catered more to a middle-class audience. This diversity of attitudes and representations within minstrelsy and abolitionism made it possible that, given a finite ideological space, these two rather different phenomena would share some common ground.

Fortunately, some of the recent scholarship on minstrelsy and abolitionism has shown that despite their apparently divergent cultural forces, they were not always dichotomous but were complementary and similar in some ways. As Sam Dennison has noticed, "Even the most ardent abolitionists were influenced to some degree by the image of blacks exhibited on the minstrel stage" (155). Several scholars have complicated the popular notion of minstrelsy as irredeemably racist by emphasizing its racial ambivalence, its nods to antislavery sentimentalism, and its carnivalesque attacks on the bourgeoisie during its early period.[2] These studies not only make it more difficult to dismiss minstrelsy as consistently racist, but also reveal how it dovetailed with abolitionism. Despite the value of this scholarship, however, its focus on early minstrelsy often has resulted in a tendency to downplay the racist elements of minstrelsy's depictions of African Americans during its peak of popularity around midcentury. I try to avoid this tendency by focusing on the 1850s and 1860s, when minstrelsy became more aggressively proslavery and derogatory toward black people, as well as the 1830s and 1840s, when minstrelsy was more ambiguous and edgy.[3] In addition, I sometimes examine how minstrel tropes and images were used in critiques of philanthropy, as in Charles Dickens's novel *Bleak House* and Thomas Carlyle's essay "Occasional Discourse on the Nigger Question." Although the anti-abolitionism and racism of later minstrelsy are more obvious today than the genre's earlier antislavery impulses, they are just as important and worthy of analysis.

Despite the recent scholarly insights into these two subjects, most studies focus primarily on one or the other of them. So far the only book-length analysis of the common ground between minstrelsy and abolitionism in the United Kingdom and the United States is Sarah Meer's recent *Uncle Tom Mania: Slavery, Minstrelsy and Transatlantic Culture in the 1850s.* Meer offers an excellent analysis of the connections between blackface minstrelsy and the various cultural permutations of Stowe's novel in both nations; however, I attempt to examine minstrelsy's connections to abolitionism more broadly than Meer, who focuses more on cultural responses to Stowe's work than on abolitionism as a whole. This book also covers a longer period, so that readers can better understand how abolitionism and minstrelsy changed over time. More specifically, this book addresses several questions about the relations between minstrelsy and abolitionism in the United States and the United Kingdom. For instance, what did minstrelsy mean in Britain, a nation with a history of blackface entertainment, a strong abolitionist movement, and a tiny black population? Why did minstrelsy, an imported entertainment form that celebrated American nationalism, flourish in a nation that American minstrel performers often ridiculed? Why did many British people turn away from abolitionism after midcentury, and what did that shift have to do with minstrelsy's popularity there? How were minstrelsy and slave narratives—the signature literary genre of American abolitionism—linked to the cultural nationalism of the American Renaissance? How did white Americans and Britons use the representations of black people in minstrelsy and abolitionism to bolster their national identities?

In attempting to answer these and other questions, I use a transatlantic perspective that reveals how the conflicts and affinities between the two nations were often played out on the minstrel stage and in the antislavery lecture hall. This transatlantic approach has largely been informed by Paul Gilroy's theory of the Black Atlantic. In *The Black Atlantic: Modernity and Double Consciousness*, Gilroy points to the repeated crossings of the Atlantic Ocean (both forced and voluntary) by black people over the past five centuries and urges us to replace our nationally oriented paradigm of studying modern black culture and identities with a framework that considers the Atlantic and its surrounding continents as a single geographical and cultural unit. Gilroy also argues that black people living in the Atlantic World shared a hybrid culture that resists national categories. Though I am indebted to Gilroy's transnation focus on the Atlantic World, my canvas is smaller than his, in that I do not include Africa and the Caribbean. The focus of this book also differs from *The Black Atlantic* in that Gilroy is concerned with the hybrid identity and consciousness of persons of African descent in the Atlantic World, whereas I concentrate on the representations of black people in abolitionism and minstrelsy as they floated back and forth between both nations. This transatlantic traffic of racial representations formed an iconic and ideological network that I call the Blackface Atlantic. The meanings of the Blackface Atlantic were influenced by the travels of abolitionists and minstrel performers between the United States and the United Kingdom and were linked to British and American nationalisms, to the cultural relations between the two nations, and to ideologies of class in both nations. Although this term would seem to pertain more to minstrelsy than abolitionism, I also use it to include the transatlantic exchange of abolitionist representations of black people, which were often in conversation or debate with blackface minstrelsy.

Gilroy's focus on the Atlantic World is part of a larger scholarly trend in transatlantic studies that has influenced my thinking about minstrelsy and abolitionism. My understanding of minstrelsy's transatlantic nature grows out of the work of scholars such as John Blair, J. S. Bratton, Jennifer DeVere Brody,

W. T. Lhamon, and George Rehin. In particular, I find Lhamon's analysis of blackface entertainment as Atlantic popular culture to be useful in revealing how the relationship between the United States and the United Kingdom forged the meanings of minstrelsy, though it is important to notice the differences between the two nations in how they received and gave meaning to minstrelsy, as Blair, Rehin, and Bratton have shown. Like minstrelsy, abolitionism was a transatlantic phenomenon, and my study of this international movement builds upon the work of R. J. M. Blackett and Audrey Fisch, as well as Clare Taylor's collection of correspondence between abolitionists of the two nations.[4] This book attempts to extend such scholarship by studying Anglo-American abolitionism alongside minstrelsy in order to understand why and how they coexisted in both nations and how they shaped each other. For example, I analyze the British precursors of American blackface minstrelsy, American minstrelsy's hostility toward British abolitionism, and British receptions of American minstrelsy and African-American abolitionists. Because these two phenomena were so closely interrelated and played such important roles in Anglophone Atlantic culture, we can understand their representations of African Americans only by jointly examining them on both sides of the Atlantic.

An analysis of the transatlantic phenomena of minstrelsy and abolitionism necessitates an examination of their intersections with British and American nationalisms and with ideologies of class and gender. As Lhamon, Dale Cockrell, Eric Lott, David Roediger, and Robert Toll have demonstrated, early blackface performances in the United States and United Kingdom were largely a working-class and male affair, both in content and audience. These performances celebrated lower-class masculinity through their underdog, trickster-figure endmen and mocked the bourgeois elitism embodied in their genteel straight-man interlocutors. Early minstrelsy's often sympathetic representations of slaves also enabled comparisons between black chattel slaves on stage and white wage slaves in the audience. In this respect, minstrelsy may have done more to stir up antislavery sentiment among the working classes during this period than abolitionism did. Abolitionism was largely middle class in leadership, membership, and orientation, especially in the United States, and many workers (even those with antislavery sympathies) looked askance at the movement. They often argued that as wage laborers, they were as oppressed as—or more oppressed than—chattel slaves, and they accused abolitionists of condoning such exploitation. Abolitionists were compelled to counter these arguments by asserting that slavery was more brutally dehumanizing than industrial capitalism, but in doing so they ran the risk of understating the oppression of poor wage laborers and thereby alienating potential working-class supporters. American minstrelsy was also deeply nationalist and anti-British, and this Anglophobia was fueled by the nationalist elements of British abolitionism, which portrayed its own nation as morally superior to the United States regarding slavery. Therefore, American minstrel audiences often laughed at Britain, abolitionism, and the bourgeoisie at the same time. For proletarian American audiences, embracing the nationalist theatrical genre of minstrelsy and spurning British abolitionism allowed them to declare both their cultural independence from Britain and their rejection of abolitionism's bourgeois and Anglophilic elements, even if they were not proslavery. Indeed, it would not be too much of a stretch to imagine the debates over slavery between bourgeois abolitionism and proletarian early minstrelsy as an interlocutor-endman dialogue.

In addition to the working-class and frontier masculinity that figured into early minstrelsy, gender shaped minstrelsy —and abolitionism—in several important ways. Although minstrelsy in both nations began to appeal to a mixed-gender audience by the late 1840s, it was frequently misogynist in its stump speeches, jokes, and song lyrics. Abolitionism, in contrast, was more welcoming toward women, not only as members but even as leaders. Some women were attracted to the movement because they saw parallels between patriarchy and slavery, and in fact abolitionism was in some ways the birthplace of the women's movement, offering women a rare chance to influence the public sphere by exhibiting the moral virtue ascribed to them by the Cult of True Womanhood. Abolitionism's strong female element and its ties with the women's movement, along with its strong support in Britain, made it an irresistible target of satire in American minstrelsy.

The anti-abolitionist elements of American minstrelsy were linked not only to class and gender ideologies, but also to nationalism, which figures into the Blackface Atlantic in numerous ways. Until the late 1840s, minstrelsy was frequently described in the United States and United Kingdom as distinctly American, and many American minstrel performers and songwriters ridiculed the British. Despite this anti-British nationalism, minstrelsy became nearly as popular in the United Kingdom as in the United States. This fact raises two questions: How much of minstrelsy was American and how much of it had roots in earlier English blackface traditions? And how did the meanings of minstrelsy in Britain and the United States compare to each other? In abolitionist circles, nationalism also factored into comparisons between the two nations regarding slavery and racism. British abolitionists often cited the 1833 Emancipation Act as evidence of their nation's ethical superiority over the United States and pointed to southern slavery as exposing the hollowness of America's egalitarian tradition. In this light, anti-British blackface patriotism in the United States might be seen as a reaction against British abolitionist nationalism. Yet some critiques of British abolitionism's moral smugness came from abolitionists themselves, on both sides of the Atlantic. These critiques revealed how British racism, the exploitation of British industrial workers, the imperialist and economic motives of British abolitionism, and Britain's neutrality during the American Civil War partly deflated the notion of British moral superiority over its slaveholding former colony. Nationalism also emerged in American abolitionism—though to a lesser degree than in Britain—in discussions of slave narratives, which Theodore Parker and Ephraim Peabody claimed were the first distinctly American literary genre. Nevertheless, these nationalisms—both in American minstrelsy and British abolitionism—were undermined by the fact that each transatlantic movement created a common culture that helped to unify the two nations. Central to this Anglophone transatlantic culture were the racial ideologies that informed minstrelsy and abolitionism and were symbolized by characters such as Jim Crow and Uncle Tom. In their frequent figurative crossings of the Blackface Atlantic, these two characters—as well as the racial discourses they represented—influenced each other deeply.

1

Strange Bedfellows
Blackface Minstrelsy and Abolitionism in America

Halfway through the fifth act of George Aiken and George Howard's 1852 stage version of *Uncle Tom's Cabin*, Uncle Tom (played in blackface by G. C. Germon, formerly of the Ethiopian Serenaders, a popular minstrel troupe) sings Stephen Foster's sentimental minstrel classic "Old Folks at Home" after being bought by Simon Legree (Riis 48). Tom's nostalgia for his life on the Shelby and St. Clare plantations is not far from his counterpart's love of his indulgent masters in Stowe's novel. Earlier in the play, Topsy breaks into a song titled "Oh! I'se So Wicked!" (Riis xv, 64–67) which uses dialect and employs the minstrel stereotype of the mischievous black child in much the same way that Stowe's characterization of Topsy did. These moments encapsulate the propinquity between antislavery sentiment and minstrelsy in mid-nineteenth century America. The former scene encouraged white viewers to pity poor, humble Tom rather than recognize him as an equal. In this sense, the characterization of Tom in the play, and to some extent in Stowe's novel, typifies the condescension that many white American abolitionists expressed toward African American slaves—an attitude shaped by the romantic racialism that permeated northern white culture. The racism of the latter scene featuring Topsy's song was not as typical of white American abolitionism as was patronizing pity, but the inclusion of this scene in this play reveals how white antislavery representations of African Americans were informed by some of the same racial ideologies that were played out on the minstrel stage.

Aside from exhibiting many of the racial attitudes that informed minstrelsy, white abolitionist representations of African Americans shared other concerns with blackface entertainment. First, minstrel shows often borrowed the antislavery tropes of the separated slave family and the overworked slave, while white abolitionists often subscribed to the romantic racialism that permeated minstrelsy, such as the belief in innate black musicality.[1] Second, white abolitionists, like minstrel performers and audiences, often showed a nearly pornographic fascination with black bodies. Third, white abolitionists and minstrel performers claimed or implied that their representations of African Americans were genuine, and in both cases this authenticity was constructed through conventionalized performative rituals. This chapter traces these links between abolitionism and minstrelsy in mid-nineteenth-century America.[2] It begins by examining how the racial attitudes of white abolitionists interacted with those attitudes that underlay minstrelsy, and then turns to an analysis of how abolitionism and minstrelsy addressed the issues of black physicality and sexuality, miscegenation, performativity, and authenticity in ways that were often startlingly similar.

Abolitionist Condescension and Zip Coon

White American attitudes toward African Americans during the mid-nineteenth century were mostly limited to romantic racialism, condescension, pity, ambivalence, and resentment against black assertions of equality or expressions of pride. Such sentiments often structured minstrel shows and songs, but they also surfaced to some extent in the abolitionist movement. These attitudes frequently influenced how white abolitionists interacted with ex-slaves and African American abolitionists. Though Frederick Douglass's white mentor Gerrit Smith apparently treated Douglass on equal terms (McFeely 151), this behavior was not typical of all white American abolitionists. Douglass complains in *My Bondage and My Freedom* that "when I first went among the abolitionists of New England, . . . I found this prejudice very strong and very annoying. The abolitionists themselves were not entirely free from it" (393). Although white abolitionists were ultimately successful in eliminating slavery in the United States, most of them failed to recognize how deeply their racial attitudes were shaped by ideologies of black inferiority.

White abolitionists may have seen themselves as more enlightened than blackface performers in their hatred of slavery, but both groups shared condescending attitudes toward African Americans, whom they often regarded as docile, passive objects of pity or as wards to be protected by paternalistic white benefactors. In *Uncle Tom's Cabin*, Stowe typifies this sentiment among abolitionists by describing "the African" as "naturally patient, timid and unenterprising" (83). Likewise, in his Preface to Douglass's 1845 narrative, Garrison's emphasis on Douglass's humility at his first antislavery meeting encouraged a paternalistic pity from white readers: "He came forward to the platform with a hesitancy and embarrassment. . . . After apologizing for his ignorance, and reminding his audience that slavery was a poor school for the human intellect and heart, he proceeded to narrate some of the facts in his own history as a slave" (4). This attitude was etched onto the famous Wedgwood medallion featuring the kneeling, chained slave with the caption "Am I Not a Man and a Brother?" which was popular in both the United States and the United Kingdom.[3] On the one hand, this image encourages whites to recognize black humanity, because the implied answer to the slave's appeal is obviously affirmative. On the other hand, the slave does not assert his manhood and brotherhood with whites, and his posture emphasizes his subservience and passivity. Indeed, abolitionism allowed whites to prove their moral virtue through acts of noblesse oblige toward people whom they saw as unjustly oppressed yet inferior. Although northern whites were not united about whether African Americans should be viewed with pity or derision, there was considerably more agreement that black people were to be looked down upon, and white abolitionists often shared this perspective.

Early minstrelsy often paralleled white abolitionist paternalism by expressing pity toward slaves, as can be seen in the lyrics of songs like "Old Uncle Ned" and "Old Folks at Home." Such condescension often echoed antislavery sentiment, despite minstrelsy's antagonism toward the abolitionist movement. Toll mentions minstrelsy's hostility toward slavery during the Civil War (118) and points out that "until the mid-1850's, minstrels condemned the destruction of black families, the theft of black women by white men, the long hours blacks had to work without pay, and the brutal and senseless beatings they had to endure" (118–19). Alexander Saxton seconds this argument regarding early minstrelsy's antislavery impulses:

> There appeared a scattering of anti-slavery expressions that entered the genre in two different ways. First, the early borrowings of African American music and dance carried anti-slavery connotations that sometimes persisted subliminally in traditional verses. . . . Subversive

sentiments might be negated in chorus or verses, perhaps added later. . . . A second and later means of entry for anti-slavery content was through the essentially white identity of romantic and nostalgic songs, European in tradition and style, which quickly became a staple of minstrel repertory. Performed in blackface, yet dealing seriously with themes of parted lovers, lost children and so forth, these songs both invited identification with the situation of the slave and suggested that slavery might have been the cause of separation or loss. (176–77)

As Sarah Meer notes, by the 1850s minstrelsy had exchanged its rowdy image for a more sentimental one (14), and this sentimentality had a wider appeal for middle-class and mixed-gender audiences than its earlier proletarian roughness. The combination of blackface and sentimentalism during this decade enabled minstrelsy to co-opt abolitionist sentimentality without urging audiences to agitate against slavery.

As Saxton points out, one sentimental image that minstrelsy borrowed from abolitionism was the separation of slave couples and families by their masters. A typical abolitionist depiction of severed slave families is the slave auction scene in *Uncle Tom's Cabin*, in which Susan is separated from her daughter Emmeline:

Down goes the hammer again,—Susan is sold! She goes down from the block, stops, looks wistfully back,—her daughter stretches her hands toward her. She looks with agony in the face of the man who has bought her . . . . the young girl mounted the block, and looked around her with a frightened and timid glance.

The blood flushes painfully in her otherwise colorless cheek, her eye has a feverish fire, and her mother groans to see that she looks more beautiful than she ever saw her before. (290)

Such emotionally charged descriptions encouraged white readers to feel not only sorrow for divided slave families, but also outrage that would lead to abolitionist action.

Minstrelsy recognized the emotional power of such scenes and tried to disarticulate such sentiment from the abolitionist agenda while still appealing to its audience's sentimentality and antislavery attitudes. One example of this strategy is "Miss Lucy Neale, or the Yellow Gal" (1844), one of the most popular minstrel songs of the 1840s. In one version by the Ethiopian Serenaders, the singer laments:

> My Massa he did sell me,
> Because he thought I'd steal,
> Which caused a separation
> Of myself and Lucy Neale. (SSMC)

Another version by the Virginia Serenaders paints slavery in even harsher tones by replacing the heartless "Massa" with a crueler slave trader:

> Oh, dars de wite man comin, To tear you from my side;
> Stan back you wite slave dealer, She is my betrothed bride.
> De poor nigger's fate is hard; De wite man's heart is stone.
> Dey part poor nigga from his wife, An brake dare happy home.
> (qtd. in Toll 80)

The same trope appears in Peter Swift's 1850 song "Juney at the Gate" and in the third verse of T. B. Prendergast's 1850 song "The Negro's Departure, or Dinah Broom": "But massa he did sell me it almost broke my heart, / And when I left my Dinah dear in tears we both did part; . . . " (SSMC). These lyrics could appeal to antislavery listeners, who were familiar with the image of divided slave families. Yet unlike abolitionist rhetoric, this song does not follow the description of the separated slave couple with an attack on slavery or an explicit or implicit call for abolition. The same is true of William Clifton's 1849 song "Dearest Lilla," which typifies many minstrel songs in its description of a slave couple being broken up when a master moves away:

> Come come my dearest Lila [sic],
> I'm going far away;
> My massa he now take me,
> To California;

I hab but dese few moments,
To bid a last farewell;
De grief dat dis poor darkie feel,
Dis heart alone can tell. (SSMC)

In this song the antislavery trope of the divided slave couple is disconnected
from abolitionist activism. Instead, the song employs sentimentality and Gold
Rush fever by having the brokenhearted slave singer transported to California,
even though slavery did not exist there and slaves were not welcome there as
prospectors. In general, minstrel songs using this antislavery trope did not
seriously threaten the moral basis of slavery or argue for abolition; rather,
they demonstrate how minstrelsy shared tropes and rhetoric with abolitionism
without committing itself to the movement.

While these songs used some of the sentimental language and imagery
of abolitionism, other songs focused on another common antislavery theme:
forced and unpaid labor. This issue crops up in the first verse and chorus of the
Christy's Minstrels' 1852 song "Hush-a-Bye Baby":

When but a little fellow, I'd nothing much to do
But run about of errands and black young massa's shoe,
The case is very diff'rent now, I have to hoe and rake,
With scarcely time of mornings for to eat my cornmeal cake.
CHORUS: But I dig dig dig, dig dig a dig,
Dig all the live long day,
The worst of all trouble to a darkey is to dig,
Tho' he aint troubled much with the pay. (SSMC)[4]

The proslavery image of childlike slaves who laze about on the plantation is
linked to the singer's childhood in this song, while his adult life is more typical
of antislavery depictions of slave life. Although this song is not representative of minstrelsy's depiction of slavery, it is one of many minstrel songs that
overlap with abolitionism in portraying the endless drudgery of bondage.

Sentimental representations of black slaves in minstrelsy and abolitionism
allowed white Americans to look down on these victims with pity, but success-

ful and assertive African Americans were often not shown respect by white abolitionists and were invariably ridiculed on the minstrel stage. The ideology of white superiority that governed blackface representations also informed much of the hostility that many white abolitionists expressed toward their black colleagues who tried to assume leadership in the movement rather than play the role of the passive slave waiting to be liberated. While white abolitionists wanted to emancipate African American slaves, they often wanted black abolitionists to take subordinate roles in the movement. McFeely writes that "Douglass, [Charles Lenox] Remond, and the other black antislavery speakers were always treated as visiting artists in a production of which the white Bostonians never dreamed of losing the direction" (108). Garrison's resentment toward Douglass for breaking away from his organization and philosophy in the late 1840s is well documented,[5] and Maria Weston Chapman felt that Douglass rose above his proper place in founding his own newspaper (McFeely 147). McFeely adds that for Chapman, "It was bad enough when white Abby Kelley spoke her exceedingly active mind; for black men [Douglass and Remond] to challenge their betters in public simply would not do" (108). Another white abolitionist warned Chapman of the dangers of inflating the egos of black speakers: "These men talented and glorious specimens of 'fallen' humanity as they are, still are but unregenerate men. . . . The circumstances which continually surround our speakers are calculated to foster self-esteem— to get pride where humility is needed."[6] Other white American abolitionists, such as Edmund Quincy and Samuel J. May, Jr., expressed their displeasure with independent-minded black abolitionists in their correspondence.[7] Such antagonism was not necessarily evidence of racism, and black abolitionists were not always beyond reproach. Nevertheless, much of the resentment that white abolitionists expressed toward their strong-willed black colleagues was based on the premise that the latter should be foot soldiers rather than generals in the war against slavery.

While minstrelsy obviously did not endorse organized philanthropic efforts to help African Americans, the white resentment toward black freedom and prosperity that fueled minstrelsy's mockery of black northern "dandies" somewhat resembled white abolitionists' hostility toward their assertive black colleagues. Such ridicule is apparent in visual representations of these characters and in the songs bearing their names. The 1834 song "Zip Coon," for example, contains the sarcastic line "Old Zip Coon is a very larned scholar" and describes Zip's ludicrous presidential fantasy: "If I was de President of dese United States, / I'd suck lasses candy and swing upon de gates, / An dose I didn't like I'd block em off de dockett" (qtd. in Dennison 61). Though white abolitionists did not deride black social ambitions in the way "Zip Coon" did, many of them did not recognize the intellectual potential and achievements of black people and probably viewed the prospect of an African American in the White House as unthinkable. Other minstrel songs belittling proud, free black people include: "Dandy Jim from Caroline" (1844), which features a black man overly pleased with his own good looks; "Jim Brown" (1835), which mocks a black bandleader in military uniform; and "The Colored Fancy Ball" (1848), which ridicules free blacks for trying to imitate upper-class white people. Likewise, the black dandy in "Long Tail Blue" (1827) looks silly when bragging about his fancy clothes:

> Some Niggers they have but one coat,
> But you see I've got two;
> I wears a jacket all the week,
> And Sunday my long tail blue. (qtd. in Dennison 76)

Minstrelsy's denigration of free black people may seem at odds with the efforts of white abolitionists on behalf of enslaved black people. Nevertheless, many white abolitionists had little more tolerance for assertive free black people than did the minstrel audiences who enjoyed the ridicule of northern black dandies expressed in these songs.

While minstrelsy derided aspiring and assertive free blacks, it nearly ignored slaves who considered resorting to violence to gain their freedom. Even though many minstrel songs reveal the hardships or injustices of slavery, the slave patiently endures the suffering or resists it through deception. These songs rarely hint at the possibility of a slave revolt; no doubt, white audiences would not find such a subject to be funny. In this sense, minstrelsy was not at odds with white abolitionists who opposed the use of violence as a means of liberation for slaves. One interesting exception to minstrelsy's avoidance of slave revolts is "Uncle Gabriel the Negro General" (1848), which conflates Gabriel Prosser's 1800 conspiracy in Richmond with Nat Turner's 1831 revolt. Instead of denouncing slave rebellion, which would hardly be entertaining, the song contains the subversiveness of its subject with a lighthearted air and with violent retribution against the slave rebels. Below are four stanzas from the song:

> Oh dont you know Old Uncle Gabriel,
> Oh! He war a niger [sic] General,
> He war de Chief of de Insurgents,
> Way down in Southampton.
>
> The whites dey fought him and dey caught him,
> To Richmond Court House dey did brought him,
> Twelve men sot up on de jury,
>
> Dey took him down to de Gallows,
> Dey drove him down, wid four grey horses,
> Brice's Ben, he drove de wagon,
>
> And dare dey hung him an dey swung him,
> And dey swung him and dey hung him,
> And that war the last of the Niger [sic] General. (SSMC)

Aside from denigrating the black "general" with the word "niger," this song makes him seem less fearsome with the words "Old" and "Uncle," which remind listeners of harmless, elderly male slaves. "Uncle Gabriel" also seems less dangerous because there is no mention of the planned or actual murder of whites, and the song emphasizes white power by describing the swift punishment of the slave rebels.[8] Despite the song's containment of the threat of black insurrection, however, such a topic seems surprising for minstrelsy, which at its worst glorified slavery and at best employed maudlin sentimentality to critique slavery or celebrated black trickster figures who deceived their masters. Although white abolitionists did not make fun of slave revolts in the way "Uncle Gabriel" did, most of them expected slaves to wait patiently for their white benefactors to emancipate them rather than use violence to gain their freedom, and they did not sanction such insurrections any more than minstrel songwriters did.

Abolitionism in Blackface

The parallels between minstrelsy and abolitionism go much further than a shared condescension toward black people and hostility toward black assertiveness. Both rose to prominence during the second quarter of the nineteenth century in the United States and the United Kingdom; both were associated with crossing racial boundaries; and, as I demonstrate in Chapter 4, both minstrelsy and the slave narrative—one of the main literary weapons of abolitionism—were often described as distinctly American. Abolitionist meetings and minstrel shows sometimes even took place in the same venues. These locales included New York's Chatham Street Chapel, where an antislavery meeting in 1834 was disrupted by an anti-abolitionist mob, and which later featured minstrel shows (Lhamon, *Raising* 30–31), and the Bowery Theatre, where Rice played as Jim Crow in 1832 and as Uncle Tom in 1854. Because of the synergy between minstrelsy and abolitionism, minstrel songs and characters borrowed from and "signified" on abolitionism, including its signature literary genre, the slave narrative. For instance, the subtitle of the Ethiopian Serenaders' 1844 song "My Old Aunt Sally" is "Composed by Herself" (SSMC), and Lhamon points out that Rice's memoir *The Life of Jim Crow* was "Written by Himself," à la the slave narratives of Douglass and Olaudah Equiano (*Raising* 197).

The relationship between minstrelsy and abolitionism worked the other way as well, and some abolitionists recognized and exploited minstrelsy's antislavery potential. Lhamon observes that minstrelsy's fugitive slave characters left their mark on slave narratives: "Because of the enormous popularity of the Jim Crow character as a free black figure on the lam, as the 1820s became the 1830s, white actors in blackface were important codeterminants in the molding of the runaway narratives" (*Raising* 207). These narratives, such as William Wells Brown's, included black trickster elements that were common in early minstrelsy. In a speech to the Rochester Ladies' Anti-Slavery Society in 1855, Douglass also recognized minstrelsy's potential usefulness for abolitionism: "It would seem almost absurd to say it, considering the use that has been made of them, that we have allies in the Ethiopian songs; those songs that constitute our national music, and without which we have no national music. . . . 'Lucy Neal,' 'Old Kentucky Home,' and 'Uncle Ned,' can make the heart sad as well as merry, and can call forth a tear as well as a smile. They awaken the sympathies for the slave, in which anti-slavery principles take root, grow and flourish" (Foner, *Life* 2: 356–57). Despite the racist and proslavery elements that were increasingly prominent in minstrelsy by 1855, Douglass implies that minstrelsy's more sentimental songs could be co-opted by abolitionism, even though they did not necessarily convert listeners to the cause. In addition to blackface sentimentality, minstrel humor was not always at odds with abolitionism, as we see in Stowe's depiction of clownish slaves in *Uncle Tom's Cabin* and in Brown's comical anecdote about a slave's ridiculously inept attempt at dentistry in his novel *Clotel*. Rather, the representations of slavery and African Americans in both abolitionism and minstrelsy often mirrored each other in their use of sentimentalism, humor, and music—elements that in each context encouraged a variety of emotions and racial attitudes for different purposes. These common features were part of the ambiguity of abolitionism and early minstrelsy but also served as sites of ideological conflict between them.

Indeed, the parallels between minstrel shows and antislavery lectures were sometimes used by anti-abolitionists to denigrate abolitionism, and hecklers at antislavery meetings sometimes mockingly compared them to minstrel shows. For instance, Martin Delany's speech in Marseilles, Ohio, was broken up by a man who called it a "darkey burlesque," and a mob taunted Delany and his friend with the minstrel-show instruments of castanets, tambourine, fiddle, and jaw-bone (Emerson, *Doo-Dah!* 122). The similarities between abolitionism and minstrelsy could also cause confusion among white audiences, as was the case for an anonymous person quoted in Colonel T. Allston Brown's series "Negro Minstrelsy": "'Ive [sic] often paid a quarter to see a white man blacked up, but it's the first and last I shall ever shell out to see a regular blackamoor,' said a friend of ours who went to see Fred Douglass the other night" (HTC).[9] Even after abolitionism faded following the passage of the Thirteenth Amendment, white audiences often saw any stage performance by African Americans as a minstrel show, as was the case of the Fisk Jubilee Singers during the 1870s (Ward 120, 128–29). While their purpose was not abolition, much of their music resembled antislavery songs by revealing the suffering of slaves, and the conflation of their singing with blackface minstrelsy suggests the extent to which the latter shaded white thinking about slavery.[10] Abolitionism was partly responsible for this confusion, however, because it was heavily influenced by minstrelsy and frequently borrowed some of the images, attitudes, and strategies that were gaining popularity on the minstrel stage.

Conversely, minstrel shows that encouraged antislavery sentiments in their audiences were influenced by abolitionism, though perhaps only temporarily and superficially. In describing the performance of Aiken's *Uncle Tom's Cabin* at the National Theatre (formerly the Chatham Street Chapel), the antislavery *New York Daily Tribune* commented on "the great change of public opinion which allows an Anti-Slavery meeting to be held every night at the National Theater, for such is the performance of Uncle Tom's Cabin dramatized." The crowd of "b'hoys," who formed a major portion of early minstrelsy's audience, was deeply affected by the play's antislavery sentiments. During the famous scene depicting Eliza's escape across the frozen Ohio River, "the pit and boxes were unanimous in their applause. The 'b'hoys' were on the side of the fugitives. The pro-slavery feeling had departed from among them. They did not wish to save the Union. They believed in the higher law" ("Abolitionism Dramatized"). The b'hoys' support for the stage slaves is not simply a matter of minstrelsy inciting antislavery sentiment, but also a result of being adapted by it. The b'hoys' reaction supports Michael Rogin's point that in the stage versions of *Uncle Tom's Cabin,* "blackface was not only embracing slaves but also supporting antislavery politics. There was considerable overlap, to be sure, between the proslavery and sentimental abolitionist structures of feeling, for maternalist abolitionism embedded itself in plantation nostalgia" (*Blackface* 41). Rogin's comment that "blackface abolition is the exception that proves the rule: burnt cork contaminated every white American political perspective on race" (43) also helps us understand how antislavery theatre could appeal to early minstrelsy's white male proletarian constituency. This statement was especially true in the North, where many whites had limited, if any, encounters with African Americans but had ample opportunity to attend minstrel theatres, which often shared neighborhoods with abolitionist lecture halls.

While the *Tribune* article mentions the b'hoys' sympathy for Eliza, other "Tom shows" that employed blackface conventions made Uncle Tom a more tame character and exploited Topsy's comical appeal. Stowe's portrayal of black characters and her use of comic dialogue already incorporated minstrel elements, so in a sense minstrelsy was taking back from Stowe what she had copied from it. These borrowings from minstrelsy are also obvious in sheet music covers of songs used in stage versions of *Uncle Tom's Cabin,* as well as Tom's singing of "Old Folks at Home" and Topsy's song "Oh! I'se So Wicked!" Thus, it is fitting that Rice began his blackface career as Jim Crow and finished it as Uncle Tom. Eric Lott remarks that "*Uncle Tom's Cabin* onstage was in one sense minstrelsy's logical antebellum conclusion, and by the 1850s casting Rice as Uncle Tom followed a train of thought. It confirms the equivocal character of racial representation—of blackface minstrelsy and *Uncle Tom's Cabin* both—just prior to the Civil War" (211). One might add that blackface versions of Stowe's novel—especially their depictions of Uncle Tom—were also a logical conclusion of sentimental antislavery representations of black people as passive victims of slavery.

The results of mixing antislavery sentiment and minstrelsy in Tom shows were unpredictable and complicated because of their inherent ambivalence and ideological diversity. Lott sees these plays as both "a break from but also a continuation of blackface minstrelsy" (212), and concludes that "a peculiarly fissured text in all of its dramatic versions, *Uncle Tom* relied on strategies of blackface representation that unsettled the plays even as the differing dramas put such stage conventions to largely conflicting uses" (233). Meer also comments on the ideological ambivalence of *Uncle Tom's Cabin* and minstrelsy, arguing that it led to the success of both:

> Part of the key to *Uncle Tom's* success thus lies in its debts to blackface, which had pioneered the ambivalent and contradictory racial politics that allowed the minstrel show—and *Uncle Tom's Cabin*—to appeal to very wide audiences. . . . Like minstrel show audiences, *Uncle Tom's* readers sometimes responded to subtle or subversive appeals for sympathy and sometimes ignored them, choosing only to see black characters as crude racial types. Stowe's antislavery message was couched in a form so ambiguous about race, and at times so explicitly demeaning in its representation of black people, that it both advocated emancipation and licensed a plethora of racist imitators. (12–13)

Blackface humor and antislavery sentiment were a powerful combination in mid-nineteenth-century America, and the differences between them became blurred in Stowe's novel and even more so in its blackface stage versions. However, while the novel *Uncle Tom's Cabin* probably contributed to abolitionist activism, minstrel shows that incorporated antislavery sentiment almost certainly did not. According to Meer, "By turning the end man-interlocutor dialogues into conduits for disguised and ambivalent sympathy for slave characters, they may have made its antislavery message palatable for the cautious and scarcely noticeable for the indifferent" (12). Unfortunately, such cautious and indifferent readers were unlikely to agitate against slavery. And because Stowe could not (or chose not to) disentangle minstrelsy from its racism, her uses of its conventions may have done as much to confirm racist stereotypes among these readers as it did in convincing them of slavery's injustice.

Because of minstrelsy's ambivalence and complexity, its uses in stage productions of Stowe's novel evinced a wide ideological range of racial representation that enabled different stage versions to serve various cultural purposes. Lott argues that minstrelsy had an even greater influence on Howard J. Conway's proslavery adaptation of the book than on Aiken and Howard's stage version, but the contrasts between these Tom shows were not just due to how much they borrowed from minstrelsy; they also resulted from the various strains of minstrelsy deployed in different productions. Lott observes that "Aiken and Conway each took up one of the minstrel show's contradictory representational strategies in regard to blacks—Conway its hard-edged ridicule, Aiken its sentimentalism" (220) and concludes that "Conway left the minstrel show's worst contributions intact, while Aiken brought out the radical uses lurking in it. . . . *Uncle Tom's Cabin* onstage was the site of competing attempts to capture the authority of blackface" (220).[11] Once again, though, we should remember that because these various threads of minstrelsy—sentimentality and ridicule—were already running throughout Stowe's novel, the differences between the numerous Tom shows merely amplified the ideological ambivalence of minstrelsy that informs Stowe's depictions of slave characters.

Black Bodies, Sexuality, and Miscegenation in Abolitionism and Minstrelsy

While abolitionism and minstrelsy shared an ideological uncertainty in their representations of black people, their ambivalence was partly brought under control by a rigid set of conventions. Abolitionism overlapped with formulaic minstrel shows in the scripted performances that white abolitionists expected from former slaves at meetings; whites often discouraged ex-slaves from expressing opinions and asked them merely to relate the horrid details of their experiences. For instance, Douglass writes in *My Bondage* that John Collins, the general agent of the Massachusetts Anti-Slavery Society, instructed him: "Give us the facts . . . we will take care of the philosophy" (367). Moreover, while describing the horrors of slavery, ex-slaves were often expected to speak with a slave dialect rather than more educated speech. William Andrews writes that the ex-slave Lewis Clarke "learned early on the antislavery platform that 'the uncouth awkwardness of his language had a sort of charm' to northern whites, and with [white abolitionist Joseph C.] Lovejoy's aid he exploited that vernacular uncouthness self-consciously and with rhetorical success in his dictated autobiography" (*To Tell* 139–40). Likewise, Douglass states in *My Bondage:* "It was said to me, 'Better have a *little* of the plantation manner of speech than not; 'tis not best that you seem too learned'" (367). In fact, his intelligence and articulateness became a liability when many whites refused to believe that such a skilled and intelligent speaker and writer had been a slave. In this sense, white abolitionist ideas about black authenticity dovetailed with the notion of black intellectual and linguistic inferiority that often surfaced in minstrelsy, and the dialect that whites wanted ex-slave witnesses to speak resembled the accents of the minstrel stage. Although white abolitionists did not actually black up and impersonate African Americans, their control over how black people would be represented somewhat resembled the power of white minstrel performers in determining popular representations of African Americans.

Judith Butler's theory of gender as performance offers a helpful analogue in understanding how ex-slaves were expected to perform white abolitionist notions of blackness at antislavery meetings. In speaking of gender, Butler writes that

> *gender* is not a noun, but neither is it a set of free-floating attributes, for . . . the substantive effect of gender is performatively produced and compelled by the regulatory practices of gender coherence. Hence, within the inherited discourse of the metaphysics of substance, gender proves to be performative—that is, constituting the identity it is purported to be. In this sense, gender is always a doing, though not a doing by a subject who might be said to preexist the deed. . . . There is no gender identity behind the expressions of gender; that identity is performatively constituted by the very "expressions" that are said to be its results. (24–25)

In a parallel fashion, white abolitionists expected ex-slaves to perform blackness, even though they viewed that blackness as essential rather than performative. Ex-slaves were also expected to perform their former slave identities. For example, Henry "Box" Brown reenacted his escape from Richmond to Philadelphia in a box by having himself sent from Bradford to Leeds in a crate while touring England during the early 1850s (Blackett, *Building* 15).[12] Like gender, blackness (and, by association, slave status) was inscribed onto the slave's body, a site that was represented as natural or essential but was always constructed. The status of slaves was literally scripted onto their bodies in the shape of branded letters, whip scars, and other markings and mutilations that were displayed and "read" at antislavery meetings. In this sense, the black body in abolitionist contexts was constructed or written as a slave body.

Abolitionists' obsession with black bodies and performances of "blackness" was shared by white minstrel performers and audiences. J. Martin Favor sheds some light on the performativity of race in minstrelsy: "Minstrelsy suggests at its root that 'race' is performable, if not always already performed. That is, with the proper makeup, a white person could be 'black,' and by removing pigmentation, a black person could become 'white.' 'Race' is theatrical—it is an outward spectacle—rather than being anything internal or essential" (123). The performative nature of minstrelsy's staging of blackness was coupled with its exhibition of black bodies, a practice also used in abolitionism. Paul Gilmore has recognized how abolitionism and minstrelsy showcased black bodies for different reasons: "The minstrel show spectacularized black bodies for commercial purposes; antislavery groups put former slaves on display— 'curiosit[ies] from the South,' 'specimen[s] of the fruits of the infernal system of slavery'—primarily for political ends. Yet both forums staged black bodies precisely because they did draw" (40–41). The display of black bodies for white consumption at minstrel shows and antislavery meetings proved to be a very versatile tactic because it lacked a single, stable meaning. Such exhibitions served several emotional functions within minstrelsy—pity, identification, and fascination—that could be easily co-opted by abolitionism. For example, Gilmore argues that William Wells Brown "is able to use minstrelsy for his antislavery purposes because of the ambivalence within the form itself, because the minstrel show, in both negative and positive ways, mirrored the representational logic and problematic of the abolitionist platform" (46). One parallel between these two forms of representing blackness was that they both reduced millions of black people to a representative black body that could serve several ideological functions. In early minstrelsy, for instance, white male laborers could identify with the endman in terms of gender and class, but they could also see him as inferior in racial terms. Likewise, whites attending antislavery meetings could view ex-slaves with condescending pity or with respect, since abolitionism required two conflicting forms of black identity and performance, as Gilmore points out: "The professional fugitive was, in essence, required to embody the social meanings of blackness and whiteness simultaneously, to be both the illiterate plantation slave of the minstrel stage and an eloquent defender of his race" (38). Such a demand was virtually impossible for ex-slaves to meet. Many of them preferred the latter role while repudiating the former, and some whites probably admired them for it. Yet their eloquence often did not inspire pity and went against white abolitionists' interest in their disfigured black bodies rather than in their minds.

The exhibitions of mutilated black bodies at antislavery meetings and the depictions of rape and flogging in abolitionist propaganda often gratified an almost salacious interest among white attendees and readers. Many abolitionists described the physical and sexual abuse of slaves in arguing against slavery, but they may have reached audiences on a sexual as well as a humanitarian level. While describing the sexual exploitation of slaves in abolitionist literature could be seen as morally compromising the movement, it may have also broadened its appeal. Audrey Fisch argues that slave narratives offered a legitimate venue for exciting, sometimes titillating, reading (54), and Andrews writes: "Given abolitionism's ready linkage of the South with Sodom, rhetorically accomplished slave narrators must have felt some temptation to exploit the prurient appeal of their knowledge of patriarchalism's perversities" (To Tell 243).[13] Andrews cites the 1861 account Louisa Picquet, the Octoroon; or, Inside Views of Southern Domestic Life by white abolitionist Hiram Mattison as an example of antislavery pornography. Mattison's interview with Picquet reveals that she was whipped by her master with a cowhide about the shoulders while wearing clothes that were "very thin; with low-neck'd dress" (12). He later declares that "there is not a family mentioned [in this account], from first to last, that does not reek with fornication and adultery" (51), and he claims that the South is even more sexually depraved than the seraglios of Orientalist pornography:

We may shudder at the "heathenism" of a Turkish harem, and send missionaries to convert the Mohammedans; we may stand aghast at the idea of twenty thousand Syrian women sold to supply the harems of the Mussulmans, and pour out our money like water to relieve or release them; but wherein is all this a whit worse than what is constantly practiced, with scarce a word of unfavorable comment, in our own "Christian" (?) land? If there is any difference, it is certainly in favor of the Turk; for neither his concubines nor his children by them are slaves; while, in this country, our chivalrous "southern gentlemen" beget thousands of slaves; and hundreds of the children of our free white citizens are sold in the southern slave markets every year. (51–52)

Passages such as these may have done more to arouse white readers' sexual curiosity than to spur them to agitate for abolition. In discussing *Louisa Picquet*, Andrews observes that "this scandalized white man made sure that whatever else we might discover therein, the first thing we associate with the slave woman is 'fornication and adultery'" (*To Tell* 244). Many other white abolitionists, like Mattison, were not always motivated solely by altruism in describing the abuse of female slaves, nor did they always appeal exclusively to the sympathy of white readers. They also revealed their ambivalence toward African Americans by representing the sexual and physical abuse of black bodies as a cause for both fascination and moral outrage.

These ambiguous representations of black physicality, sexuality, and suffering are evident not only in the antislavery tracts by white men such as *Louisa Picquet* but also in several narratives written by ex-slaves. While some narratives, such as those of Moses Roper and Harriet Jacobs, avoided graphic descriptions of the sexual abuse of slaves so as not to offend the delicate sensibilities of their readers, many others depicted such brutality explicitly. Henry Bibb's narrative, for instance, includes illustrations and detailed descriptions of whites flogging slaves (especially white men whipping partially nude black women) in ways that implied rape. One such illustration includes two scenes of slave women being physically abused by whites—one by a white man, the other by a white woman (see Figure 1). Unlike the left-hand scene, which occurs outside, the scene on the right shows the white woman beating a slave woman in a domestic setting with what appears to be a coal shovel—a domestic instrument, but one which a slave mistress would normally not handle except as a weapon against a slave. Though this scene frames the white woman

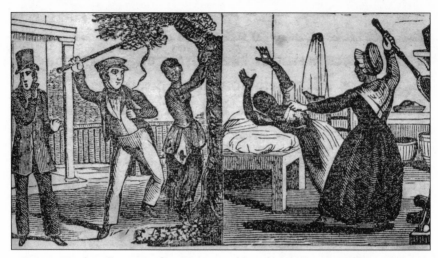

Figure 1: Woodcut illustration from *Narrative of the Life and Adventures of Henry Bibb, an American Slave, Written by Himself* (1849). Used with Permission of Documenting the American South, The University of North Carolina at Chapel Hill Libraries.

in a traditionally feminine domestic setting, it subverts the notions of feminine domesticity and morality by showing how slavery obliterates them. The fact that the slave woman is falling back on what appears to be a bed gives an added sexual dimension to this scene, which either places the white woman in the position of the white male rapist or suggests that she is unleashing her jealous rage against the sexually exploited slave woman at the site where this exploitation may have occurred. While the two-part illustration shows that slavery corrupts the "angel of the house" as well as the morally weaker man, it also provides white women with a possible sadistic fantasy. The fact that the illustrations in Bibb's narrative were borrowed from previously published abolitionist sources (Wood 118)[14] points to the pervasiveness of sadomasochistic imagery in antislavery literature and its usefulness in simultaneously sensationalizing slavery and promoting abolitionism.

The multiple meanings of these sexually charged abolitionist texts and images were largely determined by the gender, racial identities, and interests of their intended readers. Mary Favret points out that pornographic antislavery accounts of flogging offer readers "a range of positions: they could participate as inflamed malefactor, abject victim, and tortured witness. At the same time that the flogging scenario offered up these roles for identification, it also masked these roles though the differences of place, gender, and most distinctively, race" (31–32).[15] Favret's argument helps us understand the ambiguity of Douglass's description of the whipping of his aunt Hester by his master, Captain Anthony, in his 1845 *Narrative:*

> I have often been awakened at the dawn of day by the most heart-rending shrieks of an own aunt of mine, whom he used to tie up to a joist, and whip upon her naked back till she was literally covered with blood. No words, no tears, no prayers, from his gory victim, seemed to move his iron heart from its bloody purpose. The louder she screamed, the harder he whipped; and where the blood ran fastest, there he whipped longest. He would whip her to make her scream, and whip her to make her hush; and not until overcome by fatigue, would he cease to swing the blood-clotted cowskin. (18)

Douglass removes himself emotionally from Hester by switching from "an own aunt of mine," a phrase emphasizing her relation to him, to the distanced, isolated "his gory victim." Such distancing encourages readers not to identify with Hester, but rather to see her as a passive object of pity. This torture, Douglass explains, is motivated by Anthony's jealousy when Hester refuses to stop seeing her slave lover on a nearby plantation. When Douglass retells the experience two paragraphs later, he foregrounds the sexual aspects of the whipping even more:

> Before he commenced whipping Aunt Hester, he took her into the kitchen, and stripped her from neck to waist, leaving her neck, shoulders, and back, entirely naked. He then told her to cross her hands, calling her at the same time a d——d b——h. After crossing her hands, he tied them with a strong rope, and led her to a stool under a large hook in the joist, put in for the purpose. He made her get upon the stool, and tied her hands to the hook. She now stood fair for his infernal purpose. Her arms were stretched up at their full length, so that she stood upon the ends of her toes. He then said to her, "Now, you d——d b——h, I'll learn you how to disobey my orders!" and . . . he commenced to lay on

the heavy cowskin, and soon the warm, red blood (amid heart-rending shrieks from her, and horrid oaths from him) came dripping to the floor. (19)

Douglass says nothing more about Hester after these passages, nor does he offer any information about her earlier in the text; in that respect, his description of her here discourages readers from placing themselves in her situation. Moreover, male readers would be even less inclined than female readers to empathize with a slave woman. White male readers could, however, identify with Douglass's sadistic master, since he belongs to their racial and gender group, though of course such identification by abolitionist white men would have to be secret if not subconscious. Readers, especially men, could also identify with Douglass himself as a witness to this scene, channeling their voyeuristic sexual excitement or vicarious sense of humiliation into hatred of slavery and ultimately into abolitionist action.[16]

Of course, what set Douglass apart from his white readers, and from white abolitionists who depicted whipping with sexual overtones, was that he had also been a slave who was whipped. Although he distances himself in some ways from Hester in the passages above, he obviously did not take the subject position of Captain Anthony or that of a voyeuristic white reader, and being whipped in some ways places him in the same position as Hester. Moreover, while sexual abuse of male slaves is not represented as widely in slave narratives and abolitionist discourse as that of female slaves, male slaves were sometimes depicted as sexual victims of white women and men.[17] Marcus Wood's discussion of British antislavery pornography focuses on the whipping of male as well as female slaves, and Roper's narrative mentions that his mistress whipped him while he was naked (495). Similarly, William Wells Brown describes the sexual humiliation of young male slaves dressed before their mistress in "that unmentionable garment that buttons around the neck, which we all wore, and nothing else," and who engaged in gymnastic competition for the coveted post of house servant: "Old mistress sat on the piazza, watching our every movement—some fifteen of us, each dressed in his one garment, sometimes standing on our heads with feet in the air—still the lady looked on" (*The Black Man* 11). Sexual abuse of male slaves in abolitionist literature could be homosexual as well as heterosexual. Jacobs (writing as Linda Brent) mentions a slave named Luke whose master was "a mere degraded wreck of manhood" and a "cruel and disgusting wretch," who "took into his head the strangest freaks of despotism. . . . Some of these freaks were of a nature too filthy to be repeated" (Brent 197). This passage, combined with Jacobs's account of her own sexual victimization, exemplifies how both male and female slaves were often represented in sexual terms in antislavery literature.

The sexuality of slaves was not represented or viewed by abolitionists solely in relation to sexual abuse, however. For example, Douglass's sexual attractiveness was often noticed by his white audiences. McFeely quotes one American's description of Douglass as "more than six feet in height, and his majestic form, . . . straight as an arrow, muscular, yet lithe and graceful" (124), and reports a comment made by one Margaret Fox that "Frederick is as fine looking as Ever" (163). White abolitionist interest in black sexuality extended to visual representations of slaves as well as to actual slaves and ex-slaves. For instance, Brian Wallis has commented that the eroticized female figure of Hiram Powers's sculpture "The Greek Slave" was popular among abolitionists, even though the slave was not black (53). Moreover, the fact that Louis Agassiz, whose daguerreotypes of naked bodies of black slaves became famous, opposed slavery (Wallis 44) suggests that black bodies were sites of white abolitionist fascination.[18] The potential of antislavery representations of black bodies to titillate white readers and viewers, shock them into agitating against slavery, or both is one of the clearest examples of white abolitionist ambivalence toward African Americans.

Despite the differing aims of abolitionism and minstrelsy, the emphasis on black physicality and sexuality in some abolitionist literature, illustrations, and meetings somewhat paralleled the display of sexualized black bodies on the minstrel stage, though abolitionism was less vulgar than early minstrelsy in depicting black sexuality. Lott has pointed out that the sheet music covers of songs such as "Coal Black Rose" and "Jim Brown," as well as the lyrics of minstrel songs like "Lubly Fan," "Now Hold Your Horses, Will You!" and "Astonishing Nose" foregrounded black sexuality (117, 120, 145–47, 162). Unlike the passive suffering of slaves in sadomasochistic abolitionist rhetoric and imagery, minstrelsy often depicted black people as sexual agents. Lott demonstrates that this sexual aggressiveness was often manifested in voracious appetites and ridiculously large body parts that stood for excessive sexual drive and large genitals. Regarding the lyrics of "Lubly Fan," Lott notes the emphasis on the enormous feet and lips of the black "wench":

> I stopt her an I had some talk,
> Had some talk,
> Had some talk,
> But her foot covered up de whole side-walk
> An left no room for me
> . . . .
> Her lips are like de oyster plant,
> De oyster plant,
> De oyster plant,
> I try to kiss dem but I cant,
> Dey am so berry large. (qtd. in Lott 146)

Certainly, this is not the same depiction of black sexuality that one sees in antislavery rhetoric and imagery, which focus more on sin and victimization than on ludicrous exaggeration. This difference between minstrelsy and abolitionism can be seen in representations of black women as well as black men, and minstrelsy's wench characters combined exaggerated black sexuality with misogyny, an element that was much weaker in abolitionism, partly because of female participation in the movement. Despite these differences, both minstrelsy and abolitionism were often concerned with black physicality and sexuality, and their different methods of representing black bodies and carnality can be seen as two sides of the same coin.

The issue of black sexuality raised anxieties among white abolitionists and minstrel audiences regarding miscegenation, a subject that surfaced in minstrel shows as well as antislavery and proslavery rhetoric, albeit in different ways. The spectacle of the handsome Douglass promenading on Broadway with Julia and Eliza Griffiths[19] fueled anti-miscegenation hysteria among anti-abolitionists, who claimed that abolition would lead to interracial marriage or the rape or seduction of white women by black men emboldened by freedom and their sense of social equality with whites (assuming, of course, that black men would prefer white women). In response, white abolitionists argued that slavery encouraged miscegenation through the rape of black women by white men. By implying that racial mixing was a calamity to be avoided, they either showed their own fears of miscegenation or catered to those of their white audience. Harriet Martineau, for instance, writes in *Society in America* (1837) that "these planters, who sell their own offspring to fill their purses, who have such offspring for the sake of filling their purses, dare to raise the cry of 'amalgamation' against the abolitionists of the north, not one of whom has, as far as evidence can show, conceived the idea of a mixture of the races" (328–29). Like many other white abolitionists who linked slavery to miscegenation, Martineau does not make it clear whether she herself opposes such mixing or is simply playing the miscegenation card for antislavery purposes. At any rate, white abolitionists were careful not to promote miscegenation, because doing so would have turned away many potential white converts.

Minstrel shows, predictably, took a more comical approach to miscegenation than did abolitionists and their opponents, though they did not always present it in negative terms. One minstrel song, "She's Black, But That's No Matter" (1853), seems to endorse white male interest in black women. The chorus states: "But she's black! / I know she is, but what of that, / You'd love, could you look at her, / I'd have her just the way she is" (SSMC).[20] Minstrelsy also dealt with black male and white female miscegenation, including "Long Tail Blue" ("Jim Crow is courting a white gall, / And yaller folks call her Sue; / I guess she back'd a nigger out, / And swung my long tail blue")[21] and "Zip Coon" ("O my ole mistress is very mad at me, / Because I wouldn't go wid her and live in Tennessee") (qtd. in Dennison 76, 61). The humorous context of these verses helped white viewers to quell their anxiety about miscegenation, but fascination may have lurked underneath their nervous laughter. Lott observes that in minstrel shows, "White men were routinely encouraged to indulge in fantasies about black women—which, however, highlighted, and implicitly identified them with, the salacious black male characters who 'authored' the fantasies, confusing the real object of sexual interest" (119–20). The fact that such eroticized black female characters were played by white men partly negated the miscegenation taboo, though it added a new layer of prohibited desire. Minstrelsy's staging of cross-racial desire is somewhat ironic, given its consistently anti-abolitionist stance and the proslavery argument linking abolitionism to miscegenation. Yet early minstrelsy, like abolitionism, was fraught with ideological ambivalence, which explains why the representations of miscegenation and black sexuality in both contexts intersected so much with each other.

Conventionality, Performance, and Authenticity

The powerful anxieties and desires that white abolitionists and minstrel audiences felt about black sexuality and miscegenation needed to be controlled. Perhaps this need partly explains the highly structured and conventionalized nature of minstrel shows and antislavery meetings and literature. Abolitionism developed its own conventions, including the ex-slave's use of dialect, the spectacle of mutilated black bodies, the horrific tales of whipping and rape, the heart-wrenching anecdotes of divided slave families, and the attacks on hypocritical Christians who owned or traded slaves or supported slavery. Regarding these conventions, Dwight McBride borrows Michel Foucault's theory of discursive formations in arguing that ex-slaves testifying at antislavery meetings were both empowered and confined by abolitionist discourse. He points out that "the slave narrator . . . [must] be able to speak the codes, to speak the language that preexists the telling of his or her story. Hence the story has to conform to certain codes, certain specifications that are over-determined by the very discursive terrain into which the slave narrator is entering or inserting himself or herself" (3–4). One convention developed by white abolitionists to authenticate their attacks on slavery was the testimony of ex-slaves, but such authentication did not give these ex-slaves the authority to change the discursive conventions set by the movement's white leaders. They had to adhere to these conventions if they wanted their voices to be heard in abolitionist circles. Wilson Moses analyzes how these expectations discouraged Douglass from describing events, ideas, and feelings that were important to him but that did not fit into the antislavery agenda established by white leaders: "Douglass soon got tired of restricting himself to the theatrical display of his stripes and the dramatic mimicking of his erstwhile masters and overseers. He wanted to express himself on a variety of subjects, including but not restricted to slavery and the race problem in the United States. In his early years, Douglass struggled against confining himself to the narrative tradition on the podium" (66–67). Although white abolitionists enabled Douglass to make his voice heard, they also contained his voice by demanding that he focus solely on the evils of slavery and the passive virtue of slaves. In this sense, ex-slave abolitionists like Douglass may have felt somewhat like African American minstrel performers who were pressured to conform to the stage conventions that were established by white men in order to appeal to the racial fantasies of white audiences.

The highly mediated nature of abolitionism, including the ritual performances that white abolitionists expected from former slaves, resembled the rigidly structured forms of representing black people that developed in minstrelsy. Although early minstrelsy was rather unpredictable, during the 1840s a set three-part structure evolved, consisting of jokes and songs in the first part, an "olio" of "stump speeches" and other variety acts in the middle, and a burlesque skit (replaced by a plantation skit in later years) in the final section. This structure, as well as the comic dialogues between interlocutors and endmen, became more predictable as minstrelsy developed. Like antislavery meetings and slave narratives, minstrelsy became discursively overdetermined—not only in its general depiction of black stupidity, mendacity, and laziness, but also its Jim Crow and Zip Coon stock characters, its malapropism-laden stump speeches, and blackface. Despite early minstrelsy's ambiguity in representing black bodies, that ambiguity was eventually contained by the rigid conventions that evolved regarding its staging of "authentic" blackness.

The conventionality of minstrelsy and abolitionism that governed their performances of blackness had an uneasy relationship to both's claims of authenticity. The title of Theodore Weld's *American Slavery As It Is*, the publication of Stowe's *The Key to "Uncle Tom's Cabin,"* the prefaces by white abolitionists endorsing the truthfulness of slave narratives and the authorship of their ex-slave narrators, and the display of mutilated black bodies suggested an authenticity untainted by convention. However, while the slave narrator's presence lent authenticity to antislavery rhetoric, this implied claim of authenticity was undermined by the rules controlling that narrator's performance. McBride compares "the staging of slavery at the auction block" to "the staging of abolitionism, the carting out of black bodies onto the stage to bear witness to their authentic experiences of slavery" (4). His use of the word "staging" may bring to mind the minstrel show, another venue in which a purportedly genuine blackness was constructed through conventionalized performance. As Gilmore points out, the "staging of abolitionism" was comparable to the staging and performance of blackness on the minstrel stage.

Minstrelsy was also deeply concerned with racial performance and authenticity, though its relationship to authenticity was much more complex than was the case for abolitionism. On the one hand, minstrelsy's racial performance was based on concepts of authenticity, and white minstrels often advertised themselves as "authentic" or "genuine." This emphasis parallels the performed authenticity of ex-slaves on the abolitionist stage and their descriptions of slavery. In minstrelsy's early phase, some white audiences thought that blacked-up white performers were black. Lhamon notes that "some of the deepest Kentuckians, reported the minstrel trouper Sam Sanford, mistook white minstrels in blackface for actual black people. 'Many, many people really thought us black, . . . and would wait after the performance to see the "Niggers" come out'" (*Raising* 172). Some early troupes, such as the Virginia Serenaders, worried that their audiences would take them for black men, so they sacrificed their claim to authenticity by representing themselves on sheet music covers with and without blackface. However, as minstrelsy grew, most American audiences realized that the "black" bodies on the stage were usually blacked-up whites performing "blackness," and there was often a tongue-in-cheek quality to the performers' claims of authenticity. Moreover, the fact that most minstrel troupes (and the most popular ones) were white suggests that counterfeit was not only acceptable, but was in some ways more important than authenticity for white audiences. Roediger observes that white minstrels blacking up "served to emphasize that those on stage were really white and that whiteness really mattered" (*Wages* 117). Indeed, traveling white minstrel troupes would have been refused hotel accommodations and forced to travel in (appropriately named) Jim Crow railroad cars if they actually had been black. One reason why counterfeit was so important to white minstrel audiences was their ambivalence toward black behavior: although they did not want to be entertained by black performers, they were fascinated by performances of "black" behavior. Watching white men perform "blackness" while knowing that they were white allowed them to have it both ways.

Minstrelsy's claims of authenticity were compromised not only by racial imposture, but also by the fact that many white minstrel performers never observed black dance and musical styles carefully and extensively. However, many minstrel audiences in the North, where early minstrelsy was most popular, did not know African American culture well enough to see any inaccuracies in the performers' "delineations," except when comparing them to other, more "genuine" minstrel performances. Part of the ideological power of minstrelsy in regions with little or no African American presence was that it borrowed black images from racial discourses such as scientific racism and proslavery and abolitionist literature that were familiar to white Americans. As minstrelsy became more popular, however, it became its own frame of reference; it mattered little if minstrel performances had nothing to do with the actual speech patterns, dance, or music of African Americans. Lott is correct in arguing that "what was on display in minstrelsy was less black culture than a structured set of white responses to it which had grown out of northern and frontier social rituals and were passed through an inevitable filter of racist presupposition. . . . Minstrel performers reproduced not only what they supposed were the racial characteristics of black Americans (minstrelsy's content) but also what they supposed were their principal cultural forms: dance, music, verbal play" (101). For whites who were more familiar with black music and dance and doubted the authenticity of minstrelsy's performances of blackness, Lott suggests that minstrels' claims to authenticity were often defensive responses to such suspicion (60). In some ways, a minstrel performance's authenticity had more to do with the performer's conformity to minstrelsy's conventions than with his race or his knowledge of African American culture and behavior.

Although white minstrel companies often asserted that their representations of black people and folk culture were genuine, minstrelsy's professions of authenticity were bolstered by African American minstrel troupes.[22] White managers of African American troupes, such as Sam Hague, Charles Callender, and J. H. Haverly, relied on this rhetoric of authenticity even more than earlier white troupes had done (Toll 198–206).[23] As was the case for abolitionism, however, the authenticity of black performers was compromised by minstrelsy's conventional nature. By the time black troupes appeared in minstrelsy, it had crystallized into a set format, had become commodified, and was more consistently racist than before, and black minstrels were not allowed to introduce significant changes to its format and tone. Although Lisa Anderson is partly correct in arguing that black minstrels were "signifyin'" on and reclaiming minstrelsy (17), they were unable to break away from an entertainment form increasingly contaminated by racism, and such "signifyin'" was likely lost upon white audiences. In fact, as Toll argues, blacks' participation in minstrelsy mostly lent credence to its conventionalized racist depictions of African Americans (196).

The arrival of black performers on the minstrel stage made the issues of counterfeit and authenticity in minstrelsy even more complex than before. It also confused some audiences about the racial identities of the performers, though this confusion predated the arrival of black minstrel troupes. By the time black actors performed onstage during the 1850s and 1860s, minstrel audiences were used to the notion of counterfeit and rarely assumed that minstrel performers were black unless they were advertised as such. Thus, black performers surprised such audiences with their supposed racial authenticity, which was augmented by the fact that aside from the endmen, most African American minstrels did not use burnt cork, thereby setting themselves apart from white minstrels (Toll 200). Perhaps audiences mistook the dark skin of black performers for burnt cork and assumed that the performers were white and therefore counterfeit. Thus, the lack of makeup suggested that their performances of blackness were not constructed but real, and that, conversely, makeup signified counterfeit. Douglass relied on the latter idea when he described white minstrels in an 1848 article in the *North Star* as "the filthy scum of white society, who have stolen from us a complexion denied to them by nature, in which to make money, and pander to the corrupt taste of their white fellow-citizens" ("The Hutchinson Family"). His remarks about Gavitt's Original Ethiopian Serenaders in 1849 are less negative, but still associate makeup among purportedly black performers with inauthenticity:

> Partly from a love of music, and partly from curiosity to see persons of color exaggerating the peculiarities of their race, we were induced last evening to hear these Serenaders. The Company is said to be composed entirely of colored people; and it may be so. We observed, however, that they, too had recourse to the burnt cork and lamp black, the better to express their characters, and to produce uniformity of complexion. Their lips, too, were evidently painted, and otherwise exaggerated. Their singing generally was but an imitation of white performers, and not even a tolerable representation of the character of colored people. (Foner, *Life* 5: 141)

The use of blackface leads Douglass to guess that the blackness of the performers "may be so." This ambiguous comment highlights the complex and constructed nature of race in minstrelsy, in which African Americans black up for the stage and mimic white imitations of black singing. Complicating this notion of constructed blackness even more is Douglass's later statement in this article that these black minstrels "must cease to exaggerate the exaggerations of our enemies; and represent the colored man rather as he is, than as Ethiopian Minstrels usually represent him to be" (142). While he seems to hold out the possibility of authenticity for African American minstrels, that authenticity is something to be represented and performed; it cannot simply be.

The case of the African American minstrel dancer William Henry Lane (known as "Juba"), who performed in P. T. Barnum's troupe in the early 1840s, also problematizes the concepts of authenticity, counterfeit, and racial performance in minstrelsy. Gilmore notes that early in Lane's career, Barnum made him blacken his face to avoid offending white audiences who would object to watching a black performer. By blacking up, Lane ironically could pass for a white minstrel performer. Gilmore writes of this incident that "although 'a genuine negro'—'the genuine article'—Lane needed to become a 'seeming counterfeit' in order to gain a place on the minstrel stage. This description highlights the way in which the minstrel show produced authenticity through counterfeits. . . . In order to appear real—and gain commercial success—Lane had to perform the blackness that he supposedly embodied naturally" (49). Lane's ability to pass for white through blackface and "acting black" reveals the importance of the "seeming counterfeit" in minstrelsy. For Lott, this double layer of cross-racial imitation did not necessarily preclude the possibility of authenticity. By blacking up, he argues, Lane showed that "it was possible for a black man in blackface, without a great deal of effort, to offer credible imitations of white men imitating him. That is to say, some blackface impersonations may not have been as far from this period's black theatrical self-presentation as we tend to believe" (113). The problem with this statement is the implied belief in a black theatrical self-presentation unmediated by conventions of blackface performance that were developed before Lane. Because we cannot know what such an unmediated, authentic black performance style looked like (if it actually existed), we cannot judge the authenticity (or lack thereof) of its white imitations, nor of black imitations of those white imitations. The ideological swirl of authenticity and counterfeit that engulfed Lane's minstrel performances, and those of black minstrel performers generally, was even more intense and confusing than that which surrounded white minstrel performance.

As was the case in Lane's blackface performances, the notions of authenticity and imitation regarding African Americans singing minstrel songs were hopelessly tangled in much of the discourse surrounding minstrelsy. For instance, a letter published in 1853 in *Dwight's Journal of Music* about minstrelsy's southern origins describes the multiple levels of imitation in "Negro Melodies" and muddles the issues of performativity, authenticity, originality, and appropriation: "Although first published at the North, you there know nothing of the power and pathos given them here [the South]. The whites first learn them— the negroes catch the air and words from once hearing, after which woods and fields resound with their strains—the whites catch the expression from these sable minstrels—thus Negro Melodies have an effect here not dreamed of at the North" ("Letter" 164). Curiously, we are not told from whom southern whites learn these songs, and because authenticity is often associated with originality, the undetermined source of these songs leaves the question of their authenticity unanswered. Moreover, the assertion that African Americans pick up these songs from whites undermines minstrelsy's claim that such songs are originally and authentically "black" and places black performances of these songs on the same level of imitation as the whites who appropriate and publish them.[24] Yet the phrase "sable minstrels" brings minstrelsy to mind and emphasizes black performance of these songs. By conflating "negroes" with "sable minstrels," the article implies that African American minstrel performers are synonymous with African Americans in general and that black minstrel performances are authentic.[25] Like many nineteenth-century commentaries on minstrelsy, this article demonstrates that minstrelsy's relationships to authenticity and imitation and to African Americans are virtually impossible to sort out. What makes its representations of African Americans even more puzzling is that they often overlapped with abolitionist images of slaves. Both sets of representations were highly conventionalized, emphasized performativity and authenticity, featured black sexualized bodies on display for white consumption, and encouraged ambivalent responses from white audiences and readers.

The messy ambiguities of minstrelsy and abolitionism and the complex relationships between them in mid-nineteenth-century America were largely tangled with the contradictions in American culture. The presence of millions of enslaved black people in a predominantly white nation that was thoroughly racist, staunchly Christian, and proudly democratic would inevitably raise questions about how to represent them: as human beings equal in intelligence, spirituality, and morality to whites; as butts of vulgar, derisive humor; as weak and humble victims of slavery; as oppressed workers who shared concerns with white "wage slaves"; as objects of erotic fascination; or as sexual threats to white racial purity. Abolitionism and minstrelsy did not divide these representations neatly. Across the Atlantic, Britain showed many of the same ideological contradictions as did its former colonies in its representation of black people, but it differed from America in two important ways. It had abolished slavery and the subsequent apprenticeship system in its West Indian colonies by 1838, thanks to an antislavery movement that was much stronger than its American counterpart, and it lacked a large black population. Despite these differences, one common bond between the two nations was the popularity of blackface minstrelsy after Thomas Rice sailed to Britain and debuted on the London stage in 1836. Both the similarities and the differences between the nations would shape Britons' complex attitudes toward African Americans, slavery, America, and Britain itself—attitudes that comprise the focus of the next chapter.

Abolitionism, Nationalism, Blackface Minstrelsy, and Racial Attitudes in Victorian Britain

In *The Uncle Tom's Almanack or Abolitionist Memento for 1853*, John Cassell declared: "England has long been distinguished by her advocacy of the Anti-Slavery Cause. To that cause have been devoted the noblest energies of her sons, who have freely lavished on it their talents, their treasures, and their lives. For years having abolished slavery in her own dominions, the aim of English diplomacy has been everywhere to bring about the same glorious result—everywhere to achieve the emancipation of the slave" (4; JJC). Although England had established slavery in its North American and West Indian colonies during the seventeenth century, Victorian Britons—especially abolitionists like Cassell—often looked to the more recent past to portray themselves as more humane than Americans regarding slavery. British abolitionists had reason to be proud. The Anti-Slavery Society, formed in 1823, had pressured Parliament into passing the 1833 Emancipation Act, and the British and Foreign Anti-Slavery Society, which grew out of the former organization, played a crucial role in agitating against the apprenticeship system in the West Indian colonies after 1833 and in working for abolition in the United States. Although the United States had outlawed the international slave trade shortly after Britain did, Britain's abolition of slavery in its West Indian colonies in 1834 and of the apprenticeship system four years later gave the nation a moral advantage over its transatlantic cousin.[1] British abolitionists were not reluctant to remind themselves and Americans of this fact, and they often contrasted a humanitarian, enlightened Britain to a slaveholding, morally bankrupt America.

However, while opposition to slavery was widespread throughout Britain, racism was far from absent. To visiting African Americans, British racism may have seemed less aggressive than its American counterpart, but notions of black inferiority mingled freely with abolitionist sentiments. As Michael Pickering observes, "Though the British may have prided themselves on having preceded America in the abolition of slavery and thus outpacing Brother Jonathan in humanitarian philanthropy, abnegation of hierarchisation and the acceptance of equality of status between black and white ethnic groups was . . . not part of that achievement" ("Mock Blacks" 229). In addition, many British antislavery nationalists neglected their nation's past and present complicity in slavery, as well as the concessions made to planters during the abolition of West Indian slavery. They also ignored the fact that abolitionism's triumph in Britain was paralleled by the growth of the British Empire and the colonialist racial attitudes supporting it. Moreover, many Britons continued to congratulate themselves on their nation's moral virtue long after the abolitionist movement itself began to dwindle during the late 1840s. This decline coincided with the growing popularity of blackface minstrelsy. In many ways, abolitionism helped pave the way for minstrelsy in Britain because it encouraged interest in black bodies, and early minstrelsy was not incompatible with the antislavery movement. Eventually, however, minstrelsy became more derogatory in its depictions of black people and less critical of slavery, and these attitudes tacitly discouraged audiences from agitating on behalf of African American slaves.

This chapter examines British attitudes toward slavery, race, nationalism, and America, offers reasons for abolitionism's triumph in Britain, and analyzes the limitations of British abolitionism and egalitarianism. It also traces abolitionism's relations to blackface minstrelsy in Britain: the growth of British minstrelsy, its meanings for British audiences, and its relationships to English blackface traditions predating Rice's 1836 London debut. The first part of this chapter examines the nationalist impulses of British abolitionism, revealing how African American visitors and white American abolitionists confirmed and challenged Britain's antislavery and antiracist reputation. It then analyzes the economic and demographic factors that enabled the triumph of British abolitionism. Understanding the ideological climate that surrounded slavery, race, and abolitionism helps us make sense of minstrelsy's vogue in Britain and the complex and dynamic meanings of the minstrel mask among Britons. I argue that Britons welcomed American minstrelsy during the 1830s and 1840s because of its working-class appeal and antislavery impulses, and because blackface and clown traditions were already in place in Britain before

Rice's arrival. I also point out that the hardening of British racial attitudes and the decline of abolitionist sentiment roughly coincided with a corresponding shift within minstrelsy after mid-century.

"Slaves Cannot Breathe in England": Britain as the Land of Liberty

Despite the differences between the United States and the United Kingdom regarding their involvement in slavery and their respective abolitionist movements, both nations professed to be the land of liberty. Often this shared claim was expressed in terms of competition rather than amity, with white Americans viewing Britain as a domineering, elitist, monarchical colonial power and Britons pointing out the hypocrisy of a nation that sanctioned slavery yet claimed to be a democracy. In contrast to their white compatriots, many African Americans saw Britain not as an oppressor but as a liberator. In this respect, the year 1776 was less important than 1772, when Lord Mansfield declared in the Somerset case that slaveowners could not force their slaves to leave England (Fryer 125).[2] While many people misconstrued the ruling to mean that slavery was abolished on British soil (Fryer 125–26),[3] it remained legal until the 1833 Emancipation Act, though it gradually disappeared before then. Moreover, the British slave trade continued for another thirty-five years and slavery itself continued in Britain's West Indian colonies for six more decades. Mansfield's decision (and its subsequent misinterpretation), along with Lord Dunmore's 1775 proclamation promising freedom to American slaves who fought for the British army in the Revolutionary War, encouraged African Americans to associate Britain with liberty rather than tyranny, and this attitude lasted through the Civil War.

This view of Britain as the champion of slaves was often espoused by African American abolitionists, who were warmly received in Britain. As a result, they often contrasted British racial egalitarianism with American racism.[4] Both the ex-slaves and their hosts pointed out that Britain had abolished slavery and that its people did not share the prejudice of white Americans. For black abolitionists, these contrasts between the two nations served a double purpose: to elicit support from Britons by praising their abolitionist virtue and lack of racism, and to shame white Americans into proving that they were as committed to freedom and egalitarianism as Britons were (Blackett, *Building* 7–8). For instance, Douglass writes in *My Bondage and My Freedom:*

> It so happened that the great mass of the people in England who attended and patronized my anti-slavery meetings, were, in truth, about as good republicans as the mass of Americans, and with this decided advantage over the latter—they are lovers of republicanism for all men, for black men as well as for white men. They are the people who sympathize with Louis Kossuth and Mazzini, and with the oppressed and enslaved, of every color and nation, the world over. They constitute the democratic element in British politics, and are as much opposed to the union of church and state as we, in America, are to such an union. (378–79)

Unlike white Americans, who reviled Britain as an oppressive monarchy, and like many British abolitionists, Douglass depicts Britain as more democratic than America. He makes the same point about British Canada in his 1853 novella *The Heroic Slave* when the protagonist Madison Washington sends a letter from Windsor to his white benefactor that states, "I nestle in the mane of the British lion, protected by his mighty paw from the talons and the beak of the American eagle" (46). Ironically, a slave named after two of America's founding fathers (themselves both slaveholders) finds comfort in a symbol of the nation that his namesakes had repudiated, and a symbol that connoted royalty as well as Britishness. In an earlier text, Moses Roper describes his similar feelings upon arriving in Liverpool: "My feelings when I first touched the shores of Britain were indescribable, and can only be properly understood by those who have escaped from the cruel bondage of slavery" (518). Roper then includes the oft-quoted lines of William Cowper's 1785 antislavery poem "The Task," which misinterprets Lord Mansfield's ruling in the Somerset case: "Slaves cannot breathe in England; / If their lungs receive our air, that moment they are free; / They touch our country and their shackles fall" (518). Similarly, William Wells Brown compares the two nations and refers to the Revolutionary War in his 1847 narrative to point out the irony of a slaveholding democracy: "An American citizen was fleeing from a democratic, republican, Christian government, to receive protection under the monarchy of Great Britain. While the people of the United States boast of their freedom, they at the same time keep three millions of their own citizens in chains; and while I am seated here in sight of Bunker Hill Monument, writing this narrative, I am a slave, and no law, not even in Massachusetts, can protect me from the hands of the slave-holder!" (*Travels* 66). Brown contrasts the virtuous might of American colonists who defeated the British with the tyranny of American slaveholders and juxtaposes a benign British monarchy with a domineering plantocracy. The fact that leaders of the American Revolution sometimes compared themselves to slaves makes the irony of Brown's criticism of American hypocrisy even more sharp.[5] Like many slave narratives, Brown's text reminds white American readers of the nation's failure to live up to its egalitarian ideals while simultaneously appealing to anti-American sentiment among British readers.

African Americans continued to depict Great Britain as an enlightened nation free of race prejudice up to the Civil War and beyond. This image can be seen in Harriet Jacobs's description of her experience in England in her narrative *Incidents in the Life of a Slave Girl*: "My situation was indescribably more pleasant [than in America]. For the first time in my life I was in a place where I was treated according to my deportment, without reference to my complexion. I felt as if a great millstone had been lifted from my breast. Ensconced in a pleasant room, with my dear little charge, I laid my head on my pillow, for the first time, with the delightful consciousness of pure, unadulterated freedom" (Brent 188). Jacobs uses a domestic image of freedom to portray Britain as a safe, welcoming home for fugitive slaves; she is "ensconced in a pleasant room" rather than confined in the garret in North Carolina, in which she had hidden from her master for nearly seven years. Two years after the publication of *Incidents*, she wrote in a letter to the Reverend James Sella Martin, an African American minister working for London's Freedman's Aid Society, that "England has been the coloured man's boast of freedom; we will still believe our English friends true to their declared principles" (7).[6] Although the British government recognized the Confederates as belligerents and many upper-class Britons supported the Confederacy (Temperley 249), Britain's reputation as the champion of slaves was too firmly set in Jacobs's mind to be negated by these facts. Even after slavery was abolished in the United States, some African Americans still saw Britain as a refuge for slaves. Maggie Porter of the Fisk Jubilee Singers, who visited England in 1873, described Queen Victoria as "the grandest and noblest queen of them all, under whose flag . . . thousands of our race had sought and found liberty in the dark days of bondage" (qtd. in Ward 208). Despite the decline of the abolitionist movement and the increase of indifference and hostility towards black people after mid-century, Britain's reputation as a color-blind abolitionist stronghold remained firm in the minds of many African Americans.

British abolitionists were eager to prove their moral superiority over America by welcoming African American abolitionists and fugitive slaves, and they often emphasized the humanity and virtue of these black visitors in order to expose the duplicity of American egalitarian rhetoric. For example, *The Uncle Tom's Cabin Almanack or Abolitionist Memento for 1853* printed an engraving of Douglass making a speech with the following caption: "In the above engraving we see him, as, in the fulness [*sic*] of intellectual might, he stood on a British platform before thousands who listened and admired, while he pleaded his rights as a man" (7; JJC). About William Wells Brown, the *Almanack* observes, "In the land of his birth, there is no spot on which Brown, the escaped slave, may not be claimed as a fugitive, and carried back to chains and bondage; . . . In England we do not recognize the right of any to hold a property in the flesh and blood of their fellow-men" (28; JJC). The *Almanack* depicts Brown as a passive victim, in contrast to Douglass's "intellectual might," but the attitudes toward American slavery and hypocrisy are similar in both instances. Although white American abolitionists made similar arguments against American slavery, such sentiments were much more acceptable to Britons than to white Americans in general, many of whom were indifferent or hostile toward abolitionism or resented any criticism from Britons.

By using ex-slaves like Douglass and Brown to represent African American slaves, British abolitionists demonstrated the absurdity of slavery and argued that their nation had proven its humanitarianism through the Emancipation Act.[7] For example, the *North of Scotland Gazette* contrasts the two nations in an 1847 article titled "American Slavery—and How to Abolish It" in order to promote British abolitionist nationalism: "Not only is slavery sanctioned by law in America; but slaves are bought and sold as goods and chattels, and the man who is benevolent enough to help one of these degraded and oppressed creatures across the boundary line which separates the United States from Canada, is liable to be punished by death. Britain has not only abolished slavery, but made it a law, that the moment a slave sets his foot within the British dominions he is free" (RH). By choosing to focus on the present rather than Britain's past complicity in West Indian and American colonial slavery, British abolitionists proudly equated their nation with Enlightenment values. Even after slavery was abolished in the United States, British writers, orators, and politicians contrasted their own nation's history of antislavery agitation with the prolonged existence of American slavery. During the 1875 controversy surrounding the Fugitive Slave Circular (which commanded British Navy captains to surrender on demand fugitive slaves who sought protection on British ships), the *Daily Telegraph* paraphrased a speech by the British abolitionist MP William Edward Forster: "He wished well to the United States, and was glad that they had abrogated slavery among themselves; but he did not wish them to take the position we had so long occupied as champions of the slave."[8] Like many Britons who celebrated their nation's abolitionist virtue, Forster seems unwilling to let Americans share Britain's noble reputation as the enemy of slavery. These assaults on American slavery by antislavery Britons were motivated not only by sympathy for slaves and hatred of slavery, but by nationalist pride and anti-American sentiment as well (Bolt 31).

This criticism of American slavery and hypocrisy was not limited to abolitionists. For example, even though Frances Trollope's 1832 travel narrative *Domestic Manners of the Americans* is more of a critique of American society and culture than an abolitionist text, it uses the anti-American rhetoric of British abolitionism in claiming that Americans "inveigh against the governments of Europe, because, as they say, they favour the powerful and oppress the weak. You may hear this declaimed upon in Congress, roared out in taverns, discussed in every drawing-room, satirized upon the stage, nay, even anathematized from the pulpit: listen to it, and then look at them at home; you will see them with one hand hoisting the cap of liberty, and with the other flogging their slaves" (172). It is bad enough, Trollope implies, that Americans condone slavery, but even worse is their professed love of liberty, often coupled (as Trollope elsewhere points out) with attacks on the lack of egalitarianism in British society. Likewise, the English magazine *Punch,* though it did not endorse abolitionism, often excoriated America's support for slavery and its hypocrisy in calling itself the land of liberty. Its 1846 article "Punch's Political Dictionary," for instance, sharply points to American slavery and duplicity in its definition of liberty: "The Declaration of American Independence assumes that all men are equal, and that they are all entitled to life, liberty, and the pursuit of happiness. Among the results of this theory are Slavery, Lynch Law, and a disagreeable habit of making one another as uncomfortable as possible" (277). Unlike British abolitionists, other Britons who denounced American slavery seemed to be less interested in eliminating the practice than in denigrating America.

Despite occasional tensions with their British colleagues, white American abolitionists sometimes conceded Britain's moral supremacy over the United States in regard to slavery (Quarles, *Black* 118).[9] While not an actual member of any abolitionist organization (Fladeland, *Men* 353), Stowe expresses her admiration of humanitarian England in *Uncle Tom's Cabin*, describing the arrival of George, Eliza, and Harry in British Canada: "Clear and full rose the blessed English shores; shores charmed by a mighty spell,—with one touch to dissolve every incantation of slavery, no matter in what language pronounced, or by what national power confirmed" (335). In this passage, Stowe figures American slavery as an evil, linguistic, legalistic power that is not argued against, but rather silenced by the magic of the "blessed English shores."[10] American abolitionists were not content to let their nation's moral inferiority to Britain continue indefinitely, pointing to British antislavery spirit as a model for white American morality and behavior. Unlike American cultural nationalists, who chafed under the dominance of English culture and promoted a uniquely American culture, antislavery Americans often encouraged their compatriots to emulate humanitarian Britons. In an effort to hearten American opponents of slavery, Ralph Waldo Emerson proclaims in his speech marking the tenth anniversary of West Indian emancipation: "As an omen and assurance of success, I point you to the bright example which England set you, on this day, ten years ago" ("Address" 26). In fact, Emerson suggests that American abolitionists, like their British counterparts, could link their movement to nationalism. The British parliament's discussion of the slave trade, he declares, "was not narrowed down to a paltry electioneering trap"; rather, there was "a delight in justice, an honest tenderness for the poor negro, for man suffering these wrongs, combined with the national pride, which refused to give the support of English soil, or the protection of the English flag, to these disgusting violations of nature" (22). Although Emerson had elsewhere expressed skepticism toward reform movements and had urged Americans to create their own literature rather than copy British models, his statement typifies the recognition that American opponents of slavery often gave to Britain for its abolitionist leadership.[11]

Other white American abolitionists responded more ambivalently and combatively to British abolitionist nationalism. One poetic illustration of this attitude is John Greenleaf Whittier's 1846 poem "The Freed Islands," written on the twelfth anniversary of West Indian emancipation. In this poem, Whittier mixes admiration for British abolitionism with a defensive nationalism against British criticisms of America as a hypocritical, slaveholding pseudo-democracy. The poem mentions Britain's abolition of slavery and asks the reader, "What she has done can we not do?" (21). Whittier predicts that "though long delayed, and far, and slow, / The Briton's triumph shall be ours" (11–12) and compares America to Britain:

> Mighty alike for good or ill
> 　With Mother-land, we fully share
> The Saxon strength, the nerve of steel,
> The tireless energy of will,
> 　The power to do, the pride to dare. (16–20)

Rather than belittling America in comparison to Britain, Whittier emphasizes their similarity in strength and suggests that America could and should follow Britain's example in ending slavery. While his abolitionism leads him to see Britain as a model for America, his nationalism causes him to see the former nation as a rival in this regard. He rejects British abolitionists' boasts about their nation's moral superiority over America later in the poem, when he switches his focus to conflict between the two nations. His tone becomes defensive in stanza seven:

> O kingly mockers! scoffing show
> 　What deeds in Freedom's name we do;
> Yet know that every taunt ye throw
> Across the waters, goads our slow
> 　Progression towards the right and true. (31–35)

In addition to referring derisively to the British monarchy, Whittier accuses British abolitionists of belittling the efforts of their American colleagues. He also denies Britain credit for abolition by declaring that "God willed their [the slaves'] freedom" (4). While Whittier's patriotism differed from that of American anti-abolitionists who despised Britain as an aristocratic enemy, it also clashed with the nationalism of British abolitionists who denounced the United States for continuing slavery.[12] Despite Britain's strong abolitionist reputation, Whittier uses this poem to define an American identity that is both antislavery and anti-British.

Whittier's stance toward Britain and British abolitionism shifts from ambivalence in "The Freed Islands" to indignation over British hypocrisy in his Civil War era poem "To Englishmen." Here he takes Britain's ruling class to task for being "either coldly indifferent or hostile to the party of freedom" (336), as his headnote to the poem states. For Whittier, this attitude would be bad enough if Britain had always condoned slavery; what makes it worse is Britain's previous opposition toward slavery and the self-congratulatory rhetoric of British abolitionists regarding their nation's antislavery virtue. The defensiveness and bitterness of Whittier's tone in "The Freed Islands" is even more obvious here:

> You flung your taunt across the wave;
>   We bore it as became us,
> Well knowing that the fettered slave
> Left friendly lips no option save
>   To pity or to blame us.
> You scoffed our plea. "Mere lack of will,
>   Not lack of power," you told us:
> We showed our free-state records; still
> You mocked, confounding good and ill,
>   Slave-haters and slaveholders. (1–10)

In the first five lines, Whittier reluctantly agrees with British abolitionists who condemn American slavery, but he criticizes them for extending their hostility toward the United States as a whole. His resentment toward British abolitionism for its anti-American rhetoric reveals that he deeply identifies with his nation despite his own opposition to American slavery. He later charges John Bull with inconsistency by referring to a British cartoon depicting an American slaveholder who says, "Haven't I a right to wallop my nigger?":

> But yesterday you scarce could shake,
> In slave-abhorring rigor,
> Our Northern palms for conscience' sake:
> To-day you clasp the hands that ache
> With "walloping the nigger!" (16–20)

Rather than encouraging the United States to follow Britain's lead through abolition, as he did in "The Freed Islands," Whittier here reverses the nationalist rhetoric of British abolitionism by suggesting that Britain has fallen below America in moral stature.

Despite its attack on British duplicity, "To Englishmen," like "The Freed Islands," claims that white Americans and Britons share a common heritage and love of liberty. One might expect Whittier to use this similarity to urge Americans to abolish slavery as their British cousins did. In making this comparison, however, slavery strangely disappears from the picture:

> O Englishmen!—in hope and creed,
> In blood and tongue our brothers!
> We too are heirs of Runnymede;
> And Shakespeare's fame and Cromwell's deed
> Are not alone our mother's.
> "Thicker than water," in one rill
> Through centuries of story
> Our Saxon blood has flowed, and still
> We share with you its good and ill,
> The shadow and the glory. (21–30)

Whittier ignores African Americans in this passage, both as victims of slavery and as antislavery activists, and the racialist reference to the "Saxon blood" of white Americans was not unusual among white abolitionists. He also foregrounds the common antimonarchical tradition of Britain and America by invoking Runnymede and Cromwell, names from the relatively distant past, rather than William Wilberforce, Granville Sharp, Thomas Clarkson, or other British abolitionists of the more recent past. The implication that democracy (and, perhaps indirectly, abolition) is the legacy of Cromwell and the English barons at Runnymede—all men of considerable power—also evades the issues of race and slavery. This absence suggests that Whittier may be less concerned with emancipating enslaved African Americans than with pointing out the hypocrisy of a nation that prides itself on its antislavery tradition and criticizes American slavery, yet recognizes the Confederacy. Reading this poem and "The Freed Islands" alongside the works of other American abolitionists reveals a range of American abolitionist attitudes toward Britain and its antislavery legacy that include admiration, rivalry, nationalist pride, resentment, and criticism. "To Englishmen" also reveals the transatlantic nature of Anglophone abolitionism in emphasizing the similarities between America and Britain—similarities that helped each nation's abolitionists work together against slavery.

"Don't Come to England": Racial Prejudice in Britain

In contrast to white American abolitionists like Whittier, African Americans who visited Britain—especially abolitionists—generally gave glowing reports about how enlightened British society was in regard to race and slavery. Nevertheless, they did not always view or represent the nation as a utopia for African Americans. For instance, in an open letter to the *London Times* titled "Don't Come to England" (reprinted in *Frederick Douglass's Paper* and *The Liberator* as "Fugitive Slaves in England" in July 1851), William Wells Brown writes that American fugitive slaves were having difficulty in finding work in England and should consider emigration to the West Indies instead. He goes on to state: "Knowing that most of the fugitive slaves have been accustomed to the raising of cotton, sugar, rice, and such other products as are raised in the West Indies, I am satisfied that a proposition of this kind would, if made upon fair terms, meet with a favorable response from my down-trodden and enslaved countrymen, and thereby be a benefit both to the owners of the West India estates and these fugitive slaves" ("Fugitive"). Brown discourages fugitive slaves from coming to England not because they would encounter racism, but because their agricultural skills were more suited to West Indian plantations than English factories. In his book *The American Fugitive,* he also does not mention English racism while describing his visit to Britain. In this sense, neither Brown's letter nor his book contradict the accounts of most African Americans, who portrayed Britain as a land free of race prejudice.

Such silence on British racism did not prove its absence, however. Blackett surmises that African American visitors seldom commented on it because of their goal of gaining British approval for their movement (*Building* 190–91). It is also possible that African Americans were so impressed by how much better they were treated in Britain that racism did not appear to be a problem. For instance, Waldo E. Martin, Jr. argues that Douglass did not seem to notice European (including British) racism: "Douglass's analysis typically neglected the often exploitative and racist ideas, policies, and actions of Europeans toward black peoples in the New World and Africa" (115). Martin further observes: "His perception of anti-Negro prejudice among Europeans . . . left much to be desired. In fact, it was shortsighted and wrongheaded. . . . Due to the unusual nature of his European reception and travels as a favorite of some of Europe's liberal and enlightened best, Douglass developed a skewed vision of Europeans and their racial attitudes and actions" (115). Martin argues that Douglass's inability to recognize European racism was due in part to being exposed only to the most progressive segments of the European population.

As both Martin and William McFeely point out, however, Douglass sometimes was aware that he was being treated as a racial novelty. In Dublin, for example, he resented being exhibited by Lizzy Poole as an exotic black man (McFeely 122). At another point during his British tour, he joked to the white American abolitionist Francis Jackson: "It is quite an advantage to be a 'nigger' here. I am hardly black enough for the british taste, but by keeping my hair as wooly as possible—I make out to pass for at least half a negro at any rate" (qtd. in McFeely 131). This comment suggests that Douglass was able to fashion his public persona to some extent, but there would have been no need for him to play the role of the exotic Negro if there were no demand for it from British abolitionists. This exoticization was part of the colonialist view of native subjects as radically different from and inferior to the colonizers, and therefore as objects of scientific and popular curiosity. It also reflected the images of racial Others in scientific racism and minstrel shows, revealing how abolitionism could be combined with racist stereotypes in the minds of Britons as well as white Americans. Gretchen Gerzina speculates that in England, "Perhaps because the importation of black slaves slowed and finally ceased, and because the existing black English population commonly intermarried with whites, black people themselves once again acquired a kind of exoticism and sympathy when they were enslaved elsewhere" (203).[13] Although Douglass might have preferred to be treated as a curio than as a slave, the racism of many British abolitionists reduced him to an exotic racial Other in their eyes.

Douglass's references to British racism were echoed by several other African Americans who visited Britain. William Andrews points out that "more than a few black autobiographers discounted as myth the ideal of an England unblemished by racism" (*To Tell* 191), and he and Blackett cite the narratives of Zilpha Elaw, Samuel Ringgold Ward, Henry "Box" Brown, and James Watkins as examples (Andrews, *To Tell* 141, 191–92; Blackett, *Building* 158). Another narrative, John Brown's 1855 *Slave Life in Georgia*, comments, "There is prejudice against colour in England, in some classes, as well as more generally in America" (381).[14] Some visiting African American abolitionists pointed out this racism to their British hosts. The British abolitionist Mary Estlin, for instance, wrote in 1851: "Ellen Craft says nothing has astonished and pained her here so much as the amount of pro-slavery feeling among the English, the bigotry of the majority of professed Antislavery people, and the small number of actual working Abolitionists."[15]

Although British abolitionists were willing to help fugitive slaves, their hatred of slavery did not necessarily lead them to respect black people as equals or recognize individual differences among them. In her study of British antislavery female writers, Moira Ferguson notes: "As these author-agitators battled for emancipation, they wrote and spoke of Africans as a totalized, undifferentiated mass, denying the Continent and its people any authentic heterogeneity. Despite antislavery beliefs, they retained the view of slavers: they imagined slaves as essentially different from themselves. In fact, they drew on stereotypes of slaves and slavery, as well as Africans and Africa, that had become part of an orthodox perspective during one hundred and fifty years of antislavery protest. Slaves had become near-fixed embodiments of a Eurocentric sense of slave reality" (4). The presence of African Americans in Britain was important because it challenged British assumptions about black inferiority, reminded British abolitionists of who would suffer if they gave up their campaign for black freedom, and tested Britain's claim to be the friend of the slave.

In taking pride in the humanitarian virtue of their enlightened nation, many British abolitionists, like their white American counterparts, tended to overlook their own self-serving motivations and failed to interrogate their racial assumptions. In some cases they did not want to treat black people as equals so much as to show their moral righteousness by liberating them. Temperley speculates that "it would have been surprising if they had not enjoyed their sense of *richesse oblige* and the social status which indulging it brought them. Plainly many of them did. Nor does one have to look far to find traces of another element often associated with conspicuous generosity—guilt" (70). Aside from their self-righteousness, condescension, and sublimated guilt, some British abolitionists preferred to keep black people at a distance. Regarding the first wave of the British antislavery movement during the late eighteenth century, Deirdre Coleman notes: "Abolitionists were . . . alarmed by the growing black population, especially when the end of the American War of Independence brought many ex-slaves to London, swelling the numbers of black poor already living in ghettoes. The disastrous Sierra Leone scheme, drawn up by leading abolitionists like Granville Sharp and Clarkson in the mid to late 1780s, was clearly designed to rid London of its surplus blacks" (357). The abolition of West Indian slavery did not eliminate the racial attitudes that had supported bondage for over two centuries, and these attitudes left their mark on the British antislavery movement. Like their white American colleagues, many British abolitionists saw no contradiction between their opposition to slavery and their assumption that black people were fundamentally different from and inherently inferior to themselves.

British abolitionists who congratulated themselves on their antislavery virtue after the 1833 Emancipation Act not only failed to examine their racial presuppositions; they often ignored their nation's recent participation in slavery as well. One exception was Lucy Browne, who argued in an 1847 letter to the American abolitionist Maria Weston Chapman that her colleagues should recognize this complicity:

With respect to English influence on this question, it should certainly be used in destroying that slavery which was first introduced by Englishmen, and long encouraged if not enforced by our government. At the same time I think that every censure and remonstrance addressed by our nation to yours, should be sent in no spirit of self satisfied virtue but with the full consciousness of the many sins which still nationally disgrace us and with the sad remembrance of how few years have passed since, by the persevering and life long efforts of our best country men, that direst oppression ceased to find a sanction in our statute book and a place in our dominions. (qtd. in Taylor, *British* 314)

Coming from a British abolitionist, this reminder of Britain's past involvement in slavery had more credibility for other Britons than if it had come from an American. While the United States continued the "peculiar institution" after Britain had abolished it, Britons could not wash their hands of West Indian slavery easily, and while they became the foremost nation in the antislavery crusade, they had previously been the most prominent nation in the Atlantic slave trade (Walvin, *Making* 164). In addition, relatively few antislavery Britons criticized the nation's increasing commitment to colonialism.

British claims of abolitionist virtue also neglected several economic factors that both revealed the nation's complicity in slavery and enabled emancipation. First, the wealth of Liverpool and Bristol, which was based largely on the slave trade, undercut British abolitionists' boasts that their nation was unsullied by slavery. Second, the shift in Britain's economic base during the nineteenth century from plantation agriculture to industrial manufacture made abolition easier than it would have been if West Indian plantations were more central to the British economy (Martin, *Britain's* 77). Third, Britain's industrial economy included textile mills, which purchased southern cotton produced by slave labor and produced fabrics that were shipped to Africa and the West Indian slave colonies (Walvin, *Making* 159). The British public was also dependent upon other cheap slave-produced material, such as sugar, although many ardent abolitionists boycotted such morally tainted goods.[16] In addition, when West Indian slavery was abolished, planters received twenty million pounds to offset their losses, while slaves received no compensation for their unpaid labor (Fryer 43). The apprenticeship system that followed slavery in most colonies between 1834 and 1838 also benefited planters, many of whom abused the system, especially in Jamaica (Temperley 30–31, 34). These compensation and apprenticeship provisions rankled many British abolitionists, but many of them recognized that such concessions were needed to appease West Indian lobbyists before the Emancipation Bill could be approved (Temperley 17–18). Abolitionists were well aware of the economic interests of the planters and their lobbyists and MPs, and some of them catered to those interests by arguing that free labor was more profitable than slave labor.[17] Moreover, the importation of "indentured servants" from India to the British West Indies after abolition aided planters by providing cheap labor to replace emancipated slaves (Temperley 124). Cleansing their nation from the moral stain of slavery proved to be more difficult than many Britons realized.

The success of abolitionism in Britain was compromised not only by concessions to slaveholders and economic circumstances but also by its serviceability in the nation's colonization schemes. At first glance, abolititonism may appear to be antithetical to exploitative, profit-driven colonialist projects, but in fact they were often compatible. Ralph A. Austen argues that the efforts of British abolitionists in Africa pressured local economies to establish an export market that would benefit British manufacturers (130). While Austen's focus is on East Africa, he mentions that the same phenomenon would largely apply to Africa's Atlantic slave economy (132). An example of British abolitionism's connection to economic imperialism appears as early as 1789 in *The Interesting Narrative* of the Anglo-African abolitionist Olaudah Equiano. By emancipating slaves in Africa, Equiano argues, Britain could create an export market for its commodities: "As the inhuman traffic of slavery is to be taken into the consideration of the British legislature, I doubt not, if a system of commerce was established in Africa, the demand for manufactures will most rapidly augment, as the native inhabitants will sensibly adopt the British fashions, manners, customs, &c. In proportion to the civilization, so will be the consumption of British manufactures" (193). Helen Thomas sees this confluence of abolitionism and colonialist profit interests in the work of the British abolitionist poet William Cowper as well. In discussing Cowper's *The Task* (1785), she points out: "The poet's abolitionist ideology vies unresolvedly with his propagation of colonial ideology and despite his critique of the trade, the concept of empire still looms large. He therefore criticises the 'dissipation and effeminacy' which he believes has reduced the arch of the British Empire to a 'mutilated structure, soon to fall' and advances a mythic valorisation of Britain's redemptive role amongst the pagan nations" (78). Thomas's observation exemplifies Coleman's remark that "the ideology of anti-slavery is closely allied to that of colonization and imperialism" (345).[18] In this sense, abolitionism served British nationalism both morally and economically.[19] These economic and imperialist elements of British abolitionism helped the movement to thrive, though they were seldom acknowledged by the its leaders.

The success of British abolitionism was enabled not only by its compatibility with imperialism but also by the nation's tiny black population and Britain's distance from its West Indian plantations. Britain's minimal black population made it easier for its white citizens to support abolitionism than for white Americans, who feared that emancipating millions of slaves would lead to a labor surplus, competition, and lower wages. In addition, as American abolitionist John Collins argued in a letter to Garrison, because slavery never thrived on British soil, it was less difficult to be antislavery in Britain than in America: "In our country, too much, vastly too much has been made of English anti-slavery feeling and sympathy. They can talk against slavery because they have never been corrupted by its presence upon their own soil" (qtd. in Taylor, *British* 133). The fact that abolitionism faced less resistance in Britain than in America can be interpreted in two ways when comparing the two nations ethically. On the one hand, the greater acceptance of abolitionism among Britons suggests their moral superiority over Americans; on the other hand, American abolitionists were more courageous than their British colleagues because they faced more hostility. The English abolitionist Harriet Martineau concedes in *The Martyr Age of the United States* (1839) that "it is a totally different thing to be an abolitionist on a soil actually trodden by slaves, and in a far-off country, where opinion is already on the side of emancipation, or ready to be converted; where only a fraction of society, instead of the whole, has to be convicted of guilt; and where no interests are put in jeopardy but pecuniary ones, and those limited and remote" (3–4). Because slavery was extinct in Britain itself and a remote phenomenon for most Britons before the Emancipation Act, they were less emotionally and economically invested in slavery than white Americans, who were living in a nation that was based on slavery from its colonial infancy. These arguments were sometimes made by those, such as Nathaniel P. Rogers and John Greenleaf Whittier, who wished to deflate Britain's abolitionist self-image, but that image persisted nevertheless.

While abolitionism's nationalist rhetoric persisted into the late nineteenth century, the movement itself gradually faded. This decline, along with the gradual rise of a more aggressive racism in Britain, coincided with the introduction and subsequent popularity of American blackface minstrelsy and its increasingly proslavery and racist qualities, though the causal relationships among these things were by no means simple. Paradoxically, minstrelsy's triumph in Britain was enabled by both the strength and the decline of British abolitionism. That abolitionism and its critics made this triumph possible may partly be explained by minstrelsy's changing representations of slavery and African Americans during the mid-nineteenth century.

Jim Crow Jumps across the Atlantic

Although Parliament answered the Wedgwood medallion slave's question "Am I Not a Man and a Brother?" with a resounding affirmative by passing the Emancipation Act in 1833, Britain warmly welcomed a more comical black image when Rice jumped Jim Crow on the London stage three years later.[20] Rice's initial blackface performances at the Surrey Theatre appealed mainly to London laborers. They featured dancing, singing, vulgar humor, and racist ridicule, but they also voiced antislavery sentiments and allowed working-class audiences to identify or sympathize with Jim Crow (Lhamon, *Jump* 64–65, 70). The popularity of Rice's performances in London during the zenith of British abolitionism can partly be explained by early minstrelsy's attitude toward slavery. Many laborers appreciated early minstrelsy's celebration of black male tricksters and mockery of the bourgeoisie. By hinting at the darker side of slavery, mistrelsy appealed to antislavery workers and was compatible with popular antislavery sentiment in British society generally.

During the mid-1840s, the phenomenal success of the Virginia Minstrels and the Ethiopian Serenaders in Britain inspired many British performers to black up. Minstrelsy remained popular there throughout the nineteenth century, partly because it adapted to ideological shifts and tastes in British society, though its success had several other causes. Aside from its early antislavery leanings, minstrelsy might have been seen as a continuation of earlier British blackface traditions, particularly in its comedic use of the blackface mask. In the early 1820s, the English actor Charles Mathews popularized blackface comedy in Britain after his return from a visit to America. Nevertheless, during the 1830s and 1840s, minstrelsy was often described as a cultural import from the United States, which might have lent it the appeal of novelty. Another factor in minstrelsy's success was that it spread upward from the working classes to the middle and upper classes during the latter half of the 1840s (thanks in large part to the Ethiopian Serenaders), and spread outward from the stage to street busking and seaside resorts.[21]

As minstrelsy permeated British society, it increasingly shaped how Britons viewed persons of African descent and slavery. For instance, Andrew Ward writes that when the Fisk Jubilee Singers performed for Queen Victoria in 1873, "The dilemma of American freedmen was not one of Her Majesty's burning concerns. But she did love oddities and approached the Jubilee Singers' impromptu performance with the same undisguised curiosity with which she had once entertained the American midget 'General' Tom Thumb" (212–13). These "oddities," which were popularized by P. T. Barnum, shared cultural space with minstrelsy, and the queen's perception of the singers' performance was probably mediated by her familiarity with blackface entertainment. By 1873, minstrelsy offered a more consistently benign portrait of slavery and a more derogatory depiction of blacks than during abolitionism's heyday in the 1830s. This shift in minstrelsy both reflected and encouraged the drift away from abolitionism and the strengthening of earlier racist ideologies in British society after mid-century. As a result of these ideological turns in British society and in minstrelsy, Britons continued to embrace blackface entertainment, though on different terms.

The warm reception that Britons offered to both African American abolitionists and early blackface minstrelsy reveals their ambivalence toward black people, as well as the complexity and ambiguity of early minstrelsy itself. Although British attitudes toward black people in the 1830s and 1840s were not as negative as they would later become, many Britons during this time saw them as inferior, and this attitude was confirmed by Rice's depiction of the clownish Jim Crow and later comical blackface characters. However, many of early minstrelsy's depictions of black slaves were not far from the melodramatic abolitionist depictions of divided slave families or the traveling fugitive of slave narratives. Rice and his Jim Crow character took Britain by storm while West Indian slavery was in its final apprenticeship phase, a synchrony suggesting compatibility between abolitionism and early minstrelsy. Indeed, Jim Crow makes antislavery speeches in the 1836 play *Flight to America* (Lhamon, *Jump* 64), and these sentiments could be heard in Rice's song "Jim Crow's Trip to France": "De country for me, / Is de country whar de people / Hab make poor nigga free" (qtd. in Lhamon, *Raising* 205).

The ideological relations between minstrelsy and abolitionism in Britain before mid-century were further complicated by the nationalisms of British abolitionism and American minstrelsy. Britain's embrace of this American form of entertainment may seem unlikely, considering the contempt that many Britons felt toward upstart America and its purported lack of culture, the anti-British nationalism of American minstrelsy, and the conflict between minstrelsy's blackfaced clowns and British abolitionism's representations of slaves as noble heroes and pitiful victims. Despite all this, America's most unique form of entertainment soon became almost as popular in Britain as in the States. The diary entry of upper-class New Yorker Philip Hone for August 4, 1837, about Rice's success in Britain foreshadows the enormous popularity that minstrelsy would later enjoy in that country: "*'American Actors in England.'* American actors are now all the rage in England. Rice, the celebrated Jim Crow, has eclipsed the fame of Kean, Kemble, and Macready. He entertains the nobility at their parties; the ladies pronounce his black face 'the fairest of the fair,' and his bow legs and crooked shins the perfect 'line of beauty': and the wits of London have established 'the Crow Club' in honor of the Yankee buffoon" (270). Though Rice first established a working-class following at the Surrey Theatre, his fame soon spread to higher social registers, as Hone indicates, after he moved his act to the Adelphi.

Hone's attitude toward Rice and his character is equivocal at best, but the linkage between minstrelsy and America is clear, as was often the case in British discussions of early minstrelsy. Rice's American identity was foregrounded in London newspapers such as *The Spectator* and *The Observer*. Later, the American troupe the Ethiopian Serenaders and their British imitators tried to differentiate their performances from Rice by placing more emphasis on sentimentality and music while downplaying coarse humor and "Negro delineation," and these elements soon became distinguishing features of British blackface minstrelsy (Meer 150–51). As minstrelsy became more ingrained in British popular culture, some British minstrel performers de-emphasized the

American elements of the genre and claimed it as their own. In his 1928 memoir *Minstrel Memories,* for example, the English former blackface performer Harry Reynolds does not mention Charles Mathews's blackface performances, instead voicing a kind of blackface nationalism by noting that "although of American origin, the minstrel business was brought to its highest state of perfection in this country" (71). Nevertheless, the success of the more musical "British" style of minstrelsy was largely enabled by the popularity of Rice's more vulgar performances and by the success of the Virginia Minstrels during their 1843 British tour. By the late 1840s, minstrelsy's success in both nations ensured its position in Anglophone transatlantic culture.

During the late 1830s, however, Rice's "Yankee" identity, as well as the proletarian associations of his Jim Crow shtick, may partly explain the negative press that he sometimes received in several London weeklies. In July 1836, one editor wrote that Rice "is 'Jumping Jim Crow' to the tune of seventy pounds per week, and a free benefit! We saw this 'apology for a man,' a few evenings since, and notwithstanding our disgust, could not forbear laughing at the fellow's impudence. He is as great odor as ever with the carpenters, bricklayers, snobs, and sweeps of the six-penny gallery. We rejoice to hear that his days, in this country, are numbered" (qtd. in Lhamon, *Jump* 63). The *Spectator,* while initially positive toward Rice's Jim Crow performances in the autumn of 1836, had cooled toward him by the following April, deriding his "vulgar and humourless specimen of Nigger slang" ("The Theatres" 349). Likewise, during Rice's later sojourn in London, the *Theatrical Journal* excoriated him for his "very bad habit . . . of continually taking oaths" ("Metropolitan Theatres" 3). A few years later, during the heyday of the Ethiopian Serenaders, *Punch* printed several articles bemoaning the blackface mania in England inspired by the troupe and its many imitators.[22] "Mr. Punch" does not mention why he considers such entertainment a "disagreeable nuisance," except that it shows a decline in public taste, and the 1847 article "The Last of the Ethiopians" celebrates—quite prematurely—the demise of blackface entertainment in England.[23]

Despite the differences between American blackface minstrelsy and its more musical British counterpart, the class trajectory of minstrelsy in the two countries was roughly equivalent. In both nations, early blackface performances, either as solo acts or as troupes, were rowdy, proletarian, male affairs with lots of rough humor. However, the same drift that occurred in the United States in minstrel shows away from working-class crowds toward more "respectable" audiences also took place in Britain (Toll 37; Meer 24–25; Pickering, "White Skin" 73). During their 1846–47 British tour, the Ethiopian Serenaders shifted minstrelsy's focus from vulgar fun to music and senti-mentalism, and thereby helped to nudge upward the class demographics of minstrel show audiences. The *Era* contrasted Rice's "vulgar" blackface perfor-mances with those of later troupes, which were "quite above the more rough, and boisterous, and uncouth feats of Rice" ("Benefit" 12). The article assures readers that "the ETHIOPIAN SERENADERS have contrived to elevate the most primitive style of musical execution and composition to an art, a profession, and almost a fashion. . . . More perfect harmony, and better time, and more faultless melody, in the way of glee singing, have never been heard than in the composition of the Ethiopian Serenaders" (12). The article points out that this troupe aims to please a more upscale clientele than did Rice: "[They] have charmed the senses of even the *elite* of the British public for a long time past," and their performance "is likely to be free from sheer vulgarity . . . ; their good taste has secured to them the patronage of the first people of the land" (12).

By mid-century, as minstrel shows became more family-friendly and less proletarian, they also seemed to offer fewer opportunities for identification be-tween white viewers and blackface characters. By the 1860s, when minstrelsy had become ubiquitous in British theatre, its depictions of African Americans had become more denigrating and its portrayal of slavery had become less critical. One theatre notice from 1866, for example, mentions "the Brothers Dean, a particularly thick-lipped, hoarse-voiced, droll couple of darkies, who in visage and grinning as nearly resemble blacks of the coarsest grade as if they were genuine natives of Negroland" ("London Music Halls" 12). Unlike descriptions of earlier minstrelsy, this account shows no traces of working-class rebellion, cross-racial identification, or antislavery sentimentality. In this sense, British minstrelsy after mid-century tended to solidify racial boundaries rather than blur them.

Despite the racist elements of British abolitionism, this later form of min-strelsy might have ruffled some feathers during the height of the abolitionist movement in the 1830s. But by the 1860s, earlier British racial ideologies were no longer cloaked in humanitarian virtue and were fortified by the growth of scientific discourses on race that emphasized black inferiority; as a result, there were few objections to minstrelsy's denigration of black people. During visits in the 1860s, both Douglass and Sarah Parker Remond expressed concern about minstrelsy's popularity in Britain, which they implicitly linked to the rise in British racism (Blackett, *Building* 160, 191; *Divided* 43). Douglass was also perturbed by the souring of British and French racial sentiment in his 1886 European tour, of which he commented that although most Englishmen and Frenchmen remained "sound in their convictions and feelings concerning the colored race," American prejudices had begun to creep in with the blackface minstrels "who disfigure and distort the features of the Negro and burlesque his language and manners in a way to make him appear to thousands as more akin to apes than to men" (qtd. in Foner, *Frederick Douglass* 343–44).

This racism was neither simply a cause nor a result of minstrelsy's popularity. Nor was it merely indicative of the racial myopia and hypocrisy of a nation proud of its abolitionist tradition. We must also consider the apparent decline in British abolitionism after mid-century in relation to British racism. In many cases, skepticism toward abolitionism was not based on racist or proslavery sentiments but on disapproval of abolitionism's indifference toward the suffering of the British poor. But such skepticism was not solely motivated by concern for poverty in Britain. Catherine Hall argues: "Throughout the 1850s a more racist discourse became increasingly legitimate. The slow shift in public opinion can be registered in such arenas as the struggles over 'scientific' racism and the [1857] Indian Mutiny" ("Economy" 182). This racist discourse, which prevailed in both Britain and the United States, was based on previous beliefs about racial difference and included a racialist version of the Social Darwinism of Herbert Spencer, which many Britons used to predict the imminent demise of "inferior" nonwhite races and to justify the lack of organized efforts to help them. The "scientific racism" of George Gliddon, Samuel Morton, and Josiah Nott also claimed that there were inherent differences in intelligence and morality among different races. While British abolitionism of the 1830s and 1840s was limited by unexamined prejudice, the growing skepticism and indifference toward abolitionism of later decades allowed Britons to express such beliefs without being hampered by humanitarian rhetoric. A quarter century after American slavery was abolished, *Chambers's Journal of Popular Literature, Science, and Art* reflected: "A great deal was said in this country a generation or two ago, in condemnation of the sales of slaves in the United States, and in praise of our own superior virtue in this respect. Many of the persons who thus denounced their American brethren were not probably aware that it is not much more than a century since the same hateful practice was put an end to in England itself" (66; JJC). By looking back "a generation or two ago," this passage points out that abolitionist ardor had faded by the late nineteenth century, when Britain was frantically trying to paint the globe—especially Africa—as pink as possible. This imperial project was motivated not only by greed, but also by the beliefs that Africans could not govern themselves, languished in spiritual darkness, had no right to their land and natural resources, and could not be helped by humanitarian efforts.

The relationship between the rise in British racism and imperialism, the decline of abolitionism, and the vogue of minstrelsy was not one of simple causality, and it intersected with other ideological factors. Although abolitionism waned in Britain as minstrelsy became more ubiquitous, racist, and proslavery, the two phenomena rubbed elbows in British culture for decades. Here the work of Douglas Lorimer, J. S. Bratton, and John Blair helps us to untangle this convoluted knot of racial ideologies. Lorimer links these ideologies to philanthropic notions about black people, arguing that before the 1870s, "minstrels thrived upon an appeal to the antislavery sentiments of their audiences, as well as to the appreciation of their particular brand of music and comedy" (86). Bratton also traces the ideological links between abolitionism and minstrelsy in Britain, arguing that Britain's sense of moral superiority over the United States regarding slavery "dictated the reception and development of minstrel and black-face acts here. As soon as the Englishman could claim to be free of the taint of slave-holding, he turned self-righteously upon the Americans with a show of horror. The self-congratulation with which the popular audience at all levels viewed black people and put them into their songs is the strongest element in the image of the black man in British popular culture" (132). With British abolitionism's focus on American slavery after West Indian emancipation, Bratton contends, blackface minstrelsy led many Britons to associate blacks with slavery in the American South (132).

In addition, minstrelsy could confirm ethnocentric British notions of their own superiority, as Blair has argued in his comparison of the meanings of minstrelsy among the American and British publics. He points to differences resulting in part from the racial demographics of the two nations, observing that for the British public, black people were colonial subjects rather than a presence in the homeland, as was the case in the United States (60). An 1843 *London Times* article about minstrelsy argues that because Britons were further removed from black people than white Americans were, Britons could believe that America was degraded by its black population: "The spectators and auditors of the wonders exhibited at this theatre have during the week been amused by what is called an Ethiopian concert, by four Virginia minstrels, in which some of the aboriginal airs of the interior of Africa, modernized if not humanized in the slave states of the Unions, and adapted to ears polite, have been introduced by the musical conductor of the theatre" (qtd. in Blair 60). Blair asserts that the phrase "modernized if not humanized in the slave states" allows the English to "imagine themselves as having it both ways, feeling superior to the Americans as contributing merely a half-way station between Africa and civilization" (60). This interpretation is certainly plausible, given the self-congratulatory and nationalist rhetoric of British abolitionism enabled by the Emancipation Act a decade earlier.

Because of its negative representations of slavery, early minstrelsy was not only compatible with the antislavery spirit that permeated much of British society, but could even bolster it. Such compatibility enabled Britons to embrace minstrelsy alongside *Uncle Tom's Cabin*. Harry Reynolds notes that during the 1860s and 1870s, "Minstrel troupes were becoming very popular in England, and English folk were getting quite attached to the imitation nigger. In addition to this, Harriet Beecher Stowe's famous novel of *Uncle Tom's Cabin* was creating quite a sensation in this country and much sympathy was being expressed for the poor freed slave" (162). Reynolds's juxtaposition of the "imitation nigger" with *Uncle Tom's Cabin* demonstrates the ideological proximity of minstrelsy and antislavery literature, both of which had a huge impact on shaping the images of black people in a country that had outlawed slavery and contained a small black population. In fact, Henry Mayhew reported in 1862 that white beggars in London exploited antislavery sympathy by blacking up and impersonating fugitive slaves (425). While such blackface begging reveals the prevalence of minstrelsy in Britain, antislavery feeling was a crucial element of its popularity. Bratton observes that the popular sense of antislavery virtue among Britons allowed them "to extend sympathy for the oppressed slave to the black-face impersonators who were, as white Americans, more likely to be representatives of the oppressors" (133). George Rehin also links early minstrelsy to British antislavery sentiment: "In its earliest period, minstrelsy had been a contemporary of, and to an uncertain extent a reflection of, evangelical and humanitarian concern for the black slave. When anti-slavery found expression in minstrelsy, in the pathos of blackface clowns or the satire of minstrel fools, then it may have had a wider resonance, as plaint or protest, particularly among those in political bondage, e.g., the Irish or the disfranchised" ("Harlequin" 689). These parallels between abolitionism and minstrelsy were sometimes observed by the theatrical press. For example, a June 1843 article in the *Era*, printed around the time that Parliament abolished slavery in British India, described a Virginia Minstrels performance at London's Royal Adelphi Theatre and jocularly blamed the blackface craze on abolitionism: "The present rage for niggers came in, we opine, with the abolitionist bill, and if the abolitionists do but patronise the present personators of their favorite protégés, the Virginia Minstrels will make no bad thing of it" ("The Theatres" 5). Despite the facetious tone of this comment, there is some truth in the suggestion that minstrelsy's triumph in Britain was largely enabled by British abolitionists' interest in black people.

The similarities between minstrel shows and abolitionist entertainment in Britain went beyond shared rhetoric, imagery, and emotions; they sometimes also included similar structures and claims of authenticity. A playbill for antislavery panoramic entertainment performed at Royal Princess's Theatre during the 1850s offers a glimpse of how abolitionist entertainment borrowed structural and mimetic elements from minstrel shows:

NEGRO LIFE!
with the following scenes—
The African Village. The Slave Battle. The Embarkation of Prisoners. The Capture of the Slaver. The Rocks of the Coast of Cuba. The City and Harbour of Havannah (by Moonlight). A Slave Sale in the Havannah. The Sugar Plantations. Cotton Picking. Rice Plantation. The Fugitive Slave. The Forest on Fire. A Mississippi Scene. Planters House. Negro Village in the Plantation. Negro Dancing Festival.
The following Songs will be introduced:—

The African Village—The Chase of the Slave—Trader by a British Cruiser—
The Slave Sale—Come, who bids? (JJC)

Like many minstrel shows, this playbill claims to represent "Negro Life"
authentically, and it suggests the variety structure of the minstrel show. In
addition, the slave auction mentioned in one of the song titles, which was
a staple trope of abolitionist literature and drama, was also characteristic of
early minstrelsy's antislavery sentimentality.

Even the more racist elements of minstrelsy could share cultural space
with British antislavery sentiment. During the 1840s, for example, *Punch* often
criticized America for upholding slavery, even as it featured racist articles such
as "Nigger Peculiarities" and comic dialogues between black characters whose
dialect, malapropisms, and ignorance were staples of minstrel humor.[24] This
linkage reveals as much about Britain's philanthropic self-image, particularly
in relation to the United States, as it does about its attitudes toward African
Americans and West Indian blacks. Minstrelsy also left its mark on some of
the graphic depictions of African Americans in antislavery literature. This influence is especially apparent in English editions of *Uncle Tom's Cabin,* which
included illustrations of Tom, Topsy, and other dark-skinned slave characters by George Cruikshank, George Thompson, and others. Marcus Wood
explains that the English publisher John Cassell commissioned Cruikshank
to produce illustrations for an English edition of Stowe's novel, a decision
that "highlights the tensions and collusions between antislavery sentiment
and the rapidly evolving forms of Victorian racism which inflect much of the
English assimilation of the book" (173–74).[25] Many of the minstrel features of
the illustrations—like those of blackface stage adaptations of the novel—were
already present in the novel rather than being introduced by the illustrators.
For instance, in Cruikshank's illustration "Mose and Pete foil Shelby," the big
eyes, wide grins, and wild postures of the black figures are indistinguishable
from comical representations of blacks in minstrelsy and promote the notion
of black inferiority and Otherness in much the same way that minstrelsy did
(see Figure 2).

Because minstrel conventions were often used in antislavery contexts,
Britons seemed to welcome counterfeit minstrel blacks as readily as African
American abolitionists, with no apparent sense of contradiction. The Sep-

Figure 2: George Cruikshank, "Mose and Pete foil Shelby" (wood engraving). From *Uncle Tom's Cabin* (1852). Courtesy Marcus Wood.

tember 5, 1846, issue of the British *Western Times*, a paper that had already complimented Douglass and Garrison, made no distinction between black-faced white performers and African Americans in promoting a minstrel show: "The negroes of America, a light-hearted and joyous race, whenever they are treated with the least kindness, have a great love of music . . . songs, jest, and dance, beguile the brief intervals of rest from the alloted toil! Their music is unsophisticated, and their instruments simple and rude. Some of them have fine voices, and their minstrelsy occasionally exhibits traces of deep-feeling—but the grotesque and humorous are its chief characteristics" (qtd. in Blackett, *Building* 160). The fact that such romantic racialism was already so prevalent among the British public virtually guaranteed minstrelsy's success. This article was printed while the Ethiopian Serenaders were playing to packed houses in the provinces and ten years after Rice's debut in England, so most Britons were already familiar with minstrelsy. As minstrel shows confirmed British racial attitudes, including those permeating abolitionism, they did more to weaken British antislavery sentiment than to strengthen it. While the cause-effect relationship between minstrelsy and British racism is unclear, Blackett is right to emphasize minstrelsy's influence on British perceptions of visiting black abolitionists and African Americans generally.

Aside from the connections between British racism and minstrelsy, Britons embraced Jim Crow partly because they had blackened their faces long before Rice's arrival in 1836. Charles Mathews found success through blackface performance in the United States and Britain during the early 1820s, and Meer points out that his popularity paved the way for the blackface mania sparked by Rice in London during the following decade (150). Several historians have demonstrated that England's history of blackface entertainment stretches back much further than that. Rehin claims that the first recorded incident of blackface in England occurred in 1377, when mummers disguised as popes, cardinals, and African chieftains performed at the court of King Richard II ("Harlequin" 686). Later, Queen Anne ordered a black mask and participated in a performance of Ben Jonson's *Masque of Blacknesse* in 1605 and 1608 (Gerzina 69). Michael Rogin cites Anne as the "first white European in recorded history to black her face," and claims that "blackface occupies at its origins a privileged place in the conjoined histories of the English theater and the English court, imperial politics and Elizabethan culture. Courtiers had masked themselves as Moors since the early sixteenth century, as had blackface players on the English stage" (*Blackface* 19). Gretchen Gerzina speculates that the reason for blacking up in Renaissance England "was in the visual contrast and spectacle, but also probably in the assumption that more behavioural and verbal freedom could occur under the guise of a 'black' skin" (4). Hans Nathan describes the use of black masks in Renaissance and early Baroque drama, but sees the origins of American blackface in eighteenth-century England (3). The masked Harlequin of eighteenth-century English pantomime was borrowed from Italian *commedia dell'arte*, but it also recalled the masked performances of Elizabethan and Stuart England.[26] Other English precursors to nineteenth-century blackface include Thomas Southerne's 1695 stage adaptation of Aphra Behn's 1688 novel *Oroonoko*, Isaac Bickerstaffe's 1768 opera *The Padlock*, and George Coleman's 1787 opera *Inkle and Yarico* (Gerzina 7–8, 10; Cockrell 13).[27]

Thus, despite the claims of nineteenth-century American cultural critics that minstrelsy was indigenous to the United States, blackface performance was not originally American, and its existence in Britain during the seventeenth and eighteenth centuries may have contributed to its immense popularity among Britons after 1836.[28] Lhamon is correct in categorizing blackface entertainment as Atlantic culture that "grew out of the way [minstrel performers] proved those gestures in theatres across all regions of the United States and, across the Atlantic, from London to Dublin" (*Raising* 59). Regarding English minstrel show audiences, Cockrell speculates: "Could it be that audiences already possessed cultural knowledge of the tropes, even some of the structures and manners of expression? A zephyr from Great Britain, which succumbed to American minstrelsy after 1836, suggests that there might be some truth to this supposition, for English audiences were in a special position to appreciate minstrelsy: In many ways it simply brought images, symbols, and forms back home" (56). Likewise, Rogin argues, "When blackface took center stage two centuries later in the former English colony that was now the United States, it had traversed the path from Africa to England, from the Stuart court to the popular theater, to be born, in its own myth of origins, on the southern plantation" (*Blackface* 22). In that sense, blackface was not an American import to Britain, but a trope that in its repeated crossings of the ocean formed the Blackface Atlantic. Jim Crow's English heritage, along with his successful return to his ancestral homeland, gives him a transatlantic identity that undercuts American minstrelsy's chip-on-the-shoulder nationalism.

As a result of these transatlantic crossings, there is little to distinguish British minstrelsy from the American version in its depictions of black people. Comparisons between American and British minstrel show programs reveal similarities in styles of dress (either the rustic or the dandy), angular postures (especially for the banjo and bones players), and exaggerated, grotesque facial features. These overlappings show the power of minstrelsy in representing similar images of blacks, despite the varying colonial and racial histories of the two nations. Although African American minstrel troupes like Sam Hague's Georgia Minstrel Troupe and the Sable Harmonists (the former in blackface, the latter not) toured Britain after 1850 (Fryer 442), their popularity was based more on the British minstrelsy craze than on genuine interest in black performers. Harry Reynolds writes of Sam Hague: "He considered he would be giving the English people a treat by producing the genuine article direct from the plantation and showing them the difference between the real negro and the imitation, feeling satisfied that he would receive the support of all classes to witness a performance given by a troupe of real emancipated slaves, uneducated, untutored, and who only a few months before were merely considered to be goods and chattels" (162–63). However, Reynolds recalls, the English rejected the black performers as inferior entertainers. By preferring the imitation to the "real negro," Reynolds's account of Hague's black troupe points to minstrelsy's move from "authentic" delineation toward conventional entertainment, especially in a country whose tiny black population made the accuracy of such delineation rather irrelevant. Regarding the English reception of Hague's black troupe, John Blair observes, "Not even public sympathy for abolition could overcome the failure of the newly freed blacks to conform to the stereotypes and the high performance style that had long since been installed as standard on both sides of the Atlantic" (60). While Blair may be overestimating British support for abolitionism shortly after the American Civil War, he is correct to point out the conventionality of British minstrelsy. Peter Fryer points out that "on the whole, British audiences 'found the music and theatrics of the visitors from Georgia [many of whom were ex-slaves and not professionals] less entertaining than the performances of the professionals who blackened themselves for their stage appearances'" (442).[29] The preference of many British audiences for white minstrels in blackface over black performers reveals how profoundly minstrelsy had shaped the British public's theatrical expectations and racial views by the 1860s. The British fascination with blackface minstrelsy continued for another century. In fact, the BBC's *The Black and White Minstrel Show* featured white male performers in blackface as late as 1978, long past the time when such a program would have been accepted by U.S. television audiences, which included a larger proportion of black people than the BBC's audience.

Because minstrelsy was a transatlantic phenomenon, its racial meanings in Britain were formed by attitudes that were imported from the United States as well as by the connotations of blackface entertainment that were already in play in Britain before Rice's 1836 arrival. While such distinctions are virtually impossible to make with confidence, it would be a mistake to ignore these two different origins of the meanings of blackface in Britain. The valences of British minstrelsy were determined by a combination of antislavery and colonialist attitudes, pantomime and other English and European forms of entertainment, and the American mannerisms and accent of Jim Crow. Therefore, we need to recognize the complexity of British minstrelsy and examine it as part of the Blackface Atlantic. Fortunately, several scholars have recently provided valuable insights on minstrelsy as a transatlantic phenomenon.[30] Although many of these analyses rightly urge us to avoid reducing minstrelsy's popularity in Britain to racism, a few scholars erroneously downplay or ignore the ideological contexts of minstrelsy's depictions of black people. Rehin, for instance, argues: "Many modern scholars incriminate [minstrelsy] for creating or reinforcing widespread racist attitudes. Often these latter are not evidenced independently, but minstrelsy's very success is taken to demonstrate the high prevalence of racism. The assumption underlying this circular argument is that minstrelsy's primary appeal rests on an invidious racial mimicry inherent in, and essential to, the genre" ("Blackface" 34). Rehin mentions earlier English blackface traditions, such as mummers' plays (21), which may partly explain the success of blackface minstrelsy in Victorian England. Rehin later attributes much of the blackface buskers' appeal to their performative skills, concluding: "Racial prejudice does not have to be postulated as a cause or an effect of the popularity of the blackface buskers, nor was street minstrelsy in Britain so simply and directly a reinforcement of derogatory attitudes and images as many modern statements aver" (34). In an earlier article, Rehin argues that minstrelsy's appeal in Britain was not based primarily on racism, as it was for white Americans:

> The black population of Victorian Britain, which in ratio grew smaller with time, posed no social threat to the mass of ordinary folk, among whom they were largely assimilated culturally and integrated socially. . . . The appeal of "nigger minstrelsy" cannot be attributed to a defensive or aggressive racist psychology among the whole populace, as it has been in the American case. . . . The British did not have a strong emotional need for a derogatory, minstrel image of the Negro to assuage guilt, reduce fear, cope with the threats of political equality and economic competition, or otherwise defend themselves against an alien race or social system. ("Harlequin" 688–89)

Rehin goes on to claim that "blackface make-up . . . was also part of a folk tradition in which it had no racial connotation, a factor which may also help account for widespread acceptance of minstrelsy" ("Harlequin" 689). Certainly, these older folk elements formed part of minstrelsy's appeal in England, though they do not prove the absence of racial meanings of minstrelsy there.

Like Rehin, Bratton makes a valid argument that the meanings of minstrelsy in Britain differed from those in the United States partly because of the racial demographics of British society, though in doing so she also fails to investigate the impact of British racial attitudes on minstrelsy: "The most obvious difference between British and American popular consciousness and cultural needs was, of course, that the average Englishman had no need of an art form which would help him deal with complex problems of identity and confrontation with a black population. He had no such problems, and experienced no such confrontation" (128). Such would not have been the case in late eighteenth-century London, when African Americans who had fought for Britain in the Revolutionary War emigrated to that metropolis, or in Liverpool and Bristol during the early nineteenth century, when black sailors were a visible element of the population. Since then, however, Britain's black population had declined (Fryer 236), and thus there were fewer referents for British minstrel audiences than for white American audiences. As a result, British minstrel shows purported to represent African American slaves (Lorimer 90) rather than black people in Britain itself.

While we need to consider how minstrelsy's reception in Britain was shaped by its lack of a large black population as well as Jim Crow's British ancestors, it is equally important to remember the legacy of racial attitudes that permeated British abolitionism and the antislavery impulses of early minstrelsy. Despite their problematic denial that the British reception of minstrelsy was uncontaminated by racism, both Rehin and Bratton recognize the influence of antislavery on the British reception of minstrelsy. Rice's London debut occurred when one of the greatest victories of the antislavery movement was still fresh in the public mind, and the racialism structuring abolitionist depictions of slaves during this period was bound to shape British perceptions of the minstrel negro. It was also inevitable that the representations of Africans propagated by colonialism and the missionary movement influenced British responses to minstrel shows and songs. Given the anti-black racism in mid-nineteenth-century Britain,[31] Lorimer is correct to surmise that while minstrelsy did not form British racial attitudes, its popularity strengthened them (90–91).

Though some of minstrelsy's meanings in Britain were influenced by early blackface traditions, the fact that such traditions predate the arrival of American minstrelsy does not necessarily mean that they were devoid of racial meaning. Regarding the Harlequin stock character of Italian *commedia dell'arte* and English pantomime, Henry Louis Gates, Jr. cites three scholars— Jean-François Marmontel and Jean-Pierre Claris de Florian in the late eighteenth century and Pierre-Louis Duchartre in 1966—who have "attribute[d] the blackness of his mask and its patently 'negroid' features to the mask of blackness of the African" (51). Furthermore, Gates writes, "When we recall that early Harlequin figures wore a phallus, the connections between him and Western representations of the African are even stronger" (51). This claim is borne out when one compares illustrations of Harlequins from eighteenth- and early nineteenth-century English pantomime, or their Italian forerunners, with illustrations on sheet music covers for some minstrel songs, in which banjos and bats are positioned suggestively in relation to blackfaced figures. Harlequin's black mask and the phallic position of his magical bat suggest the same connection between blackness and male sexuality as do the swords and banjos and the black faces of the figures on the sheet music cover of "Old Dan Emmit's Original Banjo Melodies" (see Figures 3 and 4).

Aside from the possible racial connotations of pre-Victorian English blackface, racial attitudes played a greater role in shaping Victorian perceptions of minstrelsy itself than Rehin claims. Like Rehin, Michael Pickering refuses to reduce minstrelsy's appeal in Britain to racism, but he critiques Rehin for downplaying the role of anti-black racism in British reactions to blackface: "His location of the 'nigger' minstrel within a long clowning tradition is grossly unhistorical. Any tradition as a repository of cultural elements associated with the past, if it has any vital active force within the present, has to prove adaptable to changing conditions and circumstances, and so, if not moribund or dead, operates of necessity in a dialectical relationship with the needs of what is already new or required for the future" ("Mock Blacks" 220). Elsewhere, Pickering rejects Rehin's implication that "the coincidence of the whole blackface phenomenon in Britain with the consolidation and world-wide ascendancy of Empire was simply fortuitous, an accident of history. While it would be incorrect to assume any neatly aligned correlation, the 'nigger' minstrel show was not something hermetically cocooned, sealed off from society in its own uncontaminated space" (218). British perceptions

Figure 3: John Rich as Harlequin Dr. Faustus in *The Necromancer,* 1723. Robert Gould Shaw Collection, Harvard Theatre Collection, Houghton Library, TS 937.3.3F, vol. 1.

of minstrelsy were probably influenced by the Harlequin figure and other early blackface conventions, but we must also examine how Britons' attitudes toward African Americans, slavery, and American culture also shaped their understanding of the minstrel mask. In another article, Pickering points out that blackface minstrelsy in England distinguished itself from previous masking traditions, such as mumming, by the element of "negro impersonation," but that this element became entangled with previous masking practices and meanings in Britain ("White Skin" 70, 72, 78–79). More recently, Pickering has examined the connection between blackface clowns in minstrelsy and clowns in pantomime and circuses, arguing that while the non-blackface clown encouraged audiences to laugh at the subversion of social norms, the blackface clown emphasized racial ridicule instead ("Blackface Clown" 167). Although some of the appeal of "nigger minstrels" may be traced to earlier clown traditions in British entertainment, we cannot deny that racism played a significant part in this popularity.

For British audiences, then, blackface minstrelsy was a combination of the old and the new. One identifiable element was its brand of comedy, which Lott notes was largely derivative of the stage Irishman shtick of British theatre (95), though Britons would have been familiar with the musical and terpsichorial

Figure 4: Sheet music cover for "Old Dan Emmit's Original Banjo Melodies," c. 1843 (detail). Courtesy Lilly Library, Indiana University, Bloomington, IN.

elements of blackface minstrelsy as well. Pickering observes that the "idioms of Afro-American music and dance were in fact fused in minstrelsy with a mélange of British influences (Irish jigs, Scotch reels, English melodies, and dance tunes)" ("White Skin" 83).[32] Though the banjo originated in West Africa, the fiddle was obviously familiar to Britons, and the tambourine somewhat resembled the Irish *bodhran*. Furthermore, many American minstrel performers traced their ancestry to the British Isles. Rice was a son of an English immigrant, and Dan Emmett, Dan Bryant, Matt Campbell, Billy Emerson, George Christy, Joel Walker Sweeney, and Matt Peel were Irish-American, as was Stephen Foster (Toll 176; Lott 95). Thus, any claim that blackface minstrelsy was uniquely American sidesteps the fact that American culture included English, Irish, and Scottish influences, and that British audiences may have recognized elements of their own folk cultures returning to them in the form of minstrel shows.

Although minstrelsy's popularity in Britain was enabled partly by these earlier blackface practices and by its overlap with antislavery representations of blackness, it both reflected and encouraged the increasing virulence of racial prejudice in British society and negated whatever energy remained in the antislavery movement. These ideological shifts, as well as the common cultural terrain shared by minstrelsy and abolitionism, are apparent in several works by Victorian authors. The following chapter examines the complex relationships among abolitionism, racism, and blackface minstrelsy in the novels of William Makepeace Thackeray and Charles Dickens, the travel writings of Dickens, Frances Anne Kemble, and Anthony Trollope, and Thomas Carlyle's "Occasional Discourse on the Nigger Question."

Race, Abolitionism, and Blackface Imagery in Victorian Literature

Although Britain's black population declined throughout the first two-thirds of the nineteenth century, both abolitionism and minstrelsy propagated countless representations of black people, both in literature and throughout British culture generally. Not surprisingly, these representations were often found in works that depicted and commented on slavery and abolitionism, two issues that even after the abolition of West Indian slavery remained important for many British readers and the authors who wrote for them. In Victorian novels and travelogues that dealt with these issues, the depictions of black people were often structured by blackface imagery and minstrel conventions, regardless of whether those works were antislavery and anti-abolitionist. This fact should not surprise us when we remember that both abolitionists and their critics often revealed racial attitudes that informed minstrelsy's depictions of black people. On one end of the spectrum, Kemble's deployment of blackface conventions in depicting slaves and slave culture in *Journal of a Residence on a Georgia Plantation in 1838–39* (1863) demonstrates how minstrelsy could be used for antislavery purposes. On the other hand, the use of blackface tropes in satirizing philanthropy and abolitionism in Dickens's *Bleak House* (1852–53) and Thackeray's *Vanity Fair* (1847–48) and *The Adventures of Philip* (1862) was made possible by the emergence of anti-abolitionist and racist attitudes in minstrelsy. The fact that minstrelsy was put to use in all four works points not only to minstrelsy's ideological versatility, but also to the ideological changes within minstrelsy and British society alike. Kemble wrote her *Journal* during the late 1830s, when minstrelsy and abolitionism often shared common ground, but minstrelsy's racism and hostility toward abolitionism became more pronounced as the century progressed. Thus, minstrelsy later proved to be useful in attacking abolitionism, as can be seen in the aforementioned novels by Dickens and Thackeray, as well as in Carlyle's "Occasional Discourse on the Nigger Question" (1849) and Trollope's *The West Indies and the Spanish Main* (1859)—all of which were written while British abolitionism was gradually losing momentum. In representing and critiquing abolitionism, these authors often borrowed elements from blackface minstrelsy that were familiar to their readers. Their uses of minstrelsy were based less on the meanings of blackface in Britain before Rice's 1836 London debut and more on the meanings of blackface in American minstrelsy. While these works evince an array of attitudes toward black people, slavery, and abolitionism, they also parallel the intensification of racism and decline of abolitionism around mid-century, and they belie Britain's enduring reputation of antislavery virtue. They also reveal the ideological damage wreaked by minstrelsy's increasingly derogatory depictions of African Americans and West Indian blacks.

Although Kemble's *Journal* was first published in 1863, it demonstrates the possible uses of blackface elements in an antislavery text. Kemble and her husband, Pierce Butler, whom Kemble had married without knowing that he would inherit a Georgia plantation with slaves, moved to the plantation in 1838, and the *Journal* chronicles her sojourn there. Kemble finally decided to publish it during the Civil War in an attempt to counter rising British support for the Confederacy (Fladeland, *Men* 396–97). Her experiences on the plantation led her to oppose slavery, and while she often borrows abolitionist depictions of slaves, she also found in minstrelsy a vocabulary for representing slave behavior and culture. However, she uses her observation of "authentic" black behavior on the plantation to dismiss northern minstrel imitations of it. Kemble's deployment of minstrelsy's vocabulary is obvious in one passage, in which the lively contortions of black dancers and musicians test the limits of her descriptive abilities and leave her nearly breathless with laughter:

> I have seen Jim Crow—the veritable James: all the contortions, and springs, and flings, and kicks, and capers you have been beguiled into accepting as indicative of him are spurious, faint, feeble, impotent—in a word, pale Northern reproductions of that ineffable black conception. It is impossible for words to describe the things these people did with their bodies, and, above all, with their faces, the whites of their eyes, and the whites of their teeth, and certain outlines which either naturally and by the grace of heaven, or by the practice of some peculiar artistic dexterity, they bring into prominent and most ludicrous display.

The languishing elegance of some—the painstaking laboriousness of others—above all, the feats of a certain enthusiastic banjo-player, who seemed to me to thumb his instrument with every part of his body at once, at last so utterly overcame any attempt at decorous gravity on my part that I was obliged to secede; and, considering what the atmosphere was that we inhaled during the exhibition, it is only wonderful to me that we were not made ill by the double effort not to laugh, and, if possible, not to breathe. (96–97)[1]

Kemble's depiction of the "veritable James" reveals a fascination with black physicality (note her attention to faces, eyes, and teeth) and terpsichorean ability that was typical of minstrel audiences. The comedic element of this performance was also consistent with blackface performance. And while this drollery did not contribute to Kemble's exposé of slavery's horrors, it did not undermine her purpose either.

Although Kemble's account of the slave dancers and musicians may have seemed genuine because they were not professional performers, the purported authenticity of this performance and her description of it is undercut in several ways. Her witnessing of Jim Crow ("I have seen . . . ") validates his existence, yet her use of the word "veritable" is negated by the more formal and seemingly inauthentic "James."[2] Moreover, the possibility that "certain outlines" of the slaves' faces and bodies are not natural but due to a "peculiar artistic dexterity" suggests the artificiality of their performance. The performers might have understood that Kemble's expectations of black behavior were inflected by blackface conventions and tailored their performance accordingly in order to entertain her. Kemble's delight in minstrelsy—in fact, as an actress she later sang a minstrel song on a Liverpool stage in 1847 (Broadbent 159–60)—was not shared by all white abolitionists, British or otherwise, but she was not the only Briton who opposed slavery yet perceived and represented African Americans in terms of minstrel imagery. While her journal, like other antislavery travel narratives about the South, purports to describe "American slavery as it is" (to quote the title of Theodore Weld's famous abolitionist tract), here Kemble attempts to describe the "veritable James" Crow on the Georgia plantation. In doing so, she invokes the minstrel stage even while distancing her own description from the counterfeit depictions of African Americans by northern white minstrels. Kemble's choice of minstrel conventions to depict the slaves' performance demonstrates how minstrelsy could be co-opted in antislavery texts and how it shaped British perceptions and representations of black people, behavior, and culture.[3]

A later description of "veritable negro minstrelsy" in Kemble's journal makes an amateur attempt at ethnomusicology through the ideological lens of romantic racialism, which was prevalent throughout both minstrelsy and antislavery discourse. Here, she also inverts minstrelsy's pattern of whites imitating blacks:

> I believe I have mentioned to you before the peculiar characteristics of this veritable negro minstrelsy—how they all sing in unison, having never . . . attempted or heard any thing like part-singing. . . . That which I have heard these people sing is often plaintive and pretty, but almost always has some resemblance to tunes with which they must have become acquainted through the instrumentality of white men; their overseers or masters whistling Scotch or Irish airs, of which they have produced by ear these *rifacciamenti*. The note for note reproduction of "Ah! vous dirai-je, maman?" in one of the most popular of the so-called negro melodies with which all America and England are familiar, is an example of this very transparent plagiarism; and the tune with which Mr. ——'s rowers started him down the Altamaha, as I stood at the steps to see him off, was a very distinct descendant of "Coming through the Rye." (127–28)

Kemble's comments on the singing of slaves may bring to mind Douglass's statement in his 1845 *Narrative* that northern whites misunderstand the sorrow songs of slaves. She implies that this "negro minstrelsy" is more authentic than its white imitations on the minstrel stage, but instead of dismissing minstrelsy outright, she reverses its mimetic pattern of whites imitating blacks by describing black mimicry of whites. Her notion of the natural mimetic proclivities of blacks is paralleled by Zip Coon's ludicrous appropriation of white male fashion in minstrelsy. Her argument contradicts her earlier comment about slaves singing in unison rather than in harmony (an element of much European group singing) and negates the possibility of black originality. This is not to argue that slave music was purely African and uninfluenced by European music; rather, it is to say that Kemble neglects how slaves mixed

African and European musical traditions in creating new ones.

When Kemble moves from the tunes to the language of slave songs, her comments on their unlettered, nonsensical, and humorous nature could be based on her familiarity with the nonsense lyrics of minstrel songs:

> The words, however, were astonishingly primitive, especially the first line, which, when it burst from their eight throats in high unison, sent me into fits of laughter.
>
> > "Jenny shake her toe at me,
> >
> > > Jenny gone away; . . .
> >
> > Hurrah! Miss Susy, oh!
> >
> > > Jenny gone away; . . ."
>
> What the obnoxious Jenny meant by shaking her toes, whether defiance or mere departure, I never could ascertain, but her going away was an unmistakable subject of satisfaction; and the pause made on the last "oh!" before the final announcement of her departure, had really a good deal of dramatic and musical effect. Except the extemporaneous chants in our honor, . . . I have never heard the negroes on Mr. ——'s plantation sing any words that could be said to have any sense. (128–29)

Kemble's obtuse gloss on this song, which apparently misses the sexual innuendo of "Jenny shaking her toe," resembles Stowe's comment on "one of those unmeaning songs, common among the slaves" in *Uncle Tom's Cabin* (297). In her description of another slave song, Kemble again emphasizes its apparent lack of meaning:

> Another very pretty and pathetic tune began with words that seemed to promise something sentimental—
>
> > "Fare you well, and good-by, oh, oh!
> >
> > I'm goin' away to leave you, oh, oh!"
>
> but immediately went off into nonsense verses about gentlemen in the parlor drinking wine and cordial, and ladies in the drawing-room drinking tea and coffee, etc. (129)

Instead of describing black expression as plagiarism, Kemble implies that the language of slave songs is so unlike the English of white people that it makes no sense to her. Many minstrel songs imitated plantation singing, whose words white people often saw as nonsensical, though in this instance Kemble does not explicitly frame her description of the lyrics in terms of minstrelsy. Her focus on lyrics she can't understand distracts her from a rather obvious theme of both abolitionist and minstrel representations of slavery in the last two lines she quotes (and possibly the last line in the song about Jenny)—that is, the sentimental depiction of the forced separation of slave couples and families. Kemble also echoes the romantic racialism of minstrelsy and antislavery discourse by claiming that black people have a "peculiar musical sensibility" and "are just the sort of people over whom a popular musical appeal to their feelings and passions would have an immense power" (129). Overall, Kemble's use of blackface conventions in describing plantation dance and song reveals minstrelsy's limitations in interpreting slave culture.

Dickens's observations of African Americans are less intimate than Kemble's, and his attitudes range from antislavery to anti-abolitionism in his works, though his skepticism toward abolitionism was motivated not by support for slavery but by his perception of its hypocrisy. Like Kemble, however, Dickens was familiar with minstrelsy, as can be seen in two of his works: he describes a famous black minstrel dancer in his travelogue *American Notes*, and he relies on blackface elements in his satire of abolitionism in his novel *Bleak House*. Before turning to those minstrel moments, however, we should examine his attitudes toward African Americans, slavery, and abolitionism in his works in order to understand the ideological connotations of his references to minstrelsy. The first chapters of *Bleak House* were published serially during the same month that *Uncle Tom's Cabin* was published in the United States in book form, but it is not the first novel in which Dickens comments on abolitionism, and his earlier novels express conflicting attitudes toward it. In Chapter 7 of *The Posthumous Papers of the Pickwick Club* (1836–37), the narrator mocks abolitionists' hypocritical insensitivity to poverty in Britain by mentioning that the people of Muggleton "have presented, at divers times no fewer than one thousand four hundred and twenty petitions, against the continuance of negro slavery abroad, and an equal number against any interference with the factory system at home" (99). Dickens shifts from critiquing the moral narrowness of British abolitionism to satirizing American anti-abolitionism in *Martin Chuzzlewit* (1843–44). Here, an Anglophobic American group called the Watertoast Sympathizers support "a certain Public Man in Ireland" (360)—perhaps Daniel O'Connell—because of his criticism of England, but they are furious when they discover that he is "the advocate . . . of Nigger emancipation!" (361). Thus, it seems from these two works that Dickens was as critical of slavery and American anti-abolitionism as he was of British abolitionism and its disregard of the plight of poor wage laborers.

Dickens's antislavery beliefs emerge most strongly in the forty-four run-away slave advertisements that he includes in the "Slavery" chapter in *American Notes* (1842), though his depictions of slaves and the cruelty they suffer is indirect. His descriptions of fugitive slaves reveal that they were branded, scarred, and weighed down by iron bars and collars. He also presents and criticizes three categories of people who defended slavery, refutes the argument that "public opinion" prevents slaveholders from abusing their slaves, and claims that the brutality of slavery encourages whites to act violently against each other. While he encourages white readers to sympathize with slaves in this chapter, he distances himself from these slaves textually by quoting runaway slave notices written by their masters rather than observing slaves himself or including their voices. Overall, the chapter does more to denounce white Americans for their duplicitous egalitarian cant than to recognize the humanity of black people or endorse abolitionism. In this respect, the chapter resembles Frances Trollope's *Domestic Manners of the Americans*, which also uses antislavery rhetoric to expose American hypocrisy rather than to promote abolitionism.

This distinction between criticizing slavery and supporting abolitionism helps us understand Dickens's mockery of philanthropic endeavors in *Bleak House*. His satire is much more extensive here than in *The Posthumous Papers of the Pickwick Club*, and it parallels the shift in Britain away from abolitionism after mid-century, as well as the growing concern with the poverty of English laborers, a problem that Dickens addressed a year later in his novel *Hard Times*. Through Mrs. Jellyby and Mrs. Pardiggle, Dickens implies that female philanthropists neglect their household duties and contribute to their children's misery. Both women lack traditional feminine qualities (such as discretion and submissiveness) and bodily features. Mrs. Pardiggle is described as "a formidable style of lady, with spectacles, a prominent nose, and a loud voice, who had the effect of wanting a great deal of room. And she really did, for she knocked down little chairs with her skirts that were a quite a great way off" (94). As Timothy Carens has observed, Dickens implies that Mrs. Pardiggle's interference in public affairs and her failure as a housekeeper indicates her lack of her feminine propriety (123). Similarly, in the "Telescopic Philanthropy" chapter, Mrs. Jellyby is so obsessed with her "African project" of educating the natives of Borrioboola-Gha and establishing coffee plantations in that faraway land that her house has become "not only very untidy, but very dirty" (35).[4] Her neglected children may be read as stand-ins for the English poor, ignored by negrophilic middle-class English abolitionists. In this sense Dickens links the female philanthropist's lack of feminine domesticity with the "wage slavery" rhetoric often invoked by critics of abolitionism, even though he does not defend slavery and had criticized proslavery arguments in *American Notes* a decade earlier.

Although Mrs. Jellyby's project is not explicitly abolitionist, abolitionism was closely related to missionary work and other philanthropic movements, and many Britons of Dickens's time lumped them together (Rice, "Missionary Context" 150–51; Lorimer 71). Of this episode, C. Duncan Rice remarks that Dickens's parody of British philanthropy is

> symptomatic of a sharp change in British attitudes to helping the Negro, but it is significant that it does not imply the slightest approval of slavery. It is entirely consistent with his lifelong distrust of Exeter Hall philanthropy, and his anxiety that foreign good causes would divert attention from pressing domestic problems. Even in 1853, it did not go without bitter abolitionist criticism. However, the significance of the Mrs Jellyby episode is not that it was new for Dickens, but that the changed atmosphere of the decade made it acceptable for a respectable middle-class novelist to deride abolitionists in a way which would have been unthinkable in the 1830s or even the early 1840s. ("Literary Sources" 330–31)

Rice is correct to argue that mockery of abolitionism did not always entail support for slavery; it was sometimes a reaction to abolitionist apathy toward poverty at home. While one might surmise that Dickens reversed his views of slavery during the decade since he had exposed the evils of slavery in *American Notes*, a more plausible explanation for this apparent discrepancy is that his ridicule of philanthropy in *Bleak House* was a critique of abolitionist indifference toward domestic poverty rather than an endorsement of slavery.

Dickens excoriates British abolitionists' disregard for the suffering of the English poor in *Bleak House* by casting Mrs. Jellyby's children as "white slaves" and contrasting them to the black slaves with whom "telescopic" philanthropists are obsessed. Not surprisingly, Mrs. Jellyby's daughter Caddy resents being impressed into her mother's philanthropic project and living in an unkempt house, later declaring, "I won't be a slave all my life" (173). Carens notes that by seeing herself as a slave, Caddy "appropriates a trope often used by critics of industrialism to focus attention on the 'white' slaves, the disenfranchised workers of England's factories" (127). Because the phrase "white slavery" was often used for anti-abolitionist as well as anti-capitalist purposes, it works well in Dickens's satire of British abolitionism. He elsewhere uses Caddy to further his parody when she tells the narrator Esther Summerson, "Talk of Africa! I couldn't be worse off if I was a what's-his-name—man and a brother!" (171). Again, the rhetoric of white slavery works against abolitionist discourse. By having Caddy compare herself to a nameless abolitionist icon rather than an actual slave, Dickens points to the abstract and stereotypical nature of philanthropic sympathy toward slaves. Moreover, the fact that the Jellyby children are more closely related to their mother than are the natives of Borrioboola-Gha may remind readers that British abolitionists were ignoring the suffering of their own poor and were interested only in a distant group of racial Others with whom they had no kinship.

In *Bleak House*, "telescopic philanthropy" comes under fire for its self-righteousness and ineffectiveness as well as its damaging domestic effects and its indifference toward the English poor. Mr. Jarndyce observes that "there were two classes of charitable people; one, the people who did a little and made a great deal of noise; the other, the people who did a great deal and made no noise at all," and the narrator suspects Mrs. Pardiggle (and, we are led to infer, Mrs. Jellyby) "to be a type of the former class" (94). The sanctimonious philanthropy of these two women is dangerous because it leads them to neglect their proper gender role as housekeepers, but in Mrs. Jellyby's case, it is also unsuccessful and misplaced. Toward the end of the novel, we learn that she "has been disappointed in Borrioboola-Gha, which turned out a failure in consequence of the king of Borrioboola wanting to sell everybody—who survived the climate—for Rum" (816). Here Dickens takes a swipe not at white slave traders, but at ungrateful, dissipated African chiefs who participate in the slave trade, as well as philanthropic women who are foolish enough to try to help them. His remarks echo the belief of many mid-century Britons that the decline of Jamaica's sugar economy after emancipation signaled the failure of emancipation (Temperley 115–16). In addition, because West Indian slavery had been abolished two decades ago, Dickens, like many Britons, may have felt that abolitionism was no longer relevant to Britain.[5]

Dickens uses blackface elements in his satire of abolitionism in *Bleak House* in order to set up comparisons between black slaves and British laborers. This feature of the novel reminds us of a rather obvious point: while the racial views of British abolitionists often overlapped with those of minstrel performers and songwriters, Dickens's use of blackface tropes in *Bleak House* demonstrates how minstrelsy was easily linked to critiques of abolitionism as it lost the antislavery edge of its early phase. He invokes the minstrel mask by having the faces of some of his characters darkened, linking these blackened faces to his implied argument that British philanthropy (particularly that of women) toward black people distracted them from problems not only closer to home but also in the home. One minstrel trope that Dickens employs in his satire of philanthropy is "racechange,"[6] particularly in portraying the neglected children of the female philanthropists Mrs. Jellyby and Mrs. Pardiggle. Mrs. Jellyby's philanthropy is so "telescopic" and misguided that she inadvertently makes her daughter's skin as black as any African's. Esther describes the daughter Caddy, whom her mother compels to serve as her secretary, as a "jaded and unhealthy-looking" girl and remarks, "I suppose nobody ever was in such a state of ink" (35). The fact that Caddy needs vinegar to remove the ink suggests that her forced labor blackens her more permanently than did the burnt cork of white minstrel performers, though she can never be black enough to enjoy the attention that her mother lavishes on the natives of Borrioboola-Gha. Caddy is not the only Jellyby child whose whiteness is compromised by her mother's philanthropic zeal; she later reports that her father calls his children "Wild Indians" who "are very unfortunate in being Ma's children" (387). Likewise, Mrs. Pardiggle's son Egbert, who was coerced to give money to the Tockahoopo Indians, is so resentful that when his mother mentions his generosity, Esther remarks, "I could really have supposed Egbert to be one of the most baleful members of that tribe, he gave me such a savage frown" (95). Esther also mentions that the face of each of the five Pardiggle sons, "as the amount of his contribution was mentioned, darkened in a peculiarly vindictive manner" (95).

Dickens suggests a possible link between the racechange trope and the issue of miscegenation, a concern for anti-abolitionists as well as a frequent theme in minstrelsy. The racechanges that these young characters undergo is not always temporary; in fact, Caddy's acquired blackness even carries over to her baby, who "had curious little dark veins in its face, and curious little dark marks under its eyes, like faint remembrances of poor Caddy's inky days" (632). The baby's strange, inky heredity suggests that Caddy's enslavement and blackening by Mrs. Jellyby has become the infamous drop of "black blood" that purportedly made a person black and left its trace on one's descendants. Caddy's racechange, as well as her child's, may remind us of proslavery accusations that abolitionists promoted and even engaged in miscegenation, a charge that many abolitionists threw back at white slaveholders whom they accused of raping slave women or keeping mulatta concubines. While there is no suggestion that Mrs. Jellyby had procreated with a black man or has any African ancestry, her husband's submissiveness (implying a lack of masculinity) and her own fascination with Africans imply a possible unrealized desire for interracial sex and potent black masculinity.

Dickens's use of blackface imagery in *Bleak House* was not his first reference to minstrelsy in his works, though his description of the African American minstrel dancer William Henry Lane in *American Notes* is not linked to a satire of abolitionism. Rather, his portrayal of Lane (known as "Juba") shares more with Kemble's description of the "veritable James" in narrating the spectacular moves of a black dancer. This description of Lane's performance emphasizes his amazing energy and skill and the fun he generates, but also raises the issues of counterfeit and authenticity in minstrel performance:

> Suddenly the lively hero dashes in to the rescue. Instantly the fiddler grins, and goes at it tooth and nail; there is new energy in the tambourine; new laughter in the dancers; new smiles in the landlady; new confidence in the landlord; new brightness in the very candles. Single shuffle, double shuffle, cut and cross-cut: snapping his fingers, roll-

ing his eyes, turning in his knees, presenting the backs of his legs in front, spinning about on his toes and heels like nothing but the man's fingers on the tambourine; dancing with two left legs, two right legs, two wooden legs, two wire legs, two spring legs—all sorts of legs and no legs—what is this to him? . . . Having danced his partner off her feet, and himself too, he finishes by leaping gloriously on the bar-counter, and calling for something to drink, with the chuckle of a million of counterfeit Jim Crows, in one inimitable sound! (110, 112).

Although the end of the passage implies that Lane copies Rice's counterfeit performance of the legendary Jim Crow, he differs from Jim Crow in that he cannot be imitated by a white man. His tremendous dancing skill (and perhaps his racial identity) makes his counterfeit of Jim Crow seem authentic. Like Kemble's "veritable James," Dickens's depiction of Lane emphasizes black physicality and joy. Also like Kemble, Dickens focuses on the dancer's eyes, fingers, knees, and, most of all, his legs.

Later in *American Notes*, Dickens's portrait of a less talented and more comical African American relies more on derogatory minstrel humor, though it echoes the emphasis on counterfeit from the earlier depiction of Lane. Dickens describes a grinning, eye-rolling, black coachman who leads him across the Potomac River: "He is a Negro—very black indeed. He is dressed in a coarse pepper-and-salt suit excessively patched and darned (particularly at the knees), gray stockings, enormous unblacked high-low shoes, and very short trousers. He has two odd gloves: one of party-colored worsted, and one of leather. He has a very short whip, broken in the middle, and bandaged up with string. And yet he wears a low-crowned, broad-brimmed, black hat: faintly shadowing forth a kind of insane imitation of an English coachman!" (155). We may see irony in Dickens's comment regarding the "very black" coachman's imitation of English coachmen, since the sartorial details he provides may remind us of Rice's Jim Crow character, one of the most famous examples of white imitation of blacks. Dickens does not indicate the racial identity of the mimicked English coachman, though considering the miniscule black population in England in Dickens's day, we may assume that he probably had a white coachman in mind. Dickens's use of the word "insane" to describe the black coachman's imitation suggests the irrationality of black mimicry of whites and thus points to the fundamental differences between the two races, differences that were highlighted by ludicrous black imitations of whites in minstrelsy. A page later, Dickens includes a humorous scene in which the horses flounder on the swampy road, and the nonsense words that the coachman shouts to them—"Ally Loo! Hi. Jiddy, Jiddy. Pill. Ally Loo!" (157)—resemble the gibberish often sung by minstrel performers. Dickens does not point out the coachman's slave status, perhaps because such a reminder might have seemed unnecessary or detracted from the humor of the scene. While he does follow this episode with comments on slavery, he does not make statements against the institution until later in the book, and this passage suggests that his opposition to slavery was not based on a belief in racial equality.

Thackeray's reaction to a blackface performance he witnessed differs notably from the racist minstrel humor in Dickens's depiction of the African American coachman and the physical exuberance of Lane's many-legged dance performance. Although Thackeray apparently was not affected by abolitionist appeals on behalf of slaves, on one occasion he was deeply touched by the counterfeit blackness of a minstrel performer. Thackeray's teary homage to this singer reveals that minstrelsy had a much stronger impact on him than antislavery depictions of humble, oppressed slaves:

> I heard a humorous balladist not long ago . . . a minstrel with wool on his head and an ultra-Ethiopian complexion, who performed a negro ballad that I confess moistened these spectacles in a most unexpected manner. I have gazed at thousands of tragedy-queens dying on the stage and expiring in appropriate blank verse, and I never wanted to wipe them. They have looked up, be it said, at many scores of clergymen without being dimmed, and behold! a vagabond with a corked face and a banjo sings a little song, strikes a wild note, which sets the heart thrilling with happy pity. (qtd. in Matthews 759)

In contrast to his lachrymose response to this performance, Thackeray refuses to recognize the humanity of the kneeling slave of abolitionist iconography when commenting on *Uncle Tom's Cabin* in an 1853 letter to his mother: "They are not my men & brethren, these strange people with retreating foreheads, with great obtruding lips & jaws. . . . Sambo is not my man & my brother" (qtd. in Ray 199). The "happy pity" aroused in Thackeray by the blackfaced white minstrel, with his banjo, woolly wig, and burnt-cork makeup, does not extend toward the black slaves symbolized by the famous abolitionist emblem. Like many other Britons during abolitionism's decline, Thackeray preferred the "imitation nigger" of the minstrel stage to the "genuine article" as represented in antislavery discourse. Because the blackness of the blackfaced performer was obviously artificial, this performance allowed Thackeray to distance himself from black people more easily than from an abolitionist depiction of an enslaved black person. Despite the ideological parallels between early minstrelsy and abolitionism in Britain, the contrast between Thackeray's reactions to these two representations of black people emphasizes the growing difference between those modes of representation, as well as Thackeray's hostility toward abolitionism.

Thackeray's anti-abolitionist attitude also emerges in *Vanity Fair*. While the novel does not deal extensively with slavery, its brief references to slavery and the antislavery movement go against Britain's abolitionist, anti-racist reputation. In Chapter 10, for instance, the narrator describes how the conniving Becky Sharp flatters the wealthy Pitt Crawley: "She admired, beyond measure, his speech at the Quashimaboo-Aid Society" (88). The passage suggests not only the insincerity of Becky's expression of admiration for Crawley's abolitionist speech, but also the pomposity and self-righteousness of the speech itself. The novel earlier dovetails its critiques of abolition and greed by mentioning that Crawley sold a seat in Parliament for fifteen hundred pounds a year to a "Mr. Quadroon, with *carte-blanche* on the Slave question" (83). Later, the novel implies that Rhoda Swartz, the biracial heiress from St. Kitts, is a beneficiary rather than a victim of slavery by noting that her father, a "German Jew," is a slaveholder in the "Cannibal Islands" (200). The fact that this descendant of two historically oppressed groups is an heiress downplays the suffering that her ancestors had experienced as a result of slavery and anti-Semitism. Ironically, none of the white characters benefits from slavery or is directly involved in it. The novel suggests that half-castes like Rhoda and foreign Jews like her father, rather than white Christian Britons, are responsible for slavery. Rhoda's family's wealth is derived from Mr. Swartz's slaveholdings and is associated with his Jewishness; as Charles Heglar notes, Thackeray's novel makes the common anti-Semitic association between Jews and money (337).[7] Although the novel's denial of British complicity in slavery does not undercut Britain's abolitionist reputation, its skepticism toward abolitionism obviously does.

Thackeray's racism and anti-abolitionism are even more egregious in his last novel, *The Adventures of Philip*, than in *Vanity Fair*. Like Swartz, the wealthy West Indian mulatto Captain Grenville Woolcomb marries a white person—in this case, the protagonist's cousin Agnes—and the black male/white female combination sets up frequent references to Othello and Desdemona. Unlike Othello, however, Woolcomb is stupid, stingy, and vicious, and he lacks the positive traits, such as affection, that Thackeray ascribes to Rhoda Swartz. Woolcomb's villainy counters abolitionist arguments regarding black humanity, an argument that the narrator mocks after introducing him to the reader. After speculating that Woolcomb's "dark complexion, and hair so *very* black and curly" would make him the target of discrimination in the American South, the narrator ironically declares: "But in England we know better. In England Grenville Woolcomb is a man and a brother" (184). The abolitionist slogan is sarcastically invoked by two other characters (242, 630), and it is again ridiculed near the end of the novel, when Woolcomb runs for a seat in the House of Lords. The narrator describes "a placard, on which a most undeniable likeness of Mr. Woolcomb was designed: who was made to say, 'VOTE FOR ME! AM I NOT A MAN AND A BRUDDER?'" (636). Adding to this travesty of the abolitionist motto is the fact that Woolcomb's first name, Grenville, was the surname of the prime minister who oversaw the abolition of the slave trade. The novel here suggests that British abolitionism's recognition of black humanity has gone too far by allowing an illiterate mulatto to amass a great fortune, be elevated to the House of Lords, and marry an English woman. Woolcomb's wealth enables his marriage to Agnes (whose family needs the money) and his political success, and, as in *Vanity Fair*, Thackeray reveals the dangerous power of money in overturning the "natural" racial order and corrupting Parliament. Thackeray's protagonist goes as far as to imply that white Englishmen have become "white slaves" to Woolcomb (635) and that Britain's political corruption enables Woolcomb to invert the racial hierarchy of slavery. Thackeray's suggestion that abolitionism encourages miscegenation, of which Woolcomb is both a product and a perpetrator, is consistent with much nineteenth-century proslavery and anti-abolitionist rhetoric. For Thackeray, abolitionism's purported link to miscegenation has dire political consequences at the national level. Just as Woolcomb's "drop of black blood" makes him black and therefore inferior, Britain's one black lord might taint the entire government and nation. Abolitionism's legacy, the novel implies, would entail the rise of other black men to political power in Britain and precipitate its further contamination.

Thackeray's racism and anti-abolitionism were linked to his use of minstrel conventions in *Vanity Fair* and *The Adventures of Philip* to represent black characters, such as the constantly grinning, inarticulate servant Sambo and Rhoda Swartz, "the rich woolly-haired mulatto from St. Kitt's" (4) in *Vanity Fair*. While Thackeray neither refers to nor borrows directly from minstrelsy in his novel, his characterizations of blacks are consistent with the stage minstrel.[8] His depiction of Sambo combines the bandy-legged, grinning minstrel negro and the inoffensive black servant in the margins of many of William Hogarth's eighteenth-century paintings.[9] This Sambo, as Thackeray makes clear, also "is not my man and brother," and he seems to have little to do with the tear-inducing minstrel performer that Thackeray describes in the above passage. While the narrator's descriptions of Rhoda are not entirely negative, they emphasize her habit of dressing in flashy colors and wearing large diamonds, thus mirroring the "yaller gals" of minstrelsy. George Osborne, whose father encourages him to marry the wealthy Rhoda, dismisses her as a "Belle Sauvage" (199) and a "Hottentot Venus" (210).[10] While the narrator often ridicules George (as well as most of the characters in the novel), the narrator's depictions of Rhoda are not much better than George's characterizations of her. For instance, the narrator describes her "in her favourite amber-coloured satin, with turquoise bracelets, countless rings, flowers, feathers, and all sorts of tags and gimcracks, about as elegantly decorated as a she chimney-sweep on May-day" (206). Her personality is characterized as "impetuous . . . but generous and affectionate" (5), but she is semiliterate and unable to control her "hysterical *yoops*" (6). These descriptions of Rhoda's appearance, character, intellect, and behavior are borrowed from the white racial discourse that inflected the minstrel stage, particularly the northern dandy Zip Coon and the black wench of American minstrelsy. *Vanity Fair* criticizes Victorian middle-class society for worshipping wealth, and Thackeray uses the partial acceptance of the wealthy but uncultured mulatta Rhoda by most of the other white characters as part of that critique.

In some ways, the wealthy Grenville Woolcomb in *The Adventures of Philip* is a male version of Rhoda Swartz, but because he is male, he resembles Zip Coon of the minstrel stage even more than Rhoda does. The narrator's initial description of Woolcomb emphasizes his materialism and parsimony by mentioning his "pair of the neatest little yellow kid gloves" and "a blazing red flower in his bosom" (184); later we are told that "he is a stingy Black Prince, and most averse to parting with his money except for his own adornment or amusement" (185). While these characterizations of Woolcomb lack the ludicrousness of the Zip Coon minstrel character, and Woolcomb does not speak in the black dialect of the minstrel stage, he shares Zip Coon's overdeveloped sense of fashion, and he is frequently depicted as underbred and ignorant. Moreover, the protagonist's description of Woolcomb's scowl resembles the dehumanizing depictions of black people in later minstrelsy: "I remarked that he grinned, and chattered, and showed his teeth; and remembering it was the nature of such baboons to chatter and grin, had no idea that this chimpanzee was more angry with me than with any other gentleman" (187). His surname further dehumanizes him, bringing to mind the "fright wigs" worn by many minstrel performers, and the narrator emphasizes the curliness of the hair (247). By patterning Woolcomb after the northern dandy of the minstrel stage, Thackeray's novel implies that black men have no more right to wealth, pride, and political power than Zip Coon does, and it suggests that abolitionists are largely to blame for allowing such a detestable person to have such wealth and power in English society.

One can see an even more unambiguous, extended, and vicious attack on abolitionism in Carlyle's 1849 essay "Occasional Discourse on the Nigger Question," a text that Catherine Hall sees as a watershed moment in the British middle class's drift away from abolitionism ("Economy" 177–78).[11] Although Kemble's *Journal* and Dickens's *American Notes* incorporate blackface tropes along with critiques of slavery, the racism and anti-abolitionism of Carlyle's essay intersects with the more derogatory depictions of black people that were emerging in minstrelsy around mid-century. For instance, Carlyle endorses the notion of black laziness that permeated much proslavery literature and would soon become commonplace in minstrelsy: "Where a Black man, by working about half an hour a day (such is the calculation), can supply himself, by aid of sun and soil, with as much pumpkin as will suffice, he is likely to be a little stiff to raise into hard work!" (296–97). He later writes that "with regard to the West Indies, it may be laid down as a principle, . . . That no Black man who will not work according to what ability the gods have given him for working, has the smallest right to eat pumpkin, however plentiful such land may be; but has an indisputable and perpetual *right* to be compelled, by the real proprietors of said land, to do competent work for his living" (299). This statement ignores the fact that it was West Indian planters, not their slaves, who felt entitled to sustenance and wealth without labor. Carlyle also mocks abolitionism through exaggeration, warning "our grand proposed Association of Associations, the UNIVERSAL ABOLITION-OF-PAIN ASSOCIATION" to not form "a universal 'Sluggard-and-Scoundrel Protection Society'" (293–94). Writing a decade after Emancipation, Carlyle's essay seems to long for a return to slavery.[12] He later reiterated his views of black people in 1867, this time with a reference to minstrelsy: "One always rather likes the Nigger; evidently a poor blockhead with good dispositions, with affections, attachments,—with a turn for Nigger Melodies, and the like:—he is the only Savage of all the coloured races that doesn't die out on sight of the White Man; but can actually live beside him, and work and increase and be merry. The Almighty Maker has appointed him to be a Servant" (qtd. in Fryer 172). Carlyle's reference to "Nigger Melodies" suggests that his image of the servile, resilient, loyal, good-natured Negro was largely based on minstrel characters.

Many of Carlyle's racist comments about black people are echoed in Trollope's *The West Indies and the Spanish Main,* written after his return from a visit to the West Indies on postal business in 1858 (Walvin, *Black and White* 166). Only a few examples of Trollope's statements about blacks from the chapter "Jamaica—Black Men" are needed to convey the gist of his general racial attitudes and how they overlap with the increasingly derogatory representations of African Americans in minstrelsy. He describes the Jamaican Negro as "idle, unambitious as to worldly position, sensual, and content with little. Intellectually, he is apparently capable of but little sustained effort. . . . [He] delights in aping the little graces of civilization" (56). In the next paragraph, he writes that this Negro "can seldom reason. . . . His motives are the fear of immediate punishment, or hopes of immediate reward" (57). Here, Trollope's depictions of blacks are more in line with the anti-black stereotypes of later minstrelsy and the racism of eighteenth-century colonial texts (such as Edward Long's

1774 *History of Jamaica*) than with even the most condescending abolitionist descriptions of blacks. Despite the racism of many British abolitionists, few of them would have viewed or described black people as Trollope does in *The West Indies*. His text exemplifies how abolitionism's patronizing romantic racialism parted ways with the increasingly vicious racism of minstrelsy. Trollope shares the skepticism toward philanthropy expressed by Dickens, Thackeray, and Carlyle, and his negative response to the question posed by the kneeling slave of abolitionist iconography "Am I Not a Man and a Brother?" is only slightly more sympathetic than Thackeray's seven years earlier: "He *is* a man; and, if you will, a brother; but he is the very idlest brother with which a hardworking workman was ever cursed, intent only on getting his mess of pottage without giving anything in return" (65). Both *The West Indies* and Carlyle's essay are in line with a shift from the condescending racism of the 1830s to a more hostile bigotry that depicted blacks as subhuman, a notion that became acceptable by the 1860s, the decade that witnessed Governor Eyre's violent suppression of the Morant Bay revolt (Hall, "Missionary Stories" 242). Ironically, this event occurred the same year that the Thirteenth Amendment abolished slavery in the United States, and the fact that many Britons supported Eyre's actions indicates their decreasing concern for black people and their increasing commitment to imperialism and white supremacy. It is unclear to what extent such a shifting of ideological ground in Britain led some members of Britain's upper classes to consider aiding the Confederacy during the Civil War. Nevertheless, as abolitionism lost public support in Britain after mid-century, earlier racialist attitudes, once they were no longer tempered by antislavery sentiment, became more vicious, and their blatant expression by Trollope, Carlyle, and other authors belied the notion of Britain as an abolitionist utopia unsullied by racial prejudice.

The British texts analyzed in this chapter lead us to several conclusions about the relations among blackface minstrelsy, racism, slavery, and abolitionism in nineteenth-century Britain. First, we can see the versatility of minstrelsy (including blackface as well as minstrel music, dance, and characters) in being articulated both to critiques of slavery (as in Kemble's *Journal* and Dickens's *American Notes*), to critiques of philanthropy (as in *Bleak House* and *Adventures of Philip*), and to satires of middle-class greed (as in *Vanity Fair*). Aside from early minstrelsy's ideological flexibility, however, we can partly attribute the popularity of increasingly racist and proslavery minstrel shows and songs in Britain after mid-century to the growing viciousness of British racism and a decline in abolitionist commitment, shifts that are signaled by the works of Thackeray, Carlyle, and Trollope. While George Rehin and J. S. Bratton are correct to argue that minstrelsy's appeal to the English public was partly enabled and conditioned by earlier, nonracist blackface traditions, we must not ignore British attitudes toward black people during the mid-nineteenth century and the role of minstrelsy in shaping and reflecting those attitudes. Although there was room in British abolitionism for imperialism, ethnocentrism, romantic racialism, and condescension toward blacks, the hardening of such attitudes and the elimination of slavery in the British empire drained off some of the appeal of abolitionism while enabling the popularity of a more racist form of minstrelsy. In this sense, Britain was becoming more like the United States in terms of white racism, while the United States was about to follow Britain's lead by abolishing slavery. Despite these convergences, however, many white Americans wanted to separate themselves from Britain, and their use of minstrelsy in doing so is the focus of the following chapter.

"Our Only Truly National Poets"
Blackface Minstrelsy, Slave Narratives, Cultural Nationalism, and the American Renaissance

In his 1845 essay "Who Are Our National Poets?" a mock celebration of American literary nationalism, James Kennard, Jr. argues that a truly American poet must reject European tastes, remain at home, and develop a strong provincial identity. He then asks:

> What class is most secluded from foreign influences, receives the narrowest education, travels the shortest distance from home, has the least amount of spare cash, and mixes least with any class above itself? Our negro slaves, to be sure! *That* is the class in which we must expect to find our original poets, and there we *do* find them. From that class come the Jim Crows, the Zip Coons, and the Dandy Jims, who have electrified the world. From them proceed our ONLY TRULY NATIONAL POETS. (332)

Kennard's ridicule of American literary nationalism stems not only from his Eurocentrism, racism, and contempt for blackface minstrelsy, but also from the nationalism that permeated minstrelsy and the discourses enveloping it. Thus, understanding his essay requires an awareness of minstrelsy's relationship to American cultural nationalism. While Ralph Waldo Emerson, Herman Melville, and other American authors were forging a distinctly national literature and culture, American theatres were overrun by minstrelsy, a stridently nationalistic form of entertainment that American cultural critics often described as uniquely American, even though one of its founders, Charles Mathews, was English. The working-class swagger of early minstrel characters like Jim Crow, Zip Coon, and Dandy Jim and their "updain"[1] toward British and European pretentiousness was a vulgar equivalent of Emerson's and Melville's celebration of a masculine American nationalism. Kennard's article links minstrelsy to cultural nationalism and raises the following question, even while dismissing it: can African American culture, or white representations of it, fit into American culture in ways that set America apart from Europe? As a white representation of African American culture, minstrelsy—especially in its early years—was thematically linked to the concerns of American cultural nationalism, with its coarse brand of anti-British and anti-European patriotism and lower-class ultramasculinity. By proudly proclaiming itself as a distinctively American cultural form, minstrelsy denied its British and European ancestry at a time when Americans looked for ways to define their nation and culture.

At first glance, the contemporaneous emergence of the American Renaissance and minstrelsy during the mid-nineteenth century may seem no more than a coincidence. However, revisionist scholarship on the American Renaissance over the past thirty years has made it easier to understand the forces behind this convergence. Literary historians and scholars have broadened our notion of the American Renaissance to include the works of female and African American authors, such as Harriet Beecher Stowe, E. D. E. N. Southworth, and Frederick Douglass, whose works were popular in their day but were later neglected. Other scholarship has challenged the traditional concept of a unified American Renaissance.[2] Some scholars have also examined the links between the works of the American Renaissance and slavery, including the slave narrative, but there is still much work to be done in exploring these connections.[3] Moreover, Lott, Lhamon, Eric Sundquist, Paul Gilmore, and others have analyzed American Renaissance texts in connection with minstrelsy.[4] Nevertheless, the overlapping ideological territory shared by minstrelsy and the American Renaissance remains largely uncharted and needs to be mapped out more fully in order to understand both cultural moments.

This chapter attempts to clarify these connections among minstrelsy, slave narratives, and the essays of Emerson, Melville, Sarah Margaret Fuller, and Theodore Parker regarding cultural nationalism, and it analyzes the roles played by ideologies of masculinity and class in American cultural nationalism and in minstrelsy's representations of African Americans. The nationalism expressed by Emerson and his colleagues was often paralleled by patriotic minstrel song lyrics and stump speeches. Minstrelsy's rough nationalism was frequently linked to its ridicule of abolitionism, which was often associated with the polite classes and with Britain, and its anti-abolitionist and anti-capitalist rhetoric of "wage slavery" appealed to working-class male audiences. This chapter also examines how minstrelsy and slave narratives were depicted as distinctively American, connects these discussions to the nationalist agendas of Emerson, Melville, Fuller, and Parker, and argues that both slave narratives and minstrelsy can be read as responses to calls for a distinct, anti-elitist American form of literature and culture. My approach shows how representations of African Americans in minstrel shows and slave narratives embodied values professed by many white American authors and cultural critics, including patriotism, anti-elitism, masculinity, and self-reliance.

Race played a central role in minstrelsy's relationship to nineteenth-century American cultural nationalism in that white American minstrel performers and audiences defined their nationality through and against blackfaced characters. This process can be better understood by turning to the insights of Ralph Ellison and Toni Morrison regarding white representations of African Americans and the psychological functions of those representations. Ellison suggests that we see "the whole of American life as a drama acted out upon the body of a Negro giant, who . . . forms the stage and the scene upon which and within which the action unfolds" (28). Ellison's theatrical metaphor is especially appropriate with regard to minstrelsy, and it helps us to imagine the minstrel stage as the site on which white performers acted out their concerns about slavery, race, nationalism, gender, sexuality, and class through their representations of black bodies. Early minstrelsy performed the anti-European nationalism and rough proletarian masculinity of their white audiences, enacted their fascination with and anxieties about black male physical and sexual power, and dramatized their proslavery and antislavery proclivities. Ellison's insight also helps us see how slave narratives dramatized America's concerns about freedom and self-determination through the struggles of enslaved African Americans who fought valiantly for those principles.

Morrison makes a similar point about the role of African Americans in the white American literary imagination, though her insight is more applicable to minstrelsy than to slave narratives: "The imaginative and historical terrain upon which early American writers journeyed is in large measure shaped by the presence of the racial other" (46). Her term "American Africanism" denotes an explicit or implied racial or metaphorical black presence, which white American authors use to define themselves by opposition as white, and onto which they project their own unwanted psychological traits (45, 52–53).

The blackfaced characters of the minstrel stage illustrate Morrison's theory that white Americans used black bodies and concepts of blackness to give meaning to abstractions such as humanity, freedom, civilization, and whiteness. The tropes of blackness and meditations on the role of African American people and culture in American society are central to the masculinized cultural nationalism of mid-nineteenth-century America expressed by Emerson and Melville, as well as by minstrelsy. Morrison's analysis of white literary constructions of blackness also helps us understand how whites projected characteristics like simplicity or savagery onto blacks on the minstrel stage.

Cultural Nationalism in American Renaissance Literature and Blackface Minstrelsy

Months after Rice had jumped Jim Crow in England, Emerson declared America's literary independence from Britain and Europe in his 1837 "American Scholar" address to the Phi Beta Kappa Society at Harvard. In that address, as well as in his 1844 essay "The Poet," he placed a genteel veneer on the macho nationalism more coarsely enacted on the minstrel stage. Emerson's desire for American literary independence was a national form of the self-reliance that he advocated in his essay "Self-Reliance," with America as the manly nonconformist and Europe as the effeminate, repressive society. His definition of American nationalism as a rejection of Europe demonstrates Donald Pease's statement that mid-nineteenth-century American writers extended the nation's rejection of Britain during the Revolutionary War by eschewing European literary models in their own work (8). In "The American Scholar," Emerson declares, "Our day of dependence, our long apprenticeship to the learning of other lands, draws to a close" (51) and "We have listened too long to the courtly muses of Europe" (70). In "The Poet," he laments the absence of the Great American Poet while pointing to the nation's wealth of subject matter for poetry:

> We have yet had no genius in America, with tyrannous eye, which knew the value of our incomparable materials, and saw, in the barbarism and materialism of the times, another carnival of the same gods whose picture he so much admires in Homer; then in the Middle Age; then in Calvinism. . . . Our log-rolling, our stumps and their politics, our

fisheries, our Negroes and Indians, our boasts and our repudiations, the wrath of rogues and the pusillanimity of honest men, the northern trade, the southern planting, the western clearing, Oregon and Texas, are yet unsung. Yet America is a poem in our eyes; its ample geography dazzles the imagination, and it will not wait long for metres. (261–62)[5]

We can see connections between this passage and several issues central to minstrelsy: masculinity, nationalism, performativity, ventriloquism, and appropriation. Emerson's definition of this unsung America—and the nationalism that celebrates it—is aggressively masculine; he probably did not imagine women engaged in such non-domestic activities such as log-rolling, politics, fishing, trade, planting, and clearing, not to mention wrathful roguery. Emerson's nationalism is not simply masculine in a generic way, however; rather, it is specifically white, Western, and working class. He suggests that America's genius is not to be found among genteel, articulate scholars, but among (apparently white) poets capable of giving voice to marginalized groups of people (Negroes and Indians). This unsung, nationalist poem must also be performed, but not by Negroes or Indians themselves; Emerson suggests that respectable whites could sing such songs for them, a form of ventriloquism not entirely unlike white minstrels' impersonation of African Americans and their appropriation of black culture. He further denigrates "Negroes and Indians" with the possessive pronoun "our" (suggesting their ownership by white Americans) and portrays them more as natural resources than as humans. Yet they are natural resources that Europe lacks, and they therefore help to make America unique.

The sense of ownership implied by the phrase "our Negroes and Indians" parallels a sense of white American entitlement to the North American continent in this passage, including the Oregon Territory, Texas, and Mexico. Indeed, Emerson's celebration of westward expansion in this passage appeared just two years before America's commitment to Manifest Destiny resulted in its war with Mexico and four years before the discovery of gold at Sutter's Mill precipitated the Gold Rush.[6] The expansionist note in Emerson's essay was sounded more vociferously in minstrel shows, as Eric Lott and Robert Toll have observed. David Roediger notes that minstrel shows often featured imitations of the locomotive (*Wages* 119), a powerful trope of westward expansion, but minstrel stump speeches also endorsed Manifest Destiny more explicitly. For instance, the Civil War–era stump speech "Let Her Rip" declares:

> Whar's de country wid as big ribbers, as high mountains, as broad lakes, as wide per-aries, as long canals, as fast railroads, as brave men, as handsome gals, as noisy children, as quick telegraphs, as lumptious rum-an-lasses, as wolly [sic] mokes, as fleet ships, as America? Whar? . . . . And what's we gwine to be by-and-by, when we annex Canada, Mexico, Cuba, and all de oder places. When de whole United States flag won't be big enough to hold de stars, den what we gwine to do? Why den de American eagle will spread his wings, put his craws on England, Ireland, Franceland, Spainland, Lapland, Dutchland, and be darned if we don't annex dem to [sic], and let her rip. (*Bones* 7)

Like Emerson's essays, this stump speech celebrates the immensity and natural diversity of America. Yet it takes Manifest Destiny even further by combining these notions with anti-European sentiment by imagining the expansion of America not only to other parts of the New World, but even to Europe. Another stump speech promoting Manifest Destiny, "Dat's What's de Matter," which was first performed on the eve of the Civil War, takes a historical approach:

> In de year Aunty Dominix 1776, how was dis country bounded. I'll tell you—it was bounded on de Norf by dat celebrated female Sara-toga, a brudder ob hers, by de name ob York-town, and de capture ob Andre. It was bounded on de Souf by Gin'ral Jackson and de Cotton Bales. On de East by Moll Pitcher de Salem Witchcraft and de Boston Tea Party. An' on de West by—by—a howlin' wilderness. Now, how is it bounded? It bounded on de Norf by everytin' dats good to eat and drink; its bounded on de Souf by Secession; on de East by New Jersey, Harper's Ferry, an' de Great Eastern; and on de West by Montgomery's Jay Hawks, Pike's Peak, an' Bleeding Kansas. Dat's what's de matter. (Christy 19)

Instead of a "howlin' wilderness," America's western frontier now includes a battle over the expansion of slavery (Bleeding Kansas). But rather than commenting on whether slavery should be allowed there, this passage simply applauds America's expansion past the Missouri River.

This nationalist theme of expansion was found not only in stump speeches but also in many minstrel songs. For instance, Harry Bloodgood's "Den I Was Gone" (1869), sung by Sharpley's Minstrels, begins by mentioning the means of travel that enabled westward migration: "Railroad and de river, / Steamboat and Canal" (SSMC). Geographical expansion is also implied in the travels of the singer of S. S. Steele's "Kate of Carolina" (1847):

> I travel'd o'er de west an' souf,
> Before I got my freedom,
> Clar to de Mississippi's mouf
> Before I got my freedom (SSMC)

While the singer did not travel north to freedom like most fugitive slaves, his (apparently voluntary) movement—especially west—was essential to Manifest Destiny. Similar lyrics mentioning westward movement appear in other Mexican War–era minstrel songs, such as "Brack Eyed Susianna" (1846), sung by the Nightingale Serenaders (SSMC). Lott points out that the lyrics of a more familiar minstrel song, Stephen Foster's "Oh! Susanna," were soon altered to refer to the California Gold Rush and, more generally and indirectly, to Manifest Destiny (205–07).[7] Foster's original version already mentioned travel westward from Alabama to Louisiana, though the revised version obviously extends that westward migration even further.

Another minstrel song promoting nationalism and Manifest Destiny was the Christy Minstrels' 1847 "Jim Crow Polka," which in its third and fourth stanzas celebrates General Zachary Taylor's victory in the Mexican War:

> I'se got de news 'bout Mexico,
> Where dey thought to whip us at one blow,
> But Gineral Taylor wasenent slow
> To make dem dance de Polka.

> De Mexican dere plans laid well
> De placed dere men in de chapparel,
> But Rough and Ready made 'em smell
>   Gunpowder, a la Polka.

> One Mexican General, it is said
> He got so scared, he swallowed his head,
> And a few days after he was dead
>   He danced de Jim Crow Polka! (SSMC)

The transformation of the dead Mexican general (whom Americans would not have viewed as white) into a blackfaced, polka-ing Jim Crow is a bizarre illustration of the fungibility of racial Others that was one of the racial ideologies informing Manifest Destiny. Except for the odd juxtaposition of minstrelsy with polka music (as well as the remarkable feat of swallowing one's head or the image of a polka-ing dead Mexican general), this song resembles many other minstrel songs in its nationalism. However, while America's enemy in many other patriotic minstrel songs was Britain, the enemy in "Jim Crow Polka" was a neighboring country that had gotten in the way of America's rampant geographical expansion. Manifest Destiny was an expansionist form of nationalism; thus, as Lott points out, "minstrel tunes became an outright venue for northern nationalism" (206).

Minstrelsy's celebration of Manifest Destiny peaked during the Mexican War, but other forms of blackface nationalism emerged during all three of America's major nineteenth-century wars. Minstrel songs of these periods often promoted a nationalist masculinity by emphasizing the lack of manhood among enemy officers and soldiers, especially the British. For example, Micah Hawkins's 1815 "Backside Albany," which William Mahar claims to be the first American blackface song, mocks the cowardice of a British general in a battle during the War of 1812. Mahar remarks that the song "says more about ineptness of the British than about racial matters in the United States" ("'Backside'" 10); in this sense, nationalism trumps racism. A later song, J. G. Evans's "Revolutionary Echoes" (1847), assumes an anti-British stance in describing the Revolutionary War. Like "Backside Albany," it points out the cowardice of the Redcoats and celebrates their defeat:

> He [Washington] wid his continentallers
> Would meet de red-coats fire! fire! &c.
> And a-running dey would go, . . .
> For they thought they'd got a little dose
> Ob de fire down below. (SSMC)

In a similar vein, the fourth stanza of "Revolutionary Echoes" ridicules the British commander in the battle of Dorchester Heights. This song makes the familiar connections between American nationalism and masculinity and between British tyranny and cowardice:

> When de British General saw de game
> He thought he should suspire,
> So he sent an inwitation for
> De Yankees to stop dere fire! fire! &c. . . .
> For de Yankees had found a patent way
> To make de red-coats go.[8]

Although the United States was at war with Mexico when this song was published, a reminder of America's military victory over Britain was useful in drumming up patriotic fervor for the current war. We also see anti-British attitudes in many stump speeches, such as "Let Her Rip":

> Whot am England anyhow? Look on de map in Webster's Contradic-tionary, dar you'll see a big black spot 'bout as big as de last chew in a five-cent paper ob tobacco, or de kidney ob a consumptive-chicken, dat's England. Why, my fellow bums, I've seen colored men wid moufs big enough, if dey wasn't to [sic] lazy to open 'em—big enough to swal-low it. Den look on de map and see what America am. Why, my friends, it looks as if a runaway hoss-an-wagon had started off to mark it out, and han't got cotched for a week. Pears to me dat when nature made up her mind to make America, she resolved to go in on a big scale, and so she let her rip.
>
> Againly, didn't England try to claw us at New Orleans, and didn't dey get chawed up in de transaction? Didn't we go froo 'em like Bran-dreth's pills? Didn't dey run from de cotton bales den? (*Bones* 7)

In belittling England geographically, this speaker ignores British imperialism and its similarities to American Manifest Destiny because acknowledging Brit-ish imperialism would entail recognition of British military power and, by extension, British manhood. The nationalism of this speech and others like it had a broader appeal and spoke in a rougher idiom than Emerson's essays and lectures, but the nationalism of "The Poet" and "The American Scholar" was not far removed from that of many minstrel songs and stump speeches.

During the Civil War, when there was no definite foreign threat to the United States, northern minstrel performers expressed their nationalism by supporting the Union (Toll 105–07).[9] Often, minstrel performers blamed the war on abolitionists or secessionists,[10] as in the Christy Minstrels' songs "Uncle Sam's Cooks" (Christy 6–7), "Canaan" (Christy 38–39), and "Our Union None Can Sever" (Christy 70–71), as well as their stump speech "Any Other Man" (Christy 9–11). However, in two Civil War–era songs, the Christy Minstrels' "Uncle Sam" and the Bryant's Minstrels' "Raw Recruits, or Abraham's Daughter" (1862), Britain again was the enemy when rumors circulated that it might aid the Confederacy.[11] Two verses from "Uncle Sam" promote anti-British nationalism through references to the Revolutionary War and the War of 1812:

In the year of '76, his daddy made him mad, sir,
By tryin' to impose on him, so he licked his dad, sir;
His daddy's name was Johnny Bull, who at him kept on pickin',
Until the year of 1812, when he got another lickin.'

Although he's young he's mighty big, and daily growin' bigger;
And if any of you have seen dis chap you can't mistake his figger,
His dress is made ob stars and stripes, about him dar's no sham, sir,
For what he says he's bound to do, and dat is Uncle Sam, sir. (Christy 24–25)

While the song suggests an affinity between Britain and the United States by describing Uncle Sam as Johnny Bull's son, it condemns Britain as a tyrannical father rightly overthrown by its American son. The lyrics of "Abraham's Daughter," which focus more directly on the Civil War, accuse Britain of attempting to encourage disunion and then take a jingoistic turn:

Now Johnny Bull has gone to grass,
To fatten up his calves, sir;
He talks of sending a shilling a day
Soldiers to the South, sir,

But we licked him well in Eighteen twelve,
And we can lick him weller, oh, oh, oh!

Now Johnny Bull may put on airs,
But what care we for that sir;
He's been itching now for some time
To have a little spat, sir,
But if he will but just keep cool
Till we've settled our fam'ly quarrel, oh, oh, oh! (SSMC)[12]

The references to the War of 1812 in both songs remind listeners of the possible outcome of disunion: a return to colonial status under Britain. In contrast to "Uncle Sam," which uses the Revolutionary War–era trope of Britain as a domineering parent, the Unionism of "Abraham's Daughters" figures the North and South as family members, emphasizing American unity and Britain's status as a snobbish intruder trying to break up the American family. Anti-British sentiment also found its way into minstrel stump speeches, such as "Dat's What's De Matter":

Talk 'bout de mudder country! Why, she aint a patch on Miss Columby's frock. Why in de year Aunty Dominix 1776, when de Stars and Stripes wasn't no bigger dan a dambanna hankerchief, and de American Eagle didn't hab narry quill—'cept a few pin feaders, and couldn't crow louder dan a bantam rooster wid de brownskeeters, we salivated de British Lion, till he didn't hab a tooth in his head, includin' his toe nails. Dat's what's de matter.

And in de present Aunty Dominix, we outsail dere yatches, outrun dere hosses, pick dere locks, Paul Morphy 'em, and *Belt* dere pugilists widout gittin' Belted in return. And dat's what's de matter. (Christy 18)[13]

This speech, somewhat like "Uncle Sam," posits America as the virtuous underdog David to Britain's arrogant Goliath, an image suggested by the undersized American Eagle defanging and declawing the mighty British Lion. The staunchly Unionist stance of this speech and of minstrelsy in general led minstrel performers and songwriters to oppose not only abolitionists (who were seen as threats to the Union) but also secessionists and any members of the British ruling class who considered giving help to the Confederacy to break up the Union.[14]

Anti-British minstrel songs did not always mention war; they sometimes deflated Britain's sense of supremacy and celebrated America's triumphs over its former parent in other rivalries. We can see this attitude in H. Angelo's 1863 song, "Folks That Put on Airs":

> Tis true we Yankees go ahead
> In all we undertake
> There's Ten Brock and great Rarey too
> Can British horses break
> Dar's Morphy next a Chessman he
> His laurels proudly wears
> Old Johnny Bull can't come to tea
> And needn't put on airs. (SSMC)

Even though it was written at the height of the Civil War, this song, unlike "Abraham's Daughter," does not mention the conflict or Britain's possible intervention on behalf of the Confederacy. Nevertheless, this potential threat to the Union might have occurred to many American listeners and given their hostility toward Britain a sense of urgency.

The anti-British nationalism of the minstrel stage was shared not only by Emerson, but also by other literary nationalists such as Parker, Melville, and Fuller. Ironically, one of the first forms of literature that may be seen as distinctly American was the stream of essays complaining about the very lack of a uniquely American literature and calling for its emergence. For example, Parker's 1846 speech "The Mercantile Classes" contrasts England with America and points to the lack of a national literary tradition while calling for its future development:

> Literature, science, and art are mainly in [poor men's] hands, yet are controlled by the prevalent spirit of the nation. . . . In England, the national literature favors the church, the crown, the nobility, the prevailing class. Another literature is rising, but is not yet national, still less canonized. We have no American literature which is permanent. Our scholarly books are only an imitation of a foreign type; they do

not reflect our morals, manners, politics, or religion, not even our rivers, mountains, sky. They have not the smell of our ground in their breath. . . . The real American literature is found only in newspapers and speeches, perhaps in some novel, hot, passionate, but poor and extemporaneous. That is our national literature. Does that favor man—represent man? Certainly not. All is the reflection of this most powerful class. The truths that are told are for them, and the lies. Therein the prevailing sentiment is getting into the form of thoughts. (qtd. in Davis and Gates xxi)

While Parker rejects English literature because it favors powerful institutions and the "prevailing class," he also dismisses attempts by American writers to mimic foreign literature, as well as the demotic expressions of America's subaltern majority—newspapers, speeches, and the occasional novel. In his later speech "The American Scholar" (discussed below), he points to a distinctively American literary genre that is not "poor and extemporaneous," but here he echoes Emerson's idea that American literature will grow out of its geographical grandeur.

Like Parker, Melville defines American literature by contrast to English literature, but his view of the former tradition is more optimistic than Parker's. In his 1850 "Hawthorne and His Mosses," a review of Hawthorne's *Mosses from an Old Manse*, Melville favorably compares the author to Shakespeare and attacks the notion of Shakespeare's unapproachability:

But what sort of a belief is this for an American, a man who is bound to carry republican progressiveness into Literature, as well as into Life? Believe me, my friends, that Shakespeares are this day being born on the banks of the Ohio. And the day will come, when you shall say who reads a book by an Englishman that is a modern? The great mistake seems to be, that even with those Americans who look forward to the coming of a great literary genius among us, they somehow fancy he will come in the costume of Queen Elizabeth's day,—be a writer of dramas founded upon old English history, or the tales of Boccaccio. (245–46)[15]

For Melville, Shakespeare represents Englishness, antiquity, and monarchy—the antitheses of American culture. Thus, Shakespeare's supremacy had to be overthrown as British political domination had been vanquished earlier.[16] As Michael Rogin notes, Melville here implies that America's political separation from Britain paved the way for development of an independent literary tradition (*Subversive* 74). However, Melville asserts, America has its own unrecognized Shakespeares and will create more of them in the future who will forge an independent literary tradition as great as the canon of English literature. Melville links American cultural nationalism to the future rather than the Elizabethan period, boasting, "If Shakespeare has not been equalled, he is sure to be surpassed, and surpassed by an American born now or yet to be born" (246). Like Emerson, Melville places the future cultural center of America in the West, far from the Whiggish, effete eastern dandies who still showed cultural allegiance to England (and, in fact, far from Hawthorne's Salem). By being born on the banks of the Ohio, Melville's future American Shakespeares might absorb the ultramasculinity of the legendary river boatman Mike Fink. In fact, Melville could have gone further west; he wrote this essay two years after America's victory over Mexico made Manifest Destiny seem inevitable and made it possible for future Shakespeares to be born not only on the banks of the Ohio, but even on the shores of the Rio Grande.

Melville's review positions American culture against English culture by defining the former as not only expansive and forward-looking, but also as original. For him, originality is more important than quality; indeed, originality is a new, American quality.[17] He suggests that if excellence were the standard for a national literature, authors would simply imitate the best literature that England has to offer.[18] It would be better to start with mediocre native literature and let it naturally improve with time, he implies, than to adopt an early American version of what Anthony Appiah has termed the Naipaul fallacy,[19] which posits English literature as the model of excellence for Americans to imitate. Melville's proposal amounts to a sort of literary tariff against imported (or pirated) English literature in order to foster the growth of budding American authors. His attitude toward American literature could be extended to theatre, in which minstrelsy parodied English and European music and drama and constituted what was seen as a uniquely American form of entertainment, in which performers purportedly imitated African Americans rather than Britons or Europeans.

Later in his essay, Melville defines the future American author's rejection of English and European literature as a form of literary masculinity:

We want no American Goldsmiths; nay, we want no American Miltons. It were the vilest thing you could say of a true American author, that he were an American Tompkins. Call him an American, and have done; · for you can not say a nobler thing of him.—But it is not meant that all American writers should studiously cleave to nationality in their writings; only this, no American writer should write like an Englishman, or a Frenchman; let him write like a man, for then he will be sure to write like an American. Let us away with this Bostonian leaven of literary flunkeyism towards England. (248)

Melville equates Americanness with masculinity, suggesting that English (and here, French) culture is effeminate.[20] The words "Englishman" and "Frenchman" place more emphasis on nationality than masculinity, and there is no such equivalent word, such as "Americanman," for American males. For Melville, an American is by default a man. Such gendered definitions of American identity were also prominent in the Crockett Almanacs, as well as on the minstrel stage. This masculinization of American identity was emphasized in much of the rhetoric surrounding minstrelsy, which often centered on the hypermasculine figures of Jim Crow and Zip Coon, as I discuss later. But in addition to foregrounding the masculinity of the American male writer, this author, by simply writing "like a man," is not limited by his nationality, unlike his English and French counterparts. Paradoxically, then, Melville suggests that American literature is uniquely American in that it is not limited by nationality, and that the American male author writes as a masculine Emersonian individual rather than as a citizen.

Jim Crow as Poet Laureate

The nationalism of Melville, Emerson, and Parker, as well as literary magazines such as *Putnam's Monthly* and *The Dial*, was not only expressed more roughly on the minstrel stage, but also permeated discussions about minstrelsy, which many cultural critics were quick to claim as a national form of popular culture. Minstrelsy's rise to prominence in mid-nineteenth-century America was part of a nationalist trend in theatre and music that paralleled the nationalism of the American Renaissance. Like the literary nationalists who castigated American authors for their lack of originality, music critics also lamented the lack of a distinctly American musical style or tradition. For example, the Boston periodical *Dwight's Journal of Music* reprinted an article from the *New York Courier and Enquirer* that echoed Emerson's comments on the lack of a distinctively American literature: "There has yet to be the first step taken towards the formation of an American school of music; all the music which has been composed here, worthy of the name, has been, of necessity German or Italian, whether written by Germans or Italians or Americans" ("First Performance" 203).[21] Although *Dwight's* often complained that minstrelsy corrupted American musical tastes (and observed how much money was made from minstrel songs and performances), no more American form of music could be found in the mid-nineteenth century. Minstrel shows filled a similar cultural void in American theatre. Previous to minstrelsy's rise, Lott remarks, there was "little that could stand as distinguished national drama" (89). Between 1820 and 1850, however, American theatre gradually distanced itself from its British counterpart, as Louis Gerteis argues: "New American theatres provided an expanding market for English managers and players, but they also spurred the emergence of distinctly American theatrical fare, most exuberantly represented in the work of a group of ethnic and regional 'delineators'" (33). By the late 1840s, the minstrel show had become the most popular form of theatre in America, and virtually all Americans were familiar with it. Similarly, minstrel tunes often parodied—and were contrasted with—European music, particularly that of England, Italy, and Germany,[22] and minstrel song lyrics, especially those in dialect, were compared to the verse of Robert Burns and other dialect poets. While minstrelsy also became popular in Britain after Rice brought his Jim Crow act there in 1836, and while blackface performance in Britain predated Rice's arrival, many Americans nonetheless saw it as a distinctly American form of popular culture.[23] Adding to America's nationalist claims for minstrelsy was the fact that its most prolific composer, Stephen Foster, was born on July 4, 1826, the fiftieth anniversary of the signing of the Declaration of Independence.[24]

Discussions of minstrelsy among cultural nationalists frequently mentioned—and conflated—its authenticity and its appropriation of black culture by white minstrel performers. One example of the nationalist discourse surrounding minstrelsy and its imitation of African American culture is the article "The Black Opera." The fact that the abolitionist editor Horace Greeley included this article in his *New York Tribune* reminds us of minstrelsy's potential appeal to antislavery readers. Unlike Melville, Greeley uses ancient Greek literature, not the works of Shakespeare, as the standard against which American popular culture may be measured. He thus does not share Melville's antagonism toward English literature: "If the lyricism of Stersichorus or of Anacreon may be regarded as an embodiment of the characteristic sentiments of the ancients; if the genius of Alcæus and of Sappho perpetuated the mysterious music of the olden fane, unvoiced before—why may not the banjoism of a Congo, an Ethiopian or a George Christy, aspire to an equality with the musical and poetical delineators of all nationalities?" ("The Black Opera"). This article takes the democratic, "Young American" spirit expressed in Melville's essay and extends it across racial lines, even while it conflates a notion of genuine Africanness with the appropriation of black music and dance by white minstrel performers. Indeed, this confusion of genuine African cultural origins ("a Congo, an Ethiopian") with their white imitations and appropriations is central to minstrelsy, and it enabled white American performers and audiences to define themselves against their English forebears without acknowledging African American contributions to American culture. Lott suggests that minstrelsy was a manifestation of how "'Anglo-Saxon' Americans distanced themselves from Britain as new ethnic formations combated one another in their turn. Far from being abstract inquiries, however, these movements were lived by working people who were bound up with the culture in which blackface moved and had its being. The point is that this jostle of cultures opened a national-popular space that was to be vigorously contested in the 1840s, quite fiercely as it turned out, and often in the arena of blackface minstrelsy" (91).[25] In the contested space of the minstrel stage, white Americans often parodied the literary and musical high culture of Europe, thus undermining the comparisons that the *Tribune* article—as well as Melville's essay—made between American and European culture. While some white Americans accepted English and European culture and literature as the standard of excellence to imitate, others rejected Old World culture and literature as effete, elitist, and outdated, and minstrelsy was useful in doing so.

Other American cultural nationalists who used minstrelsy to distance American culture from European culture confused African American culture with its white appropriations on the minstrel stage. Such was the case for Margaret Fuller, whose discussion of these issues in her 1842 article "Entertainments of the Past Winter" in *The Dial* rests upon some rather muddled notions of authenticity. She criticizes American whites for imitating European culture and suggests that "Jump Jim Crow" is more uniquely American than "Yankee Doodle":

> Our only national melody, Yankee Doodle, is shrewdly suspected to be a scion from British art. All symptoms of invention are confined to the African race, who, like the German literati, are relieved by their position from the cares of government. "Jump Jim Crow," is a dance native to this country, and one which we plead guilty to seeing with pleasure, not on the stage, where we have not seen it, but as danced by children of an ebon hue in the street. Such of the African melodies as we have heard are beautiful. But the Caucasian race have yet their rail-roads to make, and all we shall learn from a survey of exhibitions in the arts which exhilarate our social life, is how far, studying and copying Europe as we do, we are able to receive and enjoy her gifts in this kind. (52)

Fuller may have meant to praise African American creativity (and remove it from the English culture from which "Yankee Doodle" sprang) by comparing it to that of the disfranchised German intelligentsia. However, the example of black expression she uses—the Jump Jim Crow dance popularized by Rice—is a white appropriation, imitation, and parody of African American dance styles, regardless of whether Rice actually got the dance from the black hostler of legend. Lott writes of this passage that Fuller assumes "that the only music and dance which are *not* false coin are those found in blackface minstrelsy, which represents, Fuller hints, something like the folk culture of an American peasantry. These comments begin to suggest that when, in the decades before the Civil War, northern white men 'blacked up' and imitated what they supposed was black dialect, music, and dance, some people, without derision, heard Negroes singing" (16). But if this is so, people who "heard Negroes singing" when watching blackfaced white minstrels had a different view of black cultural authenticity than Fuller expresses.

Fuller does not see minstrel shows as authentic; rather, she favors the street dances of black children over conventionalized dances on the minstrel stage. She is more ambiguous, however, about where authenticity lies when black children imitate white stage performers who mimic black people. Perhaps she implies that minstrelsy appropriates or distorts an "authentic" black culture, but she might also mean that only when black children mimic Rice's imitation of a black man's dance does it become authentic. The latter interpretation leads to a rather complex notion of black cultural authenticity that is based on a double layer of imitation. Fuller's comments on the song "Jim Crow" exemplify Lawrence Levine's observation that "Rice helped to inaugurate the paradoxical practice by which white minstrels frequently made stage hits out of bits of black songs, spreading them through the South where they were heard for the first time by other slaves who in their turn appropriated them and reintegrated them into the black tradition" (*Black Culture* 192). Indeed, the existence of African American minstrel performers reveals a mind-bending simulacrum of irony suggested but not clearly explained by Fuller's statement, regardless of her intent. Fuller's essay appeared around the time that the African American minstrel dancer William Henry Lane began his career, but she seems less concerned here about black professional performers on the minstrel stage than about "authentic" black children, and the advent of African American minstrel troupes was still a decade away. Despite Fuller's attempts to define authenticity and separate "real" black culture from stage minstrelsy, she conflates the two. This blurring of authenticity with counterfeit was commonly made by those who claimed minstrelsy as a national cultural form.

Authenticity, counterfeit, and appropriation were again linked to the notion of minstrelsy as a distinctly American cultural form in an 1855 *Putnam's Monthly* article titled "Negro Minstrelsy—Ancient and Modern," though here these issues were related to the commodification of black music and singers. Regarding "negro minstrels," the author Y. S. Nathanson claims: "The true secret of their favor with the world is to be found in the fact that they are genuine and real. They are no senseless and ridiculous imitations forged in the dull brain of some northern self-styled minstrel, but the veritable tunes and words which have lightened the labor of some weary negro in the cotton fields, amused his moonlight hours as he fished, or waked the spirits of the woods as he followed in the track of the wary racoon [sic]" (72–73). By embracing these "genuine" songs and avoiding northern minstrel counterfeits of them, Nathanson argues, American culture could compete with English and other European cultures and also live up to its geographical grandeur. However, since the people who produce such songs are slaves, Nathanson continues, this uniquely American musical genre is as commodified as the slaves themselves. After quoting the lyrics of "Uncle Gabriel the Negro General," Nathanson states: "Those of us who have for so many years been looking anxiously forward to the advent of the coming poet who is to take away from America the sin and the shame of never having produced an epic, or a lyric, commensurate with Niagara and the Rocky Mountains, will do well to get a subscription and buy the author of this song, if his owner can be persuaded to part with him" (73–74). It is uncertain whether this song, which was sung by E. P. Christy, originated among slaves, but Christy appropriated either the song itself or the musical culture and language of slaves more generally.[26] To the extent that minstrelsy appropriated and commodified African American music, Nathanson's tongue-in-cheek suggestion of purchasing a musical slave might be seen as merely a logical extension of such an appropriation and commodification. His article continues the theme of commodifying African American music by asking in its conclusion: "Is it unreasonable to suppose that, on each of these plantations, one song may be found of undisputed genuineness and excellence? It will be a proud day for America when these thirty thousand songs are collected into several volumes, handsomely bound in Turkey morocco, and superbly embellished. Then negro minstrelsy will take its proper place in literature; then Ethiopian Serenaders, and Congo Minstrels will draw crowded houses at three dollars a seat, and one dollar for a promenade ticket" (79). Such an elegantly bound anthology of African American music, Nathanson sarcastically implies, could take its place next to Shakespeare, Milton, and Dante on library shelves. Only when white minstrel troupes are involved, however, is money mentioned. It is unclear whether the article condones such appropriation of black culture by white performers. At any rate, we see the issues of cultural nationalism, genuineness, and appropriation once again linked to minstrelsy.

Americans who admired British and European culture probably did not appreciate minstrelsy's anti-British nationalism or its early working-class vulgarity. But even some of minstrelsy's detractors associated minstrelsy with nationalism. In "Who Are Our National Poets?" James Kennard parodies the notion of literary nationalism by making minstrelsy its logical extreme. He begins his argument with conventional defensiveness: "Who says we have no American Poetry? No American Songs? The charge is often made against us, but . . . without the slightest foundation of truth" (331). Although Kennard's Whiggish cultural loyalties differed from those of most minstrel songwriters and performers, the connection he draws between minstrelsy and literary nationalism resembles the celebratory, nationalist descriptions of minstrelsy. Furthermore, he conflates African American culture with its white theatrical appropriations and misrepresentations by sliding from "negro slaves" to blackface characters performed by whites—a conflation that was central to the rhetoric of minstrelsy as America's national cultural form.

Kennard takes his parody of anti-elitist, anti-European literary nationalism so far that he implies that America lacks Culture, that is, European high culture. He concludes his essay with a tongue-in-cheek challenge to "Bryant, Longfellow, Halleck, Whittier" to

> doubt no longer that nationality is the highest merit that poetry can possess; uneducate yourselves; consult the taste of your fair country-women; write no more English poems; write negro songs, and Yankee songs in negro style; take lessons in dancing of the celebrated Thomas Rice; . . . do this, and not only will fortune and fame be yours, but you will thus vindicate yourselves and your country from the foul imputation under which both now rest! With *your* names on the list with Crow and Coon, who *then* will dare to say that America has no National Poets? (341)

Kennard discredits American literary nationalism by ironically championing the subaltern negro—or rather his blackfaced white surrogate. For Kennard, such nationalism is absurd if it means that a "negro" poet (a white American writing minstrel songs) is better than an English poet. He seems less disturbed by minstrelsy's appropriation and distortion of African American culture than by the idea that white Americans could stoop so low as to emulate black people, and he implies that their appropriation of African American culture results in the blackening of American culture. Unlike Emerson and Melville,

Kennard sees American culture as Africanized, and his racism leads him to dismiss the idea of an Africanized American popular culture altogether.

Although many American cultural critics either dismissed or praised minstrelsy for its rejection of European culture, at least one writer suggested minstrelsy's similarity to that culture. The article "Songs of the Blacks," published anonymously in *Dwight's Journal of Music* in 1856, relies heavily on romantic racialist notions of African Americans and Anglo-Americans. Like many other expressions of cultural nationalism, it distinguishes between the "American" race (that is, white Americans) and Europeans. Interestingly, however, the article also claims that southern Europeans, unlike white Americans, have the same natural musical proclivities as southern blacks (51). This juxtaposition raises some interesting questions regarding the racial classification of southern Europeans, whom native whites did not see as white in nineteenth-century America (Roediger, *Working* 5–6). Although the article does not explicitly define southern Europeans in racial terms, comparing them to southern African Americans suggests that they have more in common musically with blacks than with the "American race." The article implies that white Americans should emulate the musicality of Europeans, and asserts that southern African Americans can help them to do so: "Let us not be ashamed to learn the art of happiness [through music] from the poor bondman at the South" (51). Unlike other essays that describe minstrelsy as a musical form that culturally distinguishes America from Europe, this article suggests that the musical affinities between southern blacks and southern Europeans can bring American culture closer to European culture. Yet "Songs of the Blacks" does not make the same argument for minstrelsy; in fact, it makes only one brief, disparaging reference to blackface entertainment.

Unlike "Songs of the Blacks," many other essays about minstrelsy described it in more favorable terms and positioned it as popular nationalist music and theatre. For the most part, though, this nationalist discourse does not offer a privileged position in American culture to African Americans, the people whose music and dance culture was either appropriated or distorted by minstrel performers and songwriters. Instead, it is based on the oppression and marginalization of African Americans. As Rogin writes, "Our national culture rooted itself—by way of the captivity narrative and the frontier myth on the one hand, of blackface minstrelsy on the other—in the nationally dispossessed.

American national culture created national identity from the subjugation of its folk" (*Blackface* 47). While the belief in black inferiority and the subjugation of African Americans were central to how white Americans defined their whiteness, they saw no contradiction in claiming black speech, dance, and music as popular cultural forms that represented all of the United States. In fact, white appropriation of African American culture was contingent upon white political, economic, and social domination of African Americans. As Morrison points out, America defined itself partly by professing democracy while excluding African Americans: "What was distinctive in the New [World] was, first of all, its claim to freedom and, second, the presence of the unfree within the heart of the democratic experiment—the critical absence of democracy, its echo, shadow, and silent force in the political and intellectual activity of some not-Americans. The distinguishing features of the not-Americans were their slave status, their social status—and their color" (48). Morrison's comment about defining American freedom by enslaving and excluding African Americans in some ways echoes W. E. B. Du Bois's concept of double-consciousness, in which African Americans are torn between their dual identity of being American (free) and black (enslaved). Unlike Du Bois's focus on African American psychology, however, Morrison is interested in the psychology of white Americans, specifically the ways in which they defined themselves by denying African Americans recognition as Americans. In a similar manner, minstrelsy helped white Americans construct a uniquely American cultural identity by positing its representations of African American culture as American while categorizing those whom it represented as not American.[27]

One discursive arena that celebrated minstrelsy as a national cultural form without crediting African American culture was minstrel songbooks. In the preface to the *Negro Minstrel Melodies* songster, for instance, William James Henderson writes: "All of us take a certain pleasure in contemplating the amusements of our fathers, and among them there was none which was more specifically American than the negro minstrel performance" (iii). Moreover, he asserts, minstrel songs "were distinctively American. They could not have been written in any other country than ours. They could not have been suggested by conditions other than those which existed in the days of slavery or the years immediately succeeding" (iii). Significantly, Henderson points out that these minstrels were white, not black (iii). In doing so, he confers

American representative status not upon actual African Americans, but upon their surrogate, blackfaced white imitators. The preface to an E. P. Christy songster repeats Henderson's claim that minstrelsy is uniquely American: "After our countrymen had, by force of native genius in the arts, arms, science, philosophy and poetry, &c, &c, confuted the stale cant of our European detractors that nothing original could emanate from Americans—the next cry was, that we have no NATIVE MUSIC; . . . until our countrymen found a triumphant vindicating APOLLO in the genius of E. P. Christy, who . . . was the first to catch our *native airs* as they floated wildly, or hummed in the balmy breezes of the sunny south" (qtd. in Saxton 166). Like the "Black Opera" article mentioned above, this preface elides European tradition by comparing American culture to that of ancient Greece, represented here by Apollo. But, like Kennard's essay, it also sidesteps the people whom white minstrels purported to portray. As Alexander Saxton points out: "Ambivalent especially toward the black component of their borrowings, the minstrels coveted the power and newness of the music, yet failed to recognize its Africanness, or to perceive in it segments of an idiom distinct and separate from the European idiom" (168). White American nationalists did not want America to be associated too closely with Europe on the one hand nor with African Americans on the other. In order to have a national culture that would neither imitate European culture (which would offend American nationalists) nor be a product of black people (which would offend most white Americans), it had to be produced by white people and depict non-white people. Blackface minstrelsy met both of these conditions perfectly.

One of the main features of the nationalist discourse surrounding minstrelsy was the myth of minstrelsy's origin. Historical accounts of minstrelsy's beginnings avoided reference to English and Italian entertainments using black masks or blackface, such as mummer's plays and the Clown and Harlequin characters of *commedia dell'arte* and pantomime that predated minstrelsy. More pointedly, they also ignored the success of Charles Mathews's blackface performances and songs in the United States during the early 1820s. Instead, this myth usually featured Rice's encounter with a crippled black hostler in Cincinnati (or Louisville) who had a peculiar dance step and Rice's borrowing of clothes from a black porter in Pittsburgh. The English minstrel performer Harry Reynolds sidesteps his own country's earlier contributions to blackface entertainment and traces minstrelsy's origin to "the real Jim Crow," a slave born in 1754 (79). Another telling of this origin myth can be found in Robert P. Nevin's 1867 article, "Stephen C. Foster and Negro Minstrelsy." Nevin concludes his two-page narrative of Rice's early blackface career by declaring: "Such were the circumstances—*authentic* in every particular—under which the first work of the distinct art of Negro Minstrelsy was presented" (610, my emphasis). His emphasis on the authenticity of minstrelsy's beginnings parallels the concern with authenticity in many discussions of minstrelsy's representations of African American culture and behavior. In addition, Nevin also points to minstrelsy's Americanness in discussing its evolution from solo to ensemble performance and its addition of the banjo: "Couples presently appeared, and, dispensing with the aid of foreign instruments, delivered their melodies to the more appropriate music of the banjo. . . . The art had now outgrown its infancy, and, disdaining a subordinate existence, boldly seceded from the society of harlequin and the tumblers, and met the world as an independent institution" (611). Though he may not have realized the African origin of the banjo, Nevin points to it as the means by which American minstrels declared their musical independence from the tyranny of European instrumentation. He also refers to the European Harlequin as a character that minstrelsy moved beyond, but he does not mention the Harlequin as a possible precursor of the blackface tricksters of American minstrelsy. Earlier in the essay, Nevin also casts minstrelsy in nationalist terms by asking: "As a national or 'race' illustration, . . . might not 'Jim Crow' and a black face tickle the fancy of pit and circle?" (608). Certainly, Rice's Jim Crow and later minstrel characters had a different meaning from the previous blackface and masking traditions of England, in that Jim Crow and Zip Coon were caricatures of (though promoted as genuine representations of) African Americans. Nevertheless, in denying or downplaying American minstrelsy's English and European ancestors, white Americans such as Nevin who claimed minstrelsy as an American cultural form also wanted it to be untainted by English and European origins.

Masculinity, Anti-Abolitionism, and "Wage Slavery" Rhetoric in American Minstrelsy

One feature of early minstrelsy that made it seem uniquely American to some cultural critics was its emphasis on excessive black masculinity. While white male audiences may have identified with the sexually potent, lower-class black male minstrel character, the fear of the black man's hypermasculinity and his competition with white men for white and black women (not to mention jobs) was alleviated by also making the ultramasculine black male the butt of ridicule. Although many minstrel shows also included blackfaced "wench" characters (played by men) and female impersonators, their femininity mostly served as a target of misogynist humor and as a foil to the masculinity of the male characters.[28] This lower-class hypermasculinity was neither reserved for black men nor for the minstrel stage, however. Consider, for instance, the ludicrous machismo and dialect of "Mike Fink's Brag" from The Crockett Almanac:

> I'm a Salt River roarer! I'm a ring-tailed squealer! I'm a reg'lar screamer from the ol' Massassip'! WHOOP! I'm the very infant that refused his milk before its eyes were open, and called out for a bottle of old Rye! I love the women an' I'm chockful o' fight! I'm half wild horse and half cock-eyed alligator and the rest o' me is crooked snags an' red-hot snappin' turtle. I can hit like fourth-proof lightnin' an' every lick I make in the woods lets in an acre o' sunshine. I can out-run, out-jump, out-shoot, out-brag, out-drink, an' out-fight, rough-an'-tumble, no holts barred, ary man on both sides the river from Pittsburgh to New Orleans an' back ag'in to St. Louiee. Come on, you flatters, you bargers, you milk-white mechanics, an' see how tough I am to chaw! I ain't had a fight for two days an' I'm spilein' for exercise. Cock-a doddle-do! (Lauter 2127)

While the dialect of "Mike Fink's Brag" differs from the black dialect of the minstrel stage, its lower-class inflection is coded as both American and masculine. Apparently, no educated, weak, wealthy American man—nor any English or European man—could talk like this. And while Mike Fink is willing to travel throughout the United States, "from Pittsburgh to New Orleans an' back ag'in to St. Louiee," he shows no interest in a salt-water voyage to Britain or Europe, places that he would probably imagine as being full of effete dandies. These masculine and American characteristics of "Mike Fink's Brag" appear in blackface in the fourth and final verses of one version of "Jim Crow":

> I'm a full blooded niggar,
> Ob de real ole stock,

> And wid my head and shoulder
> I can split a horse block.
>
> . . . .
>
> An I caution all white dandies,
> Not to come in my way,
> For if dey insult me,
> Dey'll in de gutter lay. (qtd. in Lott 23–24)[29]

In depicting a black man who threatens "white dandies" (who probably affect European manners) with violence and who "can split a horse block" "wid my head and shoulder," these lyrics suggest minstrelsy's celebration of rough black masculinity, though one might argue that white men were able to allay their fears of black male violence by laughing at this personification of it. In either case, the similarities between Jim Crow and Mike Fink imply that lower-class masculinity could partially erase racial differences. This transracial, mobile masculinity is suggested by the sheet music cover for another minstrel song, "Gombo Chaff," which features a drawing of a black river boatman whom we might imagine as the black counterpart of Mike Fink (see Figure 5)

Minstrelsy's brash celebration of lower-class masculinity was linked to its anti-British nationalism as well as its ridicule of abolitionism, a movement that competed with minstrelsy in propagating popular representations of African Americans in the North but that failed to win wide support among the white working-class northerners who formed a large part of minstrelsy's initial audience. Early minstrelsy's humorous, vulgar representations of blacks and its mockery of bourgeois pretensions (which were often associated with white abolitionists) had more appeal for white male laborers than harangues about the evils of slavery made by middle-class and wealthy abolitionists. In other ways, too, minstrelsy was more successful than abolitionism in encouraging working-class white American males to identify with blacks when they weren't laughing at them. While abolitionism had strong working-class support in mid-century Britain (Martin, *Britain's* 108),[30] such was not the case in the United States, though this does not mean that white American workers were proslavery (Foner, "Abolitionism" 257; Lott 155). There were several other reasons for American laborers' lack of support for abolitionism: white working-class racism, the perceived threat of labor competition from

Figure 5: Sheet music cover for "Gombo Chaff," c. 1834. Evert Jansen Wendell Bequest, Harvard Theatre Collection, Houghton Library.

free African Americans, and the class origins and orientations of many white American abolitionist leaders. Too often, white American abolitionists showed little concern for white workers who benefited from the color of their skin and experienced oppression that paled in comparison to that of black slaves but was nevertheless real (Foner, "Abolitionism" 264–65). The hostility of working-class white men toward middle- and upper-class abolitionists was as important as racism in explaining their participation in anti-abolition riots that erupted in New York, Philadelphia, and Boston during the 1830s and 1840s. Abolitionism also overlapped heavily with temperance, a movement that many white American laborers resisted. This proletarian opposition to abolitionism was popular both among native-born laborers and immigrants. The largest immigrant group, the Irish, despite living in the same slums as black people and facing xenophobic and anti-Catholic hostility from white native-born Protestants, generally did not identify with black people and violently opposed abolitionism, partly because of abolitionism's Protestant and xenophobic leanings.

Abolitionism's bourgeois elements gave it a reputation—in many instances well earned—of not caring about poor and working-class whites, and also made it vulnerable to accusations of condoning "wage slavery." This charge was voiced in Britain as well as in the United States, despite the greater popularity of abolitionism in the former nation and the fact that many British abolitionists supported the working-class Chartist movement (Fladeland, "'Our Cause'" 69–70).[31] Abolitionists who ignored the plight of poor white laborers should not have been surprised when their opponents used the rhetoric of wage slavery to steer white laborers away from abolitionism. Poverty in northern cities was more visible to early minstrel audiences than slavery in the South, and American abolitionists who ignored the former problem and enjoyed a comfortable economic position were often dismissed as hypocrites.

Although some American abolitionists were genuinely concerned about the problems of lower-class whites, they were not always encouraged by their colleagues. The Garrisonian abolitionist John Collins, for example, felt that overthrowing poverty and classism in Britain was just as important as abolishing chattel slavery in the United States. In December 1840, he wrote to Garrison:

> The English can never condemn our prejudice against color, our negro seats & negro cars, while they are exercising the same prejudice against poverty, that we do against color. It is unphilosophical to think that the British people as a nation should be in favor of genuine freedom, for upon an analysis of the principles of the British government, as developed by its system of legislation &c it will be found to be a vast and complicated system of slavery. It is a dangerous species of slavery,

as it is subtle and intangible. It gives to the poor subject the ostensible appearance of freedom the more successfully to grind him to powder. (qtd. in Taylor 133)

At an 1843 antislavery meeting in Syracuse, when Collins advocated extending the abolitionist movement's focus from two and a half million African American slaves to laborers throughout the world who were oppressed by capitalism, Douglass and Charles Lenox Remond verbally confronted him.[32] Because many abolitionists on both sides of the Atlantic did not support Collins's concern for the oppression of white laborers, they left the movement vulnerable to accusations of indifference toward the evils of industrial capitalism.

Defenders of slavery as well as advocates for industrial reform often attacked abolitionists with the phrase "wage slavery"[33] to equate the misery of wage laborers with that of chattel slaves, since they were overworked and their meager wages were not enough to buy adequate food, clothing, and shelter. The attitudes toward slavery implied in these comparisons were rather complex, as were the purposes of such comparisons. In discussing the term "wage slavery" in its American context, Eric Foner has argued that theoretically, it could suggest opposition to chattel slavery: "The entire ideology of the labor movement was implicitly hostile to slavery: slavery contradicted the central ideas and values of artisan radicalism—liberty, democracy, equality, and independence" (257). However, Foner's argument does not address the racism of many white American laborers that would discourage them from extending the same principles to black people, and Roediger claims that in reality, the phrase was often used for proslavery purposes (*Wages* 74). This rhetoric often implied that wage laborers were even more unfortunate than chattel slaves because the slaveholders' profit motive discouraged them from killing their slaves or abusing them so brutally as to make them useless or ineffective, whereas capitalists had no economic interest in maintaining the well-being of their laborers.[34] Defenders of slavery such as George Fitzhugh who employed the rhetoric of wage slavery ignored the fact that slaves were often murdered and maimed, and they offered no solutions to the plight of these wage slaves or the capitalist economy that oppressed them.

Such rhetoric appeared in derisive references to *Uncle Tom's Cabin* on the minstrel stage. The novel's stridently abolitionist message, coupled with the fact that its female author had stepped outside her proper sphere by becoming a literary celebrity who agitated for social change, made the text too easy a target to resist. Blackface satires of Stowe's novel that mentioned wage slavery may have also been replying to her treatment of this issue in a dialogue between the slaveholder Augustine St. Clair and his Yankee cousin Ophelia; not surprisingly, the novel has Ophelia dismiss Augustine's comparison between chattel slavery and wage labor. Minstrel songs and skits that accused Stowe of condoning wage slavery in her novel were also giving voice to the more lumpen elements of minstrelsy's audience, however. This combined attack on abolitionism and capitalist oppression may be seen in the minstrel song "Aunt Harriet Becha Stowe" by Charles Soran (1853), which refers to Stowe's triumphant tour of Britain after the publication of *Uncle Tom's Cabin:*

> But dont come back Aunt Harriet in England make a fuss,
> Go talk against your Country, put money in your puss
> And when us happy niggers you pity in your prayer,
> Oh! dont forget de WHITE SLAVES dat starvin ober dare. (5)

The antislavery arguments of *Uncle Tom's Cabin* were refuted on the stage as well as in minstrel songs. The 1853 play *Uncle Tom's Cabin in England* by Marco Mingle, published in Richmond, points to the hypocrisy of English abolitionists weeping over the suffering of slaves in Stowe's novel while showing contempt toward poor people in England (Hirsch 373–74).[35]

Working-class opposition toward abolitionism was related not only to the movement's neglect of capitalist oppression and laborers' fears of job competition from emancipated slaves, but also to the strong British support for abolition and to American working-class Anglophobic nationalism, which we have seen was a major element of early minstrelsy. Among native-born whites, nationalism entailed the rejection of Britain, and this hostility was often linked to opposition to abolitionism if not outright support for slavery. Anti-abolitionist and anti-British anger erupted in a New York riot in 1834, in which a mob ransacked the house of wealthy abolitionist Lewis Tappan, as well as a Boston riot in 1835 that targeted Garrison, Wendell Phillips, and the British Garrisonian George Thompson. Regarding the 1834 riot, the anti-abolitionist *Morning Courier and New-York Enquirer* of July 10, 1834, mentions the violence at the Bowery Theatre, whose stage manager, Mr. Farren, "had indulged in some very disrespectful expressions towards the American People, [and consequently] an indignant feeling against him had taken possession of a large portion of the public." Another manager who tried to restore order in the theatre "was greeted with 'down with the English man! down with the British b——'" ("Disturbances"). During the next decade, anti-British hostility directed at the British Shakespearean actor William Charles Macready sparked the bloodier Astor Place riot in May 1849. Lawrence Levine points out that this riot was spurred not only by workers' resentment against the bourgeoisie, but also by anti-British nationalism aimed at Macready (*Highbrow* 63–66).[36] The rioters supported Macready's American rival, Edwin Forrest, who, according to Michael Rogin, was "the first actor on the American stage to impersonate a plantation slave [in 1820]" (*Blackface* 28). The rioters also connected Macready's Britishness to elitism (despite his public support for workers), abolitionism, miscegenation, and African Americans. As the *New York Herald* reported, the crowd shouted sarcastically, "Three cheers for Macready, Nigger Douglass, and Pete Williams" (qtd. in Berthold 434).[37] American nationalism in this instance was based on notions of anti-elitist, working-class machismo and white racial purity, and the Astor Place rioters believed that purity was threatened not only by abolitionism but also by Britain and aristocratic values. Because working-class American patriotism was largely defined against Britain, and because many Americans associated that country with abolitionism, especially during the 1830s and 1840s (Temperley 205), this nationalism was often anti-abolitionist and to a lesser extent proslavery. These working-class, Anglophobic, anti-elitist, anti-abolitionist elements were nowhere more prevalent than in early minstrelsy.

In contrast to abolitionism, early minstrelsy spoke to white American (and, increasingly, immigrant) laborers in their own language, as Lhamon, Lott, and Roediger have demonstrated.[38] For this reason, its representations of blacks had a powerful impact on the racial views of white workers, and those depictions were not uniformly negative. To be sure, early minstrelsy often ridiculed and dehumanized African Americans, but it also encouraged white audiences to laugh with the blackfaced, lower-class endman and at the white bourgeois interlocutor. Lhamon claims that "blackface action is usually slashing back at the pretensions and politesse of authority more than at blackness. Certainly in these earliest instances of white fascination with black performers there was little laughing at blacks, alone or even primarily" (*Raising* 22). Early minstrelsy often succeeded where abolitionism failed in encouraging white laborers to identify with African Americans, largely because it appealed to its proletarian audience's class consciousness. It was also far more attractive to working-class nationalists than abolitionism, a transatlantic movement strongly associated with Britain.

Slave Narratives and American Literary Nationalism

Despite abolitionism's failure to compete with minstrelsy for the hearts and minds of working-class whites, its most popular form of literature—the slave narrative—could also be read (and to a lesser extent than minstrelsy, was read) as an example of distinctly American literature. Slave narratives, like minstrelsy, overlapped chronologically with American literary nationalism, though they have until recently been excluded from the American Renaissance canon. They also responded to the demands of literary and cultural nationalists in ways that often conflicted with the rougher nationalism of the minstrel stage. Unlike other abolitionist literature, which was produced in Britain as well as the United States (and was more widely accepted in the former nation), the slave narrative offered America a unique literary form, one that Britain rarely produced.[39] Over a quarter of a century ago, William Andrews read the fictional works of African Americans of the 1850s within the context of the American Renaissance, writing that "those who helped to instill a parallel kind of romantic spirit and ethnic awareness in Afro-American literature have either been largely forgotten or dissociated from their roles in this important movement in black American literary history" ("The 1850s" 38).[40] In recent decades, literary scholars have studied early African American fiction as well as slave narratives alongside (or as part of) the American Renaissance canon instead of treating them as a separate, implicitly inferior tradition or as mere documentary or propaganda. Nevertheless, the connections between mid-nineteenth-century African American literature and the works of Emerson, Melville, and Fuller have not been fully explored in the decades after Andrews raised this issue.

While Fuller's 1846 essay "American Literature" does not explore the relations between slave narratives and American literature, it hints that the American "genius" (which would create a distinctly American literature) might spring from non-white races. In comparing America to Britain, she writes:

> What suits great Britain, . . . does not suit a mixed race, continually enriched with new blood from other stocks the most unlike that of our first descent, with ample field and verge enough to range in and leave every impulse free, and abundant opportunity to develope a genius, wide and full as our rivers, flowery, luxuriant and impassioned as our vast prairies, rooted in strength as the rocks on which the Puritan fathers landed.
> That such a genius is to rise and work in this hemisphere we are confident. (123–24)

Though she may only be thinking of European "races" that would later be categorized as "white," Fuller does not specify which "stocks" are mixed in America. However, the fact that they are "the most unlike that of our first [English] descent" implies a wider racial range than that offered in the "new American" as defined by Crèvecoeur in *Letters from an American Farmer,* which was a product of mixing among northern European "races." Fuller then writes of the coming of this American "genius": "That day will not rise till the fusion of races among us is more complete" (124). This passage leaves open the possibility of an American genius formed of a blend of various races. Because any distinctly American literature would be imbued by this genius, Fuller allows that such literature could be written by authors of various races or by racially mixed authors. Such a possibility may encourage us to think of the role of the slave narrative in a uniquely American literary tradition.

The connection between slave narratives and literary nationalism was recognized more explicitly by the American Transcendentalist clergymen and abolitionists Theodore Parker and Ephraim Peabody. Parker's statement about slave narratives in his 1849 speech "The Position and Duties of the American Scholar" exemplifies Joan Dayan's claim that "the development of romance in the United States was linked in unsettling ways to the business of race" (90). Parker writes: "Yet, there is one portion of our permanent literature, if literature it may be called, which is wholly indigenous and original. . . . So we have one series of literary productions that could be written by none but Americans, and only here: I mean the Lives of Fugitive Slaves. But as these are not the work of men of superior culture, they hardly help to pay the scholar's debt. Yet all the original romance of America is in them, not in the white man's novel" (128). Like Melville, Parker is less concerned with quality than originality, and he does not expect slave narratives to show "superior culture." Indeed, many abolitionists expected slave narratives to reveal the evils of slavery bluntly rather than to show literary elegance, especially if such elegance would raise suspicions that the narrative was not written by an ex-slave, and Parker made this statement before the first fictional works by African Americans appeared during the 1850s.

In the same year, Peabody also described slave narratives as original works of American literature in his essay "Narratives of Fugitive Slaves," written for the *Christian Examiner:* "America has the mournful honor of adding a new department to the literature of civilization,—the autobiographies of escaped slaves" (19). Anticipating the nationalist concerns of Melville's "Hawthorne and His Mosses," Peabody suggests that slave narratives are the American equivalent of Homeric epics: "They encounter a whole Iliad of woes, not in plundering and enslaving others, but in recovering for themselves those rights of which they have been deprived from birth. Or if the Iliad should be thought not to present a parallel case, we know not where one who wished to write a modern Odyssey could find a better subject than in the adventures of a fugitive slave" (19). These narratives, Peabody suggests, are not only as inspiring and exciting as Homer's epics, but also as original. Furthermore, one might look at how epics—the *Iliad* and *Odyssey,* the *Aeneid,* and *Beowulf*—have been appropriated for nationalist purposes throughout history and extend Peabody's argument to read the prose epics of ex-slaves as America's national literature as well as abolitionist literature.

Despite Parker's and Peabody's nationalistic enthusiasm for slave narratives, white literary nationalists may well have felt ambivalent toward positing slave narratives as the signature genre of American literature. On the one hand, for American abolitionists to claim the slave narrative as a uniquely American literary genre was something of an embarrassment. The fact that so many slave narratives emerged in the United States during the mid-nineteenth century pointed to the prevalence of slavery and the failure of abolitionists to stamp it out. On the other hand, the proliferation of slave narratives was a testament to the activity of the American antislavery movement. Also, the critiques of American hypocrisy in slave narratives, either by the ex-slave narrators themselves or their abolitionist sponsors who wrote authenticating prefaces, could be seen as patriotic attempts to cleanse America of the moral stain of slavery.

A common theme in slave narratives that emphasized their national character while simultaneously exposing American hypocrisy was the desire for freedom from oppression, often expressed by quoting or revising Patrick Henry's famous statement "Give me liberty, or give me death!" For instance, Douglass's 1845 *Narrative* (significantly subtitled "An American Slave") invokes the patriotic masculinity of the Revolutionary leader and slaveholder while also improving upon his sentiment: "In coming to a fixed determination to run away, we did more than Patrick Henry, when he resolved upon liberty or death. With us it was a doubtful liberty at most, and almost certain death if we failed. For my part, I should prefer death to hopeless bondage" (74).[41] In his preface to the *Narrative,* Garrison also compares Douglass to the American patriot in response to Douglass's speech at the Nantucket antislavery convention: "PATRICK HENRY, of revolutionary fame, never made a speech more eloquent in the cause of liberty, than the one we had just listened to from the lips of that hunted fugitive" (4). Likewise, in his introduction to his narrative, Henry "Box" Brown mentions a letter written by the man to whom Brown was sent, which describes his escape as "a verification of Patrick Henry's Speech in Virginia Legislature, March, 1775, when he said, *'Give me Liberty or Give me Death'*" (7; italics in original). The appropriation of Henry's manly declaration was not limited to male slaves. Harriet Jacobs also writes that when she escaped from her master, "I had resolved that, come what would, there should be no turning back. 'Give me liberty, or give me death,' was my motto" (Brent 101). Obviously, such comparisons between slaves and Henry can be read as attacks on the falsity of America's purported commitment to freedom, especially when they were directed toward British audiences, who also saw themselves as champions of liberty. In addition, however, these comparisons suggest that slaves could appropriate this rhetoric for themselves and signify upon it for abolitionist purposes while also forging a distinctly American literary genre.

In addition to promoting the quintessential American value of freedom, Douglass and many other authors of slave narratives, such as William Wells Brown, patterned their narratives after the most famous American autobiography, written by another Founding Father and the forefather of Emersonian self-reliance, Benjamin Franklin. Like Franklin, African Americans born into slavery could overcome their low origins and make a name for themselves in American society through hard work and determination. The influence of Franklin's autobiography is more apparent in Douglass's *My Bondage and My Freedom* and in later slave narratives like Douglass's *Life and Times of Frederick Douglass* and Booker T. Washington's *Up From Slavery*.[42] In *My Bondage*, Douglass's description of his nearly penniless arrival in New York in 1838 echoes Franklin's first day in Philadelphia in 1723: "I had very little money—enough to buy me a few loaves of bread, but not enough to pay board, outside a lumber yard" (351). The fact that Douglass and other ex-slaves who had achieved success through hard work as Franklin had is even more impressive, given that they had almost no opportunities for education and faced racial prejudice, discrimination, and the threat of being captured and remanded to slavery.

Douglass's *Narrative* also includes another trait often seen as distinctively American, the Emersonian notion of self-reliance that was central to much of American Renaissance literature. When Douglass describes his first, unsuccessful attempt to escape with his fellow slaves, he emphasizes their unity, and when he reaches New York and eventually New Bedford, he also writes about the African American and white abolitionists who supported him. Yet in one of the most important events of his life, his escape in 1838 (the details of which he includes in his 1881 *Life and Times*), he is by necessity the lone hero running toward freedom. Other moments in the *Narrative* also emphasize his individualism, thus placing him in line with much American Renaissance literature and philosophy. His attack on the Underground Railroad, while it focuses on the indiscretion of abolitionists that made it harder for slaves to escape in the future, also suggests a skepticism toward abolitionists that resembles Emerson's rejection of reform movements in "Self-Reliance." Douglass's Byronic apostrophe to the ships on Chesapeake Bay also foregrounds his individualism, and when he arrives in New York, he is "in the midst of thousands, and yet a perfect stranger; without home and without friends, in the midst of thousands of my own brethren—children of a common Father, and yet I dared not to unfold to any one of them my sad condition" (89–90). The strangely abrupt mention of his marriage to Anna Murray in the *Narrative* does little to modify his individualistic self-portrait, and he passes it over even more quickly in *My Bondage*. Douglass later describes his new job in stridently self-reliant terms that reveal his Franklinesque work ethic: "It was new, dirty, and hard work for me; but I went at it with a glad heart and a willing hand. I was now my own master. It was a happy moment, the rapture of which can be understood only by those who have been slaves" (95). Andrews notes that in *My Bondage*, in which Douglass writes about northern prejudice and his conflicts with white Garrisonians, he further emphasizes self-reliance ("The 1850s" 56–57). Not all slave narrators were as individualistic as Douglass was; for instance, Jacobs and William Wells Brown emphasize the importance of relatives and abolitionist benefactors.[43] Yet Douglass's narratives, which share the individualism of many American Renaissance texts, have often been deemed the best and most representative narratives of the genre and can be read as examples of the uniquely American literature sought by literary nationalists.

Despite the statements of Parker and Peabody regarding the "Americanness" of slave narratives, and despite the ways in which these narratives can be read as distinctly American, they were not discussed in nationalist terms as much as minstrelsy was. One obvious reason for this difference is that while minstrelsy often celebrated America, slave narratives often criticized the hypocrisy of American democracy that condoned slavery, even if such criticism was meant to improve America by encouraging abolition. Another reason may be that some white American literary and cultural nationalists were more inclined to see the product of white performers appropriating black culture and mocking black people as representative of America than the literary products of ex-slaves. Thirdly, the strong support that British abolitionists gave to the U.S. antislavery movement and their interest in African American slave narratives may have made this genre seem un-American to white anti-British American nationalists. Regardless of the British origins of blackface performance and the huge popularity of minstrelsy in Britain, white Americans were more likely to claim minstrelsy than slave narratives as their own, and until recently, literary scholars segregated slave narratives from the American Renaissance canon. However, revisionist scholars of the American Renaissance have moved slavery closer to the center of this literary tradition and are increasingly placing the narratives of Jacobs and Douglass, as well as *Uncle Tom's Cabin,* on their bookshelves next to *Moby-Dick* and *The Scarlet Letter.*

Studying the essays of Emerson, Melville, Fuller, and Parker alongside slave narratives, minstrelsy, and the nationalist discourses surrounding them may help us sort out the complex relations among nationalism, race, gender, and class in mid-nineteenth-century America. Because of the prominence of slave narratives and the immense popularity of minstrelsy during this period, and because of the nationalist rhetoric surrounding them both, scholars of American literature would benefit from thinking more extensively about the links among minstrelsy, slave narratives, and the works of these four authors. Though the traditional notion of the American Renaissance—consisting of a handful of white, mostly male, "great" authors—has been redefined in ways that examine slavery, abolitionist literature, and African American literature, there is much more work to be done in this direction. It is especially important to examine the connections between minstrelsy and the American Renaissance because minstrelsy, more so than the slave narrative, has seldom been studied in conjunction with this literary period, either the older canon or the newer, broader canon that includes slave narratives and *Uncle Tom's Cabin.* If we wish to analyze the works of authors like Melville, Emerson, Stowe, and Jacobs within their cultural context rather than in artificial isolation, one fruitful approach would be to read them alongside minstrel shows and song lyrics. By not examining how slave narratives and minstrelsy were related to these works, we run the risk of perpetuating traditional, yet unfounded, classist distinctions between the "high" culture of the text and the "low" culture of popular stage entertainment as well as fallacious divisions between art and propaganda. In addition, separating these arenas of culture prevents us from seeing how they informed and paralleled each other. A comparative analysis, in contrast, would reveal how early minstrelsy's antibourgeois and anti-British elements were echoed by canonical nineteenth-century American authors and cultural critics. Such an approach would also clarify how both minstrelsy and slave narratives, despite their popularity in Britain, met the demands for a distinct national literature and culture that were so prevalent in the American Renaissance canon. Recognizing these connections reveals how these apparently disparate cultural forms at different class registers were unified by nationalist concerns. In addition to examining these links, we might also benefit from analyzing how slave narratives and other American literature dealing with slavery and race borrowed blackface elements to explore the meanings of race and to advocate the abolition of slavery. The following chapter analyzes these uses of blackface conventions by African American authors and abolitionist white writers, reminding us of minstrelsy's availability for antislavery and antiracist literary texts.

Blackface Tropes in Nineteenth-Century American Literature

Because Jim Crow jumped into American culture and started the first national form of popular culture while Emerson, Fuller, and Melville sought a distinctly American literature, he was bound to leave his footprints on the pages of American fiction. American authors often borrowed character types from minstrelsy, referred to its songs, employed its comedic style, and used the motif of blackface in their works, and they did so for multifarious reasons. Unlike most of the British literary texts analyzed in Chapter 3, which often use minstrelsy to denounce abolitionism, most of the American works discussed in this chapter are antislavery texts, and their appropriations and revisions of minstrelsy thus show its relationship to antislavery sentiment more directly. Although Melville's "Benito Cereno" is not explicitly antislavery and his *The Confidence-Man* avoids the subject entirely, these works are also worth analyzing alongside antislavery American texts because they utilize blackface motifs to explore issues of counterfeit and racial performance and challenge notions of racial stability and racial difference. In doing so, Melville's works strike at the ideological foundation of slavery by deconstructing the derogatory representations of black people that permeated American culture. In that respect, they relate indirectly to other American works that attack slavery head-on. Other American authors with more obvious abolitionist commitments—such as William Wells Brown, Frank Webb, Harriet Beecher Stowe, Lydia Maria Child, and Thomas Wentworth Higginson—appropriate minstrel song lyrics and comedic style as well as blackface motifs in their works. The presence of blackface elements in these antislavery texts should come as no surprise, given the conflict, overlap, and mutual borrowing between minstrelsy and abolitionism. Some of these texts countered minstrelsy's proslavery and racist tendencies, while others exploited early minstrelsy's antislavery impulses. In the works of some white antislavery authors, however, the ambiguity of the

blackface motif reveals their ambivalence toward ideologies of racial difference, and the uncritical use of minstrelsy's racist humor by Stowe and Higginson reminds us that many abolitionists did not always resist the ideology of
black inferiority that supported the very institution they opposed.

"They are apt to overdo the ebony": Blackface Performance and Counterfeit in "Benito Cereno" and *The Confidence-Man*

More than any other author in the American Renaissance pantheon, Melville
was deeply interested in racial issues. "Benito Cereno" (1855) and *The Confidence-Man* (1857) are particularly worth studying because they explore the
issue of racial indeterminacy and suggest that popular representations of blackness are performed, projected, and inauthentic. Morrison's theory about the
Africanist presence in American literature and society is relevant to Melville's
use of blackface imagery in these texts, particularly her claim that Africanisms
are essential to the works of white American authors, whose "concerns—au-
tonomy, authority, newness and difference, absolute power—not only become
the major themes and presumptions of American literature, but . . . each one
is made possible by, shaped by, activated by a complex awareness and employ-
ment of a constituted Africanism. It was this Africanism, deployed as rawness
and savagery, that provided the staging ground and arena for the elaboration of
the quintessential American identity" (44). Morrison argues that these authors
project their own undesirable attributes onto black people and define their
identities in opposition to these constructed Africanisms. Her explanation of
white American literary constructions of racial blackness is much like Ralph
Ellison's idea that white Americans act out their hopes and fears on the stage
of the mythical "Negro giant," and both notions are as applicable to minstrelsy
as to the works of Melville and other white American authors. As Lott and
Roediger have observed, white minstrel performers and audiences often projected their own lust, sloth, gluttony, and other unacceptable behaviors onto
black characters, thereby reinforcing their own sense of whiteness in contrast
to these personae. Minstrelsy's ascription of such objectionable traits to black
people, as well as its concerns with authenticity and performance, figure in
"Benito Cereno" and *The Confidence-Man*. Both texts employ minstrel devices
to blur racial distinctions and to underscore the performative and counterfeit
nature of white notions of "Negro" behavior. Though Morrison's theory about

the role of blackness in white American literature is pertinent to my analysis of Melville's use of blackface tropes, Melville portrays black people, racism, and racially coded behaviors and traits in more complicated and ironic ways than did most of his white contemporaries.

Melville's depictions of the American captain Amasa Delano and the slave mutiny leader Babo highlight both the performativity of black docility and simplicity and the projection of those qualities by whites onto blacks, two elements that were central to minstrelsy. Although most of "Benito Cereno" portrays Africans through the lens of Delano's romantic racialism, it eventually discredits that perspective by showing how Delano's racism allows the Africans to dupe him. His racism also prevents him from recognizing the danger facing the Spanish captain Benito Cereno, the Spanish crew, and even himself until the story's climax. In addition, by revealing Babo's pretended servility to Cereno as a sham, the text foregrounds the performativity of Babo's behavior in playing up to Delano's romantic racialism. This notion of black docility was common in minstrelsy, and while the story is set well before minstrelsy's heyday, it was written at the height of its success during the mid-1850s, and traces of burnt cork theatricality appear throughout the narrative. On another level, Babo's counterfeit "contented darky" act can be compared to the trickster figure of minstrelsy, though his deceptions are far more menacing than those of any endman. His performance and Delano's faith in its genuineness resemble the counterfeit portrayal of black people on the minstrel stage and white audiences' belief in its accuracy, especially when the performers were black. By showing how black men can act out white notions of blackness, the story suggests that racial identity is nothing more than performance, regardless of the performer's race. At one point Delano comes close to recognizing the performativity of both Babo's and Cereno's behavior, but falls short: "To Captain Delano's imagination, . . . there was something so hollow in the Spaniard's manner, with apparently some reciprocal hollowness in the servant's dusky comment of silence, that the idea flashed across him, that possibly master and man, for some unknown purpose, were acting out, both in word and deed, nay, to the very tremor of Don Benito's limbs, some juggling play before him" (216–17). Delano is right to suspect that Babo's behavior is a performance, but his racist belief in black docility makes him suspicious for the wrong reason, and he soon dismisses his qualms. While he recognizes the theatricality of Babo's and Cereno's performances, he does not realize that he is part of a very dangerous minstrel show, in which Babo's apparent servility is merely a performative mask to hide his power over Cereno and to draw Delano himself into a deadly trap.

Delano views Babo as good-natured and simple-minded not only because of the latter's proto-minstrel performance, but also because Delano seems to project some of his own qualities onto Babo. The narrator describes Delano as "a man of such native simplicity as to be incapable of satire or irony" (184) and often refers to his naïveté and good nature. Later the narrator ironically presents Delano's romantic racialist perceptions of black people, which can be read as projections of his own personality:

> Above all [negro traits] is the great gift of good-humor. . . . a certain easy cheerfulness, harmonious in every glance and gesture; as though God had set the whole negro to some pleasant tune.
>
> . . . . When at ease with respect to exterior things, Captain Delano's nature was not only benign, but familiarly and humorously so. At home, he had often taken rare satisfaction in sitting in his door, watching some free man of color at his work or play. If on a voyage he chanced to have a black sailor, invariably he was on chatty and half-gamesome terms with him. In fact, like most men of a good, blithe heart, Captain Delano took to negroes, not philanthropically, but genially, just as other men to Newfoundland dogs. (212–13)

The narrator also relates Delano's belief in "the docility arising from the unaspiring contentment of a limited [black] mind, and that susceptibility of bland attachment sometimes inhering in indisputable inferiors" (212). As these passages imply, it is not Africans who embody the characteristics of "good-humor" and the "unaspiring contentment of a limited mind," but Delano himself; he ascribes to blacks his "native simplicity" and "good, blithe heart," never dreaming that they would kill to regain their freedom. In this sense, he attributes his own qualities to Africans in much the same way that white American authors transferred their own undesirable traits onto their representations of African Americans. Morrison analyzes this projection by white American authors, but Melville's text is interesting in its implicit, ironic comment on such projections by Delano. Through Delano, the text reveals how the attribution of certain psychological traits to Africans supports pernicious ideologies of racial difference.

This insight can easily be transferred from Delano's mindset to the minstrel stage. The docility and good humor that Delano ascribes to Babo resemble the racial traits often projected by white blackface performers onto African Americans. While Delano's perception of Babo was clouded by the kind of racist representations of African Americans that appeared in minstrelsy, minstrelsy's claims of authenticity and the pervasiveness of its depictions of black people in American culture may have made it more difficult for Melville's white readers to see past Delano's perspective and recognize Babo's behavior as a minstrel act. Delano's misperception of Babo's motive is more dangerous than mistaking a blackfaced white performer for a black person, however, because Babo, like many slaves, uses the minstrel mask to hide his rebellion. Ironically, while Delano's gullibility, racism, and projection of his simplicity onto the Africans prevent him from recognizing the situation, they also save him from the hasty death he would have suffered if he had shown any sign of comprehension. Furthermore, his simplicity is in some ways linked to his nationality, which is often mentioned in the text. To a considerable extent, Delano embodies America itself and the innocence with which it has often been associated. Thus, the story blurs popular racial distinctions by suggesting that there is little if any difference between (white) American simplicity and the romantic racialist notion of African simplicity. Of course, neither Babo nor the other Africans are as simple as Delano believes, and their "contented slave" personae are deceptive performances that match the traits that Delano projects onto them. Through Babo, the text reveals the image of the happy slave that was popularized on the minstrel stage to be a mask used by slaves as a weapon of survival or rebellion.[1]

Melville switches from a black proto-minstrel performer in "Benito Cereno" to a blackfaced white man in *The Confidence-Man,* continuing his exploration of racial indeterminacy and the notion of counterfeit in blackface performance. In Chapter 3, the narrator links inauthentic blackness to sham disability by describing Black Guinea (the white confidence man in blackface) as

a grotesque negro cripple, in tow-cloth attire and an old coal-sifter of a tambourine in his hand, who, owing to something wrong about his legs, was, in effect, cut down to the stature of a Newfoundland dog; his knotted black fleece and good-natured, honest black face rubbing against the upper part of people's thighs as he made shift to shuffle about, making music, such as it was, and raising a smile even from the gravest. It was curious to see him, out of his very deformity, indigence, and houselessness, so cheerily endured, raising mirth in some of that crowd, whose own purses, hearths, hearts, all their possessions, sound limbs included, could not make gay. (7)

Aside from repeating the comparison between black people and Newfoundland dogs that appears in "Benito Cereno," this description of Black Guinea's apparent disability may remind readers of the deformed black hostler of legend whose dance step Rice allegedly appropriated in his Jim Crow act. Like blackness, disability is a form of otherness that "normative" (in this case, able-bodied) people can perform, counterfeit, and appropriate for monetary purposes.

The performance of disability and blackness is lucrative for Black Guinea, as it was for Rice. The character's name, which denotes a British coin as well as western Africa, points to a possible connection between counterfeit and commodification, a link that was central to minstrelsy.[2] The monetary association is appropriate here. Like the rest of the novel, this episode, in which a crowd throws pennies at Black Guinea's open mouth, focuses on counterfeit, both in terms of false currency and imposture.[3] The narrator paraphrases an observer who complains about Black Guinea's deceitful and mercenary performance of disability: "While this game of charity was yet at its height, a limping, gimlet-eyed, sour-faced person . . . began to croak out something about his deformity being a sham, got up for financial purposes, which immediately threw a damp upon the frolic benignities of the pitch-penny players" (8). Later, this genuinely disabled skeptic also questions the authenticity of Black Guinea's blackness, an issue with which white blackface performers and their audiences were deeply concerned. Despite Black Guinea's "honest" face (his blackness apparently does not rub off on the thighs of the passersby), his pretended lameness and blackness are paralleled by the counterfeit pennies (many of which are actually buttons) thrown at his mouth.[4]

Melville later shifts the metaphor of racial inauthenticity from currency to the stage. When the crippled skeptic tells his interlocutor (the confidence man in another guise, this time as the "man in gray") that he suspects Black Guinea of being a "white masquerading as a black," the following exchange ensues:

> "If a white, how could he look the negro so?"
> "Never saw the negro-minstrels, I suppose?"
> "Yes, but they are apt to overdo the ebony; exemplifying the old saying, not more just than charitable, that 'the devil is never so black as he is painted.'" (27)

By distinguishing between genuine and overdone blackness, the man in gray suggests the inauthenticity of minstrelsy's depiction of blackness. The fact that easy racial distinctions and categories are problematized by the man in gray is appropriate, in that he can slip between a black persona and a white one. The man in gray, unlike the white minstrel, does not oscillate between a "real" whiteness and an artificial blackness. Rather, he refuses to hide his apparent whiteness (which his racially unmarked identity suggests), opting for a more subtle, ambiguous, gray disguise that fools the skeptic. In addition to emphasizing the performative, inauthentic nature of minstrelsy, this scene also uses the grayness of the confidence man's disguise to blur the white/black dichotomy that often shaped minstrelsy's representations of black people.

Although Melville opposed slavery as well as many of its supporting racial ideologies, he did not write on behalf of the abolitionist movement, and most of his works do not deal explicitly with slavery. But other American authors committed to abolition—both white and African American—represented slavery more directly and polemically, and they sometimes enlisted the songs, humor, and stock characters of minstrelsy to further their agenda. The blackface traces in their works testify to the pervasiveness of minstrelsy in American culture, and they chose these tropes precisely because of their familiarity and appeal to many readers. In addition, because early minstrelsy often depicted the hardships of slaves, many abolitionist authors borrowed its elements in their works. Yet as minstrelsy became more conventional and commercial from the 1850s onward, it became more racist and proslavery, and many abolitionist authors employed its conventions to create a counterdiscourse to minstrelsy's support for slavery. Analyzing these uses of minstrelsy by American abolitionist authors leads us to several interpretations. First, some of these writers signified on and resemanticized these minstrel motifs to reverse their racist and proslavery connotations. Second, abolitionist appropriations of minstrel conventions reveal the ideological versatility of early minstrelsy, which was available for antislavery and antiracist purposes. Third, the unironic use of minstrelsy's more racist elements by some white antislavery authors points to their limited racial egalitarianism.

Signifying on Stephen Foster: Black Abolitionist Revisions of Minstrel Songs

Although Douglass, Sarah Parker Remond, and other African Americans often denounced minstrelsy as irredeemably racist, some black abolitionists borrowed its features in their works and performances. Henry "Box" Brown, for example, employed minstrel conventions in his performances (Newman xxix). Another black abolitionist author, William Wells Brown, may at first appear complicit in minstrelsy's racism in his depiction of the ludicrous slave character Sam in his novel *Clotel*. One scene describes Sam as "one of the blackest of his race. This he evidently regarded as a great misfortune. However, he made up for this in his dress. Mr. Peck [his master] kept his house servants well dressed; and as for Sam, he was seldom seen except in a ruffled shirt" (135). Sam's fancy dress resembles that of the absurdly overdressed northern dandy Zip Coon of the minstrel stage. Moreover, his skin tone resembles the exaggerated blackness produced by burnt cork, he speaks in a slave dialect, and he mispronounces long words such as "insinuation" ("insinawaysion") in the tradition of minstrelsy's stump speeches. Brown continues the minstrel humor with his narration of an incident (accompanied by an illustration) in which Sam pulls the wrong tooth from the mouth of a slave suffering from a toothache. Later, though, Brown reveals that Sam is not just a minstrel clown but a trickster who uses the minstrel mask to hide his hatred of slavery and sadistic slavemasters. The "real" Sam emerges when he sings a song that points out a dead slaveholder's cruelty and rejoices in his death. Moreover, in Brown's 1858 play *The Escape; or, A Leap for Freedom*, the minstrel-like, comical stupidity of Cato is later countered by his singing of an antislavery song that reveals the United States' brutal oppression of black people.

William Wells Brown, along with Henry "Box" Brown and Martin Delany, also co-opted popular minstrel songs by using their melodies and writing new lyrics that reversed minstrelsy's racism and proslavery sentiment or exploited its early antislavery tendencies. The song Cato sings in Brown's *The Escape*, for instance, is set to the tune of the minstrel song "Dandy Jim" (67–69). Brown also collected songs for *The Anti-Slavery Harp: A Collection of Songs for Anti-Slavery Meetings* (1848) that appropriated the melodies of minstrel songs, including "Get off the Track," sung to the tune of Foster's minstrel song hit "Dan Tucker"; "The North Star," which used the melody of "O, Susannah"; and "A Song for Freedom," which borrowed the tune of "Dandy Jim" (Gilmore 37, 180 n. 3). In *Clotel*, Brown also revises the lyrics of Foster's popular song "Old Uncle Ned" (1848), which depicts Ned as a pitiable figure without suggesting that he suffered injustices from slavery:

> Dere was an old nigga dey calld him Uncle Ned
> Hes dead long ago, long ago
> He had no wool on de top ob de head
> De place wha de wool ought to grow.
> Den lay down de shubble and de hoe-o-o
> And hang up de fiddle and de bow.
> No more hard work for poor old Ned
> Hes gone wha de good niggas go. (SSMC)

Brown has Sam and his fellow slaves sing a different version of this song when they believe they are alone, though they are unknowingly overheard by Georgiana (the antislavery daughter of Sam's master) and her northern lover Carlton. Brown revises Foster's song by exposing the brutality of slavery, removing the slaves' mask of servility, and revealing their glee upon hearing of the master's death. Below are excerpts from this version:

> Old master has died, and lying in his grave,
> > And our blood will awhile cease to flow;
> He will no more trample on the neck of the slave;
> > For he's gone where the slaveholders go.

> Hang up the shovel and the hoe—
> Take down the fiddle and the bow—

> Old master has gone to the slaveholder's rest;
> He has gone where they all ought to go.
>
> We'll no more be roused by the blowing of his horn,
>   Our backs no longer he will score;
> He no more will feed us on cotton-seeds and corn;
>   For his reign of oppression now is o'er.
> He no more will hang our children on the tree,
>   To be ate by the carrion crow;
> He no more will send our wives to Tennessee;
>   For he's gone where the slaveholders go. (153–54)

In Brown's revision, the slaves "hang up the shovel and the hoe" not because they mourn the loss of a poor, humble slave or a kind master, but because they celebrate the death of their cruel owner. In this song, Brown cashes in on the popularity of Foster's minstrel air while giving it a much more subversive, antislavery meaning.

Henry "Box" Brown also adapts "Old Uncle Ned" in the 1851 edition of his narrative for antislavery purposes—in his case, to describe his escape from slavery. This version depicts a much more heroic image of black masculinity than Foster's version does:

> Here you see a man by the name Henry Brown,
> Ran away from the South to the North;
> Which he would not have done but they stole all his rights,
> But they'll never do the like again.
> *Chorus*—Brown laid down the shovel and the hoe,
> Down in the box he did go;
> No more Slave work for Henry Box Brown,
> In the box *by Express* he did go (65)

Aside from the obvious difference between the slave dialect of Foster's lyrics and the standard English of Brown's revision, Brown revises Uncle Ned's death and possible placement into a coffin by describing his own shipment in a different kind of box, one that enables his escape. Instead of going from life to death, as Ned does in Foster's song, Brown moves from the death of slavery to the life of liberty. Brown thus signifies on "Old Uncle Ned" by suggesting that a slave's life of forced, uncompensated labor could end not in death but in freedom.

Like Brown and Brown, Delany alters the lyrics of Foster's popular songs for antislavery purposes in his novel *Blake*. The chorus in his revision of "Old Uncle Ned" is much like William Wells Brown's version:

> Hang up the shovel and the hoe-o-o-o!
> I don't care whether I work or no!
> Old master's gone to the slaveholder's rest—
> He's gone where they all ought to go! (105–06)

In addition to changing the content of Foster's song, Delany, like Brown and Brown, standardizes the dialect in Foster's lyrics to emphasize the intelligence of African Americans—a major argument against slavery and racism. Delany also rewrites Foster's classic blackface tearjerker, "Old Folks at Home" (1851), which underscores the slave singer's loyalty to his master's plantation. In the first stanza of Foster's version, the singer laments:

> Way down upon de Swanee ribber,
> Far, far away,
> Dere's wha my heart is turning ebber,
> Dere's wha de old folks stay.
> All up and down de whole creation,
> Sadly I roam,
> Still longing for de old plantation,
> And for de olds folks at home. (3–4)

By foregrounding the slave's family ties in his version, Delany refutes the pro-slavery argument that slaves were not emotionally scarred when they were divided from members of their family:

> Way down upon the Mobile river,
> Close to Mobile bay;
> There's where my thoughts is running ever,

> All through the livelong day:
> There I've a good and fond old mother,
>   Though she is a slave;
> There I've a sister and a brother,
>   Lying in their peaceful graves. (100–101)

To some extent, Delany's emphasis on family separation was not a radical revision of the original "Old Folks at Home," which, like many minstrel songs, describes the sorrow of slaves lamenting the absence of their loved ones: "When I was playing wid my brudder, / Happy was I, / Oh! take me to my kind old mudder, / Dere let me live and die" (5). Thus, Foster's song was already somewhat compatible with antislavery sentimentalism.[5] Nevertheless, this separation is not blamed on a master selling any of the family members, and the song evokes nostalgia for the plantation where the singer was enslaved. At first, Delany seems content to change only the location of the singer's homeland and render the song without dialect. In the second quatrain, though, his depiction of the painful separation of slave families is more critical of slavery than Foster's lyrics were. Ken Emerson observes that Delany also signified on the refrain of Foster's "Oh! Susanna" (1848) to celebrate the escapes of slaves: "O, righteous Father / Wilt thou not pity me; / And aid me on to Canada / Where fugitives are free?" (133). Rather than simply criticizing or ignoring minstrelsy, Delany, Brown, and Brown appropriate its popular melodies, exploit the antislavery elements of some songs, and reverse the proslavery bent of others.

"Grease Dat Face an Make It Look Shiney": Blackface Motifs in American Abolitionist Literature

In addition to borrowing the tunes of popular minstrel songs and rewriting their lyrics, one of the most common ways in which American abolitionist authors incorporated and signified on minstrelsy was to depict characters who literally or figuratively are "blacked up." In some cases, whites darken the skin of racially mixed slaves in response to their fears about miscegenation and its blurring of racial distinctions. For instance, the fair-skinned slave Mary in *Clotel*, the light-complected protagonist Frado of Harriet Wilson's *Our Nig*, and

Moses Roper in his narrative are forced to work in the sun in order to darken their faces. Obviously, this is an attempt to eliminate the racial ambiguity of these characters, which threatens the dualistic logic supporting slavery, and to erase the living evidence of miscegenation, which in Mary's and Roper's cases are caused by the sexual indiscretions of white men. Roper reveals a much more painful and alarming incident of facial darkening, in which his master Mr. Gooch, upon returning from church, "pour[ed] some tar on my head, then rubbed it all over my face, took a torch, with pitch on, and set it on fire" (506). Gooch is not content to blacken Roper's face; he makes Roper suffer pain to remind him that despite his pale skin and white ancestry, he is black. Gooch apparently commits this atrocity because he is disturbed by Roper's light complexion, and in this instance Roper's artificial, involuntary blackness causes him more agony than would a naturally dark skin. In each case, whites blacken the faces of light-skinned biracial slaves in order to bolster the notions of racial difference supporting slavery, much in the same way that white minstrels used burnt cork to emphasize their difference from the black people they imitated and ridiculed.

Slaveholders had other reasons for darkening the skin of their slaves. In *Clotel*, William Wells Brown connects blacking up to issues of counterfeit and commodification. In the short version of his personal narrative originally appended to the novel, he explains that his master, Mr. Walker, was a slave trader who made Brown blacken his other slaves before selling them—a task that Roper also describes being ordered by his master to perform (508). Referring to himself in the third person, Brown writes: "On their way down to New Orleans William had to prepare the old slaves for market. He was ordered to shave off the old men's whiskers, and to pluck out the grey hairs where they were not too numerous; where they were, he coloured them with a preparation of blacking with a blacking brush. After having gone through the blacking process, they looked ten or fifteen years younger" (52). Despite the negative values that whites often ascribed to blackness, this scene foregrounds its financial worth. In this sense, counterfeit blackness was commodified for Walker, as it was for white minstrel performers who made money by blacking up. In *Clotel*, Brown again raises the issue of racial counterfeit by describing how the slave Pompey prepares other slaves for market. Although Pompey "was of real negro blood" and exclaims, "Dis nigger is no counterfeit; he is de genewine artekil" (90), he engages in counterfeit by instructing the slaves to make themselves more marketable by lying about their age. While Pompey does not employ the blacking brush as Brown did, he tells one slave to "grease dat face an make it look shiney" (90). Moreover, Brown's description of Pompey as having "eyes large, lips thick, and hair short and woolly" (90) brings to mind the exaggerated, counterfeit minstrel representations of black people. Both Brown's characterization of Pompey and his descriptions of how he and Pompey prepared slaves for market underscore the connections among slavery, minstrelsy, profit, and counterfeit. Unlike Melville's "Benito Cereno," however, the link between blackface and counterfeit in Brown's text emphasizes the power of slaveholders rather than the subversive, deceptive minstrel performances of slaves. This scene may bring to mind how the conventionalized performances of blackness by African American minstrel performers indirectly and unintentionally undermined popular notions of racial essentialism.

Frank J. Webb also signifies on the uses and meanings of blackface in his novel *The Garies and Their Friends* (1857), though he does so in order to counter minstrelsy's racism and undermine popular white notions of racial difference. Webb focuses on free African Americans in antebellum Philadelphia, one of the centers of early minstrelsy, and his description of the wealthy black land-lord Walters revises the northern urban dandy character of the minstrel stage and blurs the distinction between black and white racial characteristics. In his hair texture and skin tone, Walters looks emphatically African; the narrator observes his "jet-black complexion, and smooth glossy skin" and notes that "his head was covered with a quantity of woolly hair, which was combed back from a broad but not very high forehead. His eyes were small, black, and piercing, and set deep in his head" (121–22). Some of his other facial features, however, resemble those of northern Europeans; the narrator remarks: "His aquiline nose, thin lips, and broad chin, were the very reverse of African in their shape, and gave his face a very singular appearance" (122). While this description makes Walters seem like a blacked-up white man, his appearance suggests interracial mixture rather than racial imposture. His respectability also sets him apart from the Zip Coon minstrel caricature through which white men ridiculed free black men of the North, and the "neatness and care" (122) with which he dresses contrasts with Zip's exaggerated dandy attire. In addition, instead of being an inauthentic white man in blackface, Walters proves that he is "authentically" black through his commitment to racial uplift, which he demonstrates by helping other African Americans financially and by leading an armed resistance to a white racist mob.

Webb's depiction of the white Clarence Garie is in one sense the reverse image of his portrait of Walters. Walters is dark-skinned and respectable, while Garie is despised by white racists despite his pale skin because he is married to a biracial woman. Blackface is invoked obliquely in a scene in which Garie's enemy, the racist George Stevens, organizes an anti-abolitionist mob that attacks Garie's house and threatens him with tar and feathers, a very painful method of blacking up. For many proslavery whites in the antebellum North, other whites who married black people or supported abolitionism surrendered part of their skin privilege and therefore became less "white" because of their supposed rejection of white supremacy. Because they oppose abolitionism and assume that any white person married to a black person must be an abolitionist, members of the mob see Garie's whiteness as only skin deep, and the tar with which they threaten him would manifest the essential "blackness" represented by his interracial marriage and alleged abolitionist sympathies.

Stevens, however, is actually blackened with tar in a humorous scene occurring shortly before the riot. Webb uses the blackface motif here to ridicule Stevens and undermine the notion of permanent racial difference, which supports his racism. In an attempt to disguise himself, Stevens buys a used coat which, unbeknownst to him, was traditionally worn by members of one of Philadelphia's gang-like fire companies.[6] Soon after entering a rough neighborhood, he is surrounded by members of a rival gang who take him for an enemy, beat him, and smear his face with tar. His swollen lips and blackened skin make him unrecognizable as a white man; as one of his tormentors remarks, "'Oh! don't he look like a nigger!'" (188). The narrator adds: "His lips were swelled to a size that would have been regarded as large even on the face of a Congo negro, and one eye was puffed out to an alarming extent" (189). Stevens's blackface nightmare continues when he is discovered by a group of drunken white men, including some of his acquaintances who fail to recognize him and instead take him for a "darky." One of them smears his darkened face with a piece of lime and quips, "'I'm making a white man of him, I'm going to make him a glorious fellow-citizen, and have him run for Congress'" (191). After he reveals his identity, the men try to help him remove the tar with water, but "unfortunately, the only result obtained by their efforts was to rub it more thoroughly in" (192). When Stevens finally gets home, his wife is shocked by his appearance, and despite her arduous attempts to clean her his face, she cannot completely remove the tar. As a result, his skin is "half scraped off from his swollen face" (193).

Throughout this scene, Webb deflates Stevens's sense of whiteness and signifies on the notions of racial difference connoted by blackface. Of course, blacking up was entirely voluntary and temporary on the part of white minstrels; unlike dark-skinned African Americans, they could choose to be "black" and could wipe off the burnt cork when being "black" was no longer convenient. Although they crossed the color line in appearance, they reinforced racial distinctions by always being either white or black, but never both simultaneously, never something in between. In contrast, Stevens's blackface episode is involuntary and not as temporary or painless as he would wish; removing the tar from his face proves more difficult than taking off burnt cork. Because his attempts to wipe off the tar only succeed in rubbing it more deeply into his skin, he cannot repudiate the blackness symbolized by the tar as easily as white minstrels wearing burnt cork. As a result, he is neither entirely "white" nor completely "black." Webb also reverses the process of darkening white skin in minstrelsy by having Stevens's black skin whitened with lime, as if his whiteness were artificial rather than natural. As this ordeal reveals, his white status, upon which his race privilege and racism are based, is not as secure as he had assumed.

Blackface is also used to critique white racism and blur racial categories in Hannah Crafts's *The Bondwoman's Narrative,* an autobiographical novel recently recovered by Henry Louis Gates, Jr. Like Webb, Crafts employs blackface for a humorous purpose: to show a white racist person who is humiliated by an undesired, temporary experience with it. The narrator's mistress, Mrs. Wheeler, applies a whitening powder to her face, but it blackens her skin when it is exposed to the fumes from her smelling bottle (165–66). This unexpected racechange is especially embarrassing because it occurs when she tries to use her influence to secure a political appointment for her husband in Washington, D.C. Her attempt to whiten her face reveals her insecurity regarding her whiteness, and the powder brings out this perceived lack rather than covering it up. The narrator helps her restore the original color to her skin, implying that Mrs. Wheeler's blackness is not essential, but also suggesting that white people need black people to shore up their sense of whiteness. Despite the restoration of her skin color, her blackface episode keeps her from enjoying racial privilege among Washington's political elite and damages her reputation and her husband's so badly that they decide to leave the city. This scene shows the importance of color in advancing oneself in society and politics, but more importantly, it points out the tenuousness of whiteness and white privilege, as well as the fluidity of racial categories.

Stowe also undercuts popular notions of racial difference through her incorporation of blackface in *Uncle Tom's Cabin*. Unlike Crafts and Webb, however, Stowe focuses on the subversive uses of blackface by black characters. The description of a blackened portrait of General Washington in Uncle Tom's cabin early in the novel jocularly suggests the possibility of a black president and questions white America's reverence for white manhood in its representations of its Founding Fathers. When introducing Uncle Tom and Aunt Chloe, the narrator observes that their cabin includes "a portrait of General Washington, drawn and colored in a manner which would certainly have astonished that hero, if ever he had happened to meet with its like" (18).[7] Although the humor of this scene depends upon the unlikelihood of a black president, it nevertheless raises that possibility. Moreover, while Tom and Chloe show no trace of white ancestry or any biological relation to Washington, this scene suggests that black slaves could be the progeny of slaveholding Founding Fathers, as was the case for the descendents of Thomas Jefferson and Sally Hemings. Despite its implied reference to blacking up, this passage comments less on blackface minstrelsy than on race, paternity, and the myth of America's origins. In showing how representations of powerful white men can be literally denigrated, this passage implies that their very whiteness might also be vulnerable.

Stowe later includes a variation on the blackface trope to blur racial categories and foreground their arbitrary nature in the Kentucky tavern scene in Chapter 11 of the novel. Here she quotes a posted handbill describing George as a light-skinned fugitive slave and then introduces a brown-skinned Spaniard named Henry Butler who turns out to be George in disguise. In the handbill, George's master describes him as "my mulatto boy . . . . a very light mulatto, brown curly hair; is very intelligent, speaks handsomely, can read and write;

will probably try to pass for a white man; is deeply scarred on his back and shoulders; has been branded in his right hand with the letter H" (91). This passage encourages readers to think that a person with George's intellectual and physical attributes should neither be enslaved nor abused. Nevertheless, despite the description of George as "very light," the suggestion that he "will probably try to pass for a white man" implies that he may make his skin even lighter—in other words, that he may use "whiteface" to pass. However, the narrator describes "Henry Butler" as having "a dark, Spanish complexion, fine, expressive black eyes, and close-curling hair, also of a glossy blackness" and mentions "his well-formed aquiline nose, straight thin lips, and the admirable contour of his finely-formed limbs" (92). This seems to erase the implication of black ancestry in the former quotation; that is, the shape of George's face and body determine his racial identity in the eyes of white observers more than the color of his skin, eyes, and hair. The passage illustrates the capriciousness of racial categorization, in which certain physical traits count more than others. When George privately reveals his identity to his former employer, Mr. Wilson, he explains that "a little walnut bark has made my yellow skin a genteel brown, and I've dyed my hair black" (94). By outguessing his master and making himself darker in order to pass for white, George not only deceives anyone who is looking for him and displays his intelligence in doing so, but he also points out the arbitrary nature of racial classification. As a light-skinned person blacking up to pass for white, he reverses the method and meaning of blackface and demonstrates that whiteness is as performative as the blackness performed by white minstrels. Julia Stern observes of this scene: "What the latent narrative of *Uncle Tom's Cabin* suggests is that to believe in the definitive legibility of race is a delusion, a misconception that carries with it potentially tragic ramifications. As George Harris dramatically proves, identity is not a stable fact but a fluid and reversible category" (123). In this sense, this scene makes similar points about the indeterminacy and instability of race that Stevens's blackface episode does in Webb's novel.

Although Stowe was the most famous American abolitionist author to employ blackface motifs, she was not the first to do so. Lydia Maria Child uses this device to blur racial differences in her 1834 story "Mary French and Susan Easton," though in doing so she paradoxically seems to confirm them. Near the beginning of the story, a slave trader kidnaps the white girl Mary French and her free black playmate Susan Easton, and he blackens Mary's face before selling them both as slaves. Mary weeps after she is sold, and her tears wash off some of the black substance covering her light skin. Another slave sees this and reports it to Mary's owner, and her father brings her home. However, Susan cannot remove the blackness from her skin, despite her free status, and is permanently sold into slavery. Child's use of blackface in the story is ambiguous because it both erases and reaffirms the racial difference between the two girls and their families. Both girls are free, and their relationship in the story as playmates suggests equality. They are also treated more or less equally by the kidnapper (except that he blackens Mary but not Susan), and he sells them both into slavery. Child concludes the story by belittling the difference between the girls while also decrying the racial distinction on which slavery is based: "The only difference between Mary French and Susan Easton is, that the black color could be rubbed off from Mary's skin, while from Susan's it could not" (202). However, racial difference is crucial in the story, not just for the girls, but also for their fathers. Mr. French is able to search for Mary without running the risk of being captured, but the precariousness of Paul Easton's freedom as a black man in the South prevents him from looking for Susan, and Mr. French callously makes no effort to help him recover her.[8] The racial difference between the girls is accentuated by the fact that Susan, unlike Mary, does not cry. Susan's inability to weep off her blackness results in her enslavement and reforges the link between blackness and slavery that Child had severed in the beginning of the story. Mary, in contrast, affirms her whiteness in somewhat the same manner that white minstrel performers did when they wiped the burnt cork from their faces backstage. In addition, the fact that her darkened skin makes her look "blacker than Susan" may bring to mind the exaggerated, counterfeit blackness in minstrelsy's representations of African Americans that underscored racial difference.

Child employs blackface as a plot device again in her 1841 story "The Black Saxons," which depicts Mr. Duncan, a slaveholder who disguises himself as a slave to eavesdrop on the secret meetings of his slaves. Through Duncan's blackface episode, the story questions the notion of racial difference but also shows how a white slaveholder can use blackface to "pass for black" in order to bolster his power over his slaves and increase his profits. The story begins with Duncan reading Jacques Nicolas Augustin Thierry's *History of the Conquest of*

England by the Normans and pitying the noble Saxons who were subdued by the Normans. Duncan reflects: "'And so that bold and beautiful race became slaves! . . . The brave and free-souled Harolds, strong of heart and strong of arm; the fair-haired Ediths, in their queenly beauty, noble in soul as well as ancestry; these all sank to the condition of slaves'" (182). Duncan identifies with the Saxons, and although his Scottish name identifies him with a traditional enemy of the Saxons, he, like many Scotch-Irish residents of the Carolinas, belonged to the dominant race and was thus in a sense an honorary Saxon. His worship of the Saxons is also ironic in that British troops are invading his state, South Carolina, during the War of 1812, though perhaps one might read these troops as descendents of the overbearing Normans invading the Saxons of South Carolina.

Despite being "a proverbially indulgent master" (183), Duncan does not extend his admiration of subjugated Saxons to his slaves, and in order to control them more effectively, he darkens his skin and dresses in slave's clothes in order to spy on them. In narrating his experience as a "slave" and his observations of a mulatto slave who desires a British identity, the story's implicit commentary on conventional notions of racial difference is ambiguous, sometimes questioning them and at other times endorsing them. Duncan, the admirer of eleventh-century Saxons, finds out that some of his slaves have designs on joining the British army and acquiring the freedom that the Saxons had loved so dearly. One slave advises his listeners to "'tell you sons to marry de free woman, dat know how to read and write; and tell you gals to marry de free man, dat know how to read and write; and den, by'm bye, you be de British *yourselves!*'" (189). In comparison to Duncan's blackface act, the slave's notion of claiming another identity is less physical and more permanent and significant. After the slave meeting ends, Duncan, still apparently in disguise, comes close to admiring his slaves when he wonders: "'Was the place I saw to-night, in such wild and fearful beauty, like the haunts of the *Saxon* Robin Hoods? Was not the spirit that gleamed forth as brave as *theirs*? And who shall calculate what even such hopeless endeavours may do for the future freedom of this down-trodden race?'" (191). It seems that his blackface episode might lead him to see his slaves in a new light, not only because of the meeting he witnesses, but also because he disguises himself as a slave and subjects himself to being captured by the patrollers, which would have been an embarrassing and perhaps painful experience. However, he does not free his slaves after this experience, and he advises local judges to prevent such meetings in the future. Rather than forging a new identity or coming to understand his slaves, Duncan's use of blackface only benefits him materially by giving him better control of his slaves; in that sense he resembles white minstrel performers who profited from blackface. Likewise, his racial identity, like that of white minstrels, is emphasized by his ability to remove his black mask. Overall, the story's vacillation regarding racial distinctions parallels the act of blacking up in minstrelsy, which both affirmed and undermined ideologies of racial difference.

Thomas Wentworth Higginson's 1869 memoir, *Army Life in a Black Regiment,* is more critical of minstrelsy's representations of African Americans than *Uncle Tom's Cabin,* though it nevertheless relies heavily on blackface motifs. Higginson, a Union Army colonel in the Civil War, bases his statements about black men on his military experience in leading them, and he mimics the claims of authenticity made by minstrel performers in his representation of black speech in the chapter "Negro Spirituals": "The words will be here given, as nearly as possible, in the original dialect; and if the spelling seems sometimes inconsistent, or the misspelling insufficient, it is because I could get no nearer" (198).[9] He also contrasts the "quaint religious songs" of his black troops with the "'Ethiopian Minstrel' ditties, imported from the North" that were learned by "a few youths from Savannah," songs which "took no hold upon the mass" (221–22). Although these minstrel songs were sung by southern African Americans, he disregards them as inauthentic because of their northern origin and possibly their secular and vulgar content.

Despite this dismissal of minstrelsy's representations of black people, Higginson employs the blackface motif, and, like Child, his use of this trope both weakens and reinforces racial distinctions. In one sense, being surrounded by black men leads him to see them "just as if they were white," and, like white minstrel performers, he is able to imagine himself becoming black: "Each day at dress-parade I stand with the customary folding of the arms before a regimental line of countenances so black that I can hardly tell whether the men stand steadily or not; black is every hand which moves in ready cadence as I vociferate, 'Battalion! Shoulder arms!' nor is it till the line of white officers moves forward, as parade is dismissed, that I am reminded that my own face is not the color of coal" (9). On the one hand, the absence of white faces leads him to identify with his black men; in this respect, his sense of whiteness is unstable and contingent upon the presence of other whites. On the other hand, his exaggeration of the blackness of his soldiers' faces and hands in this passage belies his claim that he sees them "as if they were white," and "the color of coal" overstates the darkness of his soldiers' complexion in much the same way that burnt cork exaggerated the skin tones of African Americans. In spite of his imagined sooty appearance, he figuratively wipes off his blackface and restores his sense of whiteness with an authoritative posture and commands that only a white man could give, and the arrival of his white officers dispels his blackface delusion.

Minstrel Humor in *Uncle Tom's Cabin* and *Army Life in a Black Regiment*

Although many American authors used blackface motifs transgressively to confound racial categories, some antislavery texts borrowed minstrel characters, dialogue, and humor in ways that denigrated black people. Such was often the case in *Uncle Tom's Cabin*, even though Stowe frowned upon secular theatrical entertainment and probably did not attend minstrel shows.[10] Her novel begins with the slaveholder Shelby calling his young, racially mixed slave Harry "Jim Crow" and prompting him to perform a minstrel song and dance for himself and the slave trader Haley. While the class difference between Shelby and Haley is roughly equivalent to that between minstrelsy's bourgeois interlocutor and lower-class endman, this gap is briefly bridged here by their shared whiteness, which contrasts with Harry's partial black heritage and slave status, and by Harry's imitation of Jim Crow. Their enjoyment of Harry's impromptu minstrel show reflects the increasing cross-class appeal of minstrelsy in white America during this time and its displacement of class conflict with a communal sense of whiteness that contrasted with a cartoonish, debased blackness.

Stowe's use of blackface humor is more ambiguous in another early scene, in which the slaves Sam and Andy play the endmen to the interlocutor Haley during his attempt to recover the escaped Eliza and Harry. After this ludicrously failed attempt to recover the fugitives, Sam delivers a classic minstrel stump speech full of malapropisms:

"Well, yer see," said Sam, proceeding gravely to wash down Haley's pony, "I'se 'quired what yer may call a habit o' *bobservation*, Andy. It's a very 'portant habit, Andy; and I 'commend yer to be cultivatin' it, now yer young. . . . Yer see, Andy, it's *bobservation* makes all de difference in niggers. Didn't I see which way the wind blew dis yer mornin'? Didn't I see what Missis wanted, though she never let on? Dat ar's bobservation, Andy. I 'spects it's what you may call a faculty. Faculties is different in different peoples, but cultivation of 'em goes a great way." (42)

While the dialect and malapropisms indicate Sam's ignorance, they are countered by his cleverness in tricking Haley and perceiving Mrs. Shelby's covert desire to facilitate Eliza's and Harry's escape by delaying him. In this sense, Stowe's characterization of Sam copies minstrelsy's ambiguous depiction of the endman as both ignorant buffoon and sly, subversive trickster.[11] Likewise, Stowe's readers may have felt ambivalent toward Sam in much the same way that white audiences felt toward endmen—they might have laughed with him when he deceives the interlocutor Haley, but laughed at him when he delivers his ridiculous speech on "bobservation."

Stowe borrows more extensively from minstrel humor in her characterization of Topsy, which was based largely on minstrel characters such as Jim Crow. In fact, Topsy became a minstrel character in her own right in the popular stage adaptations of the novel.[12] Stowe's 1856 novel *Dred* includes the silly, mischievous slave characters Tomtit and Tiff who in some ways resemble Topsy, and Tomtit's comically contentious relationship with white Aunt Nesbit parallels that between Topsy and her master's northern cousin Ophelia.[13] But of all the black characters in Stowe's fiction, Topsy most resembles the blackface clown. When St. Clare buys her for Ophelia, he introduces her as "rather a funny specimen in the Jim Crow line" (207). Both Topsy and Harry are compared to Jim Crow, and, perhaps not coincidentally, these comparisons come at times when their status as commodities and chattels is foregrounded—right before Harry is sold and just after Topsy is purchased. Like Shelby, St. Clare tells Topsy to sing and dance for another white person's amusement, and she responds with a condensed minstrel show that would rival the best performances of Christy's Minstrels:

The black, glassy eyes glittered with a kind of wicked drollery, and the thing struck up, in a clear shrill voice, an odd negro melody, to which she kept time with her hands and feet, spinning round, clapping her hands, knocking her knees together, in a wild, fantastic sort of time, and producing in her throat all those odd guttural sounds which distinguish the native music of her race; and finally, turning a summerset or two, and giving a prolonged closing note, as odd and unearthly as that of a steam-whistle, she came suddenly down on the carpet, and stood with her hands folded, and a most sanctimonious expression of meekness and solemnity over her face, only broken by the cunning glances which she shot askance from the corners of her eyes. (207)

Later, the narrator remarks that Topsy's "talent for every species of drollery, grimace, and mimicry,—for dancing, tumbling, climbing, singing, whistling, imitating every sound that hit her fancy,—seemed inexhaustible" (215). The narrator's reference to her imitative talent echoes minstrelsy's mockery of black men who ape the fashions and language of upper-class whites, though it also parallels the racial mimicry of white minstrel performers. Stowe's depictions of Sam, Topsy, and Tomtit, along with her other nods to minstrelsy in these novels, reveal not only her racism but also her familiarity with minstrelsy and her recognition of its appeal, as well as its availability for antislavery purposes.[14]

Higginson's use of minstrelsy to translate his experiences in *Army Life in a Black Regiment* reveals some of the same racism and ambivalence that surface in Stowe's appropriations of blackface humor. His comparisons of black soldiers to stage minstrels also parallel Kemble's references to minstrelsy as a touchstone in describing the singing of plantation slaves in her *Journal*, as we saw in Chapter 3. He distinguishes the modest demeanor of his black soldiers from "that sort of upstart conceit which is sometimes offensive among free Negroes at the North, the dandy-barber strut" (29), but his statement that he expected to find among his black recruits "male Topsies, with no notions of good and plenty of evil" (244) blurs the lines between his soldiers, Stowe's Topsy, and the minstrel stage. Higginson also uses racist minstrel humor when writing about his soldiers having fun during target practice: "When some unwary youth fired his piece into the ground at half-cock, such infinite guffawing and delight, such rolling over and over on the grass, such dances of ecstasy, as made the 'Ethiopian minstrelsy' of the stage appear a feeble imitation" (11). While Higginson, like Kemble, discredits minstrelsy's delineation of black behavior, his emphasis on the comicality of black soldiers echoes the minstrel song "Raw Recruits, or Abraham's Daughter." Christopher Looby points out that an earlier version of this passage in Higginson's journal claims that such frolicking "'made the Ethiopian minstrelsy of the stage appear no caricature,'" then comments: "He previously would have thought that stage minstrelsy was a distortion or exaggeration of actual African American merriment, but after firsthand observation Higginson judges that there was no distortion" ("As Thoroughly Black" 111–12 n. 33). Of the difference between the two versions, Looby writes: "The white entertainer's blackface minstrel performance wasn't essentially an *inaccurate* imitation, only an inferior one, lacking in performative energy. While this emendation seems to promote actual black performance to the status of an inimitable object, one that a white copy can't touch, at the same time it confers upon the black soldiers a recognized talent for the ludicrous and the grotesque, a talent that (of course) no white man could match. The blacks are naturally such caricatures that a white imitation can't help but be feeble" (112 n. 33).

Although Higginson faults minstrelsy for its depictions of blacks, his use of blackface humor in describing his soldiers says as much about minstrelsy's prevalence in American culture as it does about his racism. He mentions that he and a white officer "sometimes slid" into a "semi-Ethiopian dialect" (256), and his references to the mispronunciations of his black soldiers are consistent with the malapropisms of the minstrel stage. Thus we see "expeditious" jocularly substituted for "expedition" (72/95); "condemned milk" for "condensed milk" (147) (possibly an intended pun); "amulet," "epaulet," and "omelet" for "ambulance" (a word, Higginson avers, that "Ethiopian lips were not framed by Nature to articulate") (148); and "inception" for "excepting" (260). When he tests his black sentries by encountering them incognito, his countersign "Vicksburg" fails to satisfy them because it is correctly pronounced, so he switches to minstrel speech: "'Vicksburg,' I repeated, blandly, but authoritatively, endeavoring, as zealously as one of Christy's Minstrels, to assimilate my speech to any supposed predilection of the Ethiop vocal organs" (50). Despite his knowledge of minstrelsy, his feeble imitation of a white minstrel's feeble imitation of black speech also fails to do the trick. He tries to mimic black speech by parroting the dialect of minstrel performers rather than African Americans themselves, as if both groups were identical. Higginson also mentions the comical "stump speech" of one of his black soldiers, who claims that "we hab lib under it [the American flag] for *eighteen hundred sixty-two years*" (23), and he goes on to relate several amusing anecdotes about his soldiers that would have worked on the minstrel stage. While he dismisses "Ethiopian minstrelsy" as a "feeble imitation," he shows his familiarity with it by using it as a point of contrast, revealing how much its racism had shaped his perception of black men.

The ideological ambiguity of Higginson's *Army Life* and Stowe's *Uncle Tom's Cabin* in their borrowing from minstrelsy exemplifies the complex functions of such tropes in American fiction more broadly. Some of these texts employ blackface tropes to emphasize racial indeterminacy and fluidity, some take advantage of minstrelsy's early antislavery elements, some reverse its pro-slavery tendencies, some uncritically echo minstrelsy's racism, and some perform a combination of these functions. In order to understand the uses of minstrel elements in these works, their explicit and implied commentary on minstrelsy, and the impact of minstrelsy on them, we cannot resort to any single, overarching interpretation. These texts reveal minstrelsy's complexity and its equally complicated relationship to American fiction, which was one of critique, appropriation, co-optation, reversal, and complicity. This was especially true in mid-nineteenth century American fiction that depicts African Americans and comments on slavery, because minstrelsy provided relevant tropes and conventions that were familiar to American readers and that could be used for a variety of ideological purposes.

Afterword

Much of what I have written about in this book would not have existed without ships. They enabled English people to settle in North America, carried white slave traders to the West African coast and slaves from Africa to the West Indies and North America, brought Thomas Rice and the Virginia Minstrels to Britain, and ferried white and African American abolitionists back and forth between Britain and America. They turned the Atlantic Ocean from a barrier into a bridge between these two nations. By taking all of these people from one point in the Atlantic World to another, ships also enabled the exchanges of images and meanings that shaped the development of a transatlantic anti-slavery movement and the popularity of blackface minstrelsy in Britain and America. The dynamic nature of both blackface minstrelsy and the antislavery movement was largely a result of these transatlantic crossings. Another reason for the changes within both minstrelsy and abolitionism was the fact that they were concerned with representing black people, making it nearly inevitable that they would respond to each other and develop symbiotically. Aside from their depictions of black people and slavery, however, both phenomena did other cultural work as they moved back and forth across the Atlantic. They provided forums for discussions of work and class differences by comparing chattel slavery to wage labor and by mediating class relations, especially between the working class and the bourgeoisie. They also offered ways for each nation to define itself in relation to—and often in opposition to—each other.

My analysis of the interactions between minstrelsy and abolitionism in Britain and the United States during the mid-nineteenth century will hopefully increase our understanding of how the meanings of blackness, humanity, freedom, slavery, labor, class, and nation were formed, altered, and connected to each other in the Anglophone Atlantic world at a crucial moment in its history. Perhaps no other period in American and British history was more concerned with this combination of issues. The most vigorous debates over slavery took place during minstrelsy's halcyon days, and the representations of

Africans, African Americans, and West Indian blacks in these two overlapping discursive formations enabled white Americans and Britons to determine their own racial and national identities. The images of black people generated by minstrelsy and abolitionism also mediated the often testy relationship between two nations that shared a common language and history. For instance, while white Americans and Britons often disagreed in their attitudes toward slavery or argued about which nation was more genuinely committed to freedom and equality, minstrel shows cemented bonds between them by allowing them to create a common sense of whiteness that contrasted with blackface characters. At the same time, the ideological diversity of both abolitionism and minstrelsy in their depictions of black people left plenty of room for debate among white people both within each nation and between nations. These representations of blackness also set the terms for how African Americans, black Britons, and West Indian blacks could interact with the white populations and dominant cultures of the Anglophone Atlantic world.

This complex transatlantic exchange of racial images and meanings between abolitionism and minstrelsy not only had a significant influence on the lives of black and white people in both nations during the mid-nineteenth century, but also had a considerable impact on how future generations of Americans and Britons would think about race, freedom, and oppression. While wearing blackface in public is no longer common, and while those who do so generate far more controversy than they did a century and a half ago,[1] many social critics and historians have commented on traces of nineteenth-century minstrelsy in rock and roll (such as the performances of Elvis Presley and the Rolling Stones) and hip hop, as well as in television sitcoms and standup comedy.[2] Even if one disagrees with these assessments and criticisms regarding the influence of minstrelsy on contemporary popular culture, their mere repetition suggests the enduring legacy of minstrelsy as a point of comparison for representing blackness. This legacy also shaped the reception of black musicians like Jimi Hendrix in ways that recuperated their liberatory impulses through racial stereotypes that can be traced back to minstrelsy. Abolitionism has had less of an impact on British and American popular culture than minstrelsy; aside from a few recent historical films such as *Amistad* and *Amazing Grace*, representations of nineteenth-century abolitionism are relatively rare in current British and American popular culture. Nonetheless, abolitionism lasted longer than minstrelsy in the sense that while there are no longer professional minstrel shows, the British-based organization Anti-Slavery International, its American affiliate group Free the Slaves, and the American Anti-Slavery Group are still working to eliminate slavery throughout the world. These organizations have a much smaller public profile in both Britain and the United States than their nineteenth-century predecessors, partly because they focus on slavery (including forced prostitution and child labor) in non-Western countries rather than in America or Britain's colonies. More obviously, the antiracist egalitarian ideals of nineteenth-century abolitionism profoundly shaped the civil rights movements of the twentieth century, especially in the United States. These latter movements differ markedly from abolitionism, however, in that African Americans spoke for themselves and assumed leadership roles in them to a much greater extent than in nineteenth-century abolitionism. As a result, the condescension and ambivalence of nineteenth-century white abolitionists was less prominent in twentieth-century civil rights discourse.

Despite the advances that African Americans and black Britons have made during the past century and a half in securing their civil rights and creating their own cultures, to a great extent their lives and their interactions with other Americans and Britons are constrained by racial ideologies that may be traced back to minstrelsy and the antislavery movement. Nineteenth-century African Americans had limited power in shaping their own representations in the abolitionist movement and even less influence on the minstrel stage, despite the existence of African American minstrel performers. The ideological formations developed by minstrelsy and abolitionism, symbolized by the characters Jim Crow and Uncle Tom, offered a finite number of behaviors and identities for African Americans and black Britons that white Americans and Britons would recognize and accept, such as the Noble Savage, the humble slave, the grinning clown, the brutal negro, and the hypersexual black man or woman. Probably no one expects that these restrictions will completely disappear anytime soon. Nevertheless, the Atlantic World is still as much in flux today as it was during the nineteenth century. This dynamic element of Atlantic culture leaves open the possibility that persons of African descent can alter existing representations of themselves in the Blackface Atlantic and create new ones that would more truly reflect their humanity and individuality in the twenty-first century and beyond.

NOTES

INTRODUCTION

1. For the sake of convenience and inclusiveness, this book often uses the word "black" instead of the narrower phrase "African American" in referring to persons of sub-Saharan African origin, including those living in the United States, Britain, or the British West Indian colonies.

2. For examples of recent scholarship on the ideological ambiguities of early blackface minstrelsy, see Cockrell, *Demons of Disorder*; Lhamon, *Raising Cain* and *Jump Jim Crow*; Lott, *Love and Theft*; Meer, *Uncle Tom Mania*; Roediger, *The Wages of Whiteness*; and Rogin, *Blackface, White Noise*.

3. The minstrel show as we know it is generally traced back to the debut performance of the Virginia Minstrels in early February 1843. Earlier blackface performers—such as Charles Mathews, George Washington Dixon, and Thomas Rice—were often called "Ethiopian Delineators" rather than "minstrels," and their performances were often interludes inserted into other entertainments rather than entire shows. Nevertheless, I use the term "minstrelsy" to denote blackface performances dating as far back as the 1820s, as well as those of the Virginia Minstrels and later blackface troupes.

4. See Blackett, *Building an Antislavery Wall*; Fisch, *American Slaves in Victorian England*; and Taylor, *British and American Abolitionists*.

CHAPTER ONE

1. I am borrowing the phrase "romantic racialism" from Fredrickson, *The Black Image in the White Mind*. See the chapter "Uncle Tom and the Anglo-Saxons: Romantic Racialism in the North" for more analysis of the racialist beliefs of many northern white abolitionists.

2. Although some of the parallels between abolitionism and minstrelsy traced in this chapter pertain to Britain as well as the United States, others do not. Minstrelsy in Britain gradually distinguished itself from its American version, and British abolitionism was more mainstream than in the U.S. and the problems it dealt with were more distant. Because of these differences, this chapter focuses primarily on an American context, while the following chapter concentrates on British abolitionism, minstrelsy, and racial attitudes.

3. Josiah Wedgwood was an English abolitionist and potter who designed and produced the famous slave medallion in 1787 (Oldfield 156). For more historical information about Wedgwood's medallion, see Oldfield, *Popular Politics and British Anti-Slavery* (155–59).

4. Some minstrel songs published in England, such as "So Early in de Morning" by the American Serenaders, also emphasize the brutal toil of slavery in ways that could appeal to abolitionists.

5. Garrison's bitterness toward Douglass was shared by John Collins and George Bradburn

as well as the Irish Quaker Richard D. Webb. See Collins's letter to Maria Weston Chapman, 23 Aug. 1843, and Webb's letter to Maria Weston Chapman, 22 Jan. 1854 (BPL). For more discussion of this rift, see Pease and Pease, "Boston Garrisonians and the Problem of Frederick Douglass"; Tillery, "The Inevitability of the Douglass-Garrison Conflict"; Quarles, "The Breach between Douglass and Garrison"; Foner, *Frederick Douglass* (78, 82, 136–54); Friedman, *Gregarious Saints* (187–92); McFeely, *Frederick Douglass* (146–49, 175–78); and McKivigan, "The Frederick Douglass–Gerrit Smith Friendship" (205–08).

6. See the letter by A. Brooke to Maria Weston Chapman, 5 Oct. 1843 (BPL).

7. See Quincy's letter to Caroline Weston, 2 July 1847 (BPL) and May's letter to Richard D. Webb, 16 Nov. 1859 (McFeely 202). White abolitionist conflict with African American abolitionists was not confined to the United States. Complaints about the perceived dishonesty, rudeness, ingratitude, and selfishness of Charles Lenox Remond, Henry Highland Garnet, and James W. C. Pennington also appear in letters by British abolitionist John Bishop Estlin to Eliza Wigham, 3 May 1851 (BPL), and by George Thompson to Richard [Webb?], 12 Aug. 1845 (Taylor, *British* 237).

8. Sundquist dismisses the possibility of subversion in this song: "Many years in advance of the similar fate of *Uncle Tom's Cabin*, for example, the *Amistad* mutiny and Nat Turner's revolt had been appropriated by stage minstrelsy and drained of their import in productions that obscured the deaths of whites while focusing on the comic punishment of the rebels" (*To Wake* 139). Toll makes a similar point in *Blacking Up* (83).

9. In another "Negro Minstrelsy" article, Brown points to the antagonism between abolitionism and minstrelsy: "Sanford's Minstrels have had some trouble in Lancaster City, Pa., on account of making some reference, during a performance, to the dilatory movements of the government. The Lancaster folks got highly incensed, and the abolition papers there pitched into the imitation nigs. Up that way, they like the 'genuine moke,' and will not have him or his supporters ridiculed" (HTC). Despite their anger at the minstrels, the possibility that some Lancaster abolitionists attended the show suggests that minstrelsy did not necessarily conflict with antislavery belief, as long as the minstrel performers avoided criticizing abolitionism.

10. For more information about how white perceptions of the Fisk Jubilee Singers were determined by blackface minstrelsy, see Chapters 10–13 and 19–20 of Ward, *Dark Midnight When I Rise*.

11. See Chapters 1 and 2 of Meer, *Uncle Tom Mania*, and Chapter 8 of Lott, *Love and Theft*, for analyses of the ambiguities of minstrelsy and *Uncle Tom's Cabin* and the interplay between them. These blackface appropriations of Stowe's abolitionist text continued into the twentieth century with Edwin Porter's 1903 film adaptation of the novel, which Rogin calls "the first substantial blackface film" (*Blackface* 14), and in the stage performances of the white Duncan sisters as Topsy and Eva during the mid-1920s (Leonard 191–93).

12. The fact that Brown's performance and those of other ex-slave abolitionists were often repeated also illustrates another of Butler's statements about gender performance that can be translated to racial performance: "Gender is the repeated stylization of the body, a set of repeated acts within a highly rigid regulatory frame that congeal over time to produce the appearance of substance, of a natural sort of being" (33).

13. Sánchez-Eppler does not focus on the pornographic elements of abolitionist literature and iconography in her essay "Bodily Bonds: The Intersecting Rhetorics of Feminism and Abolition," but she does comment on the complicity of readers of abolitionist literature in the brutality of slavery: "The horrific events narrated in these tales attract precisely to the extent that the buyers of these representations of slavery are fascinated by the abuses they ostensibly oppose. For despite their clear abolitionist stance, such stories are fueled by the allure of bondage, an appeal which suggests that the valuation of depictions of slavery may rest upon the same psychic ground as slaveholding itself" (98).

14. For example, this image is used in *The American Anti-Slavery Almanac, for 1840* (Lapsansky 210).

15. Explicit descriptions of sexual abuse on plantations also appeared in British antislavery literature. Examples include *The History of Mary Prince, a West Indian Slave* (1831) and Whitely, *Three Months in Jamaica in 1832* (1833). See Favret, "Flogging: The Anti-Slavery Movement Writes Pornography," for an analysis of the sadomasochistic elements of abolitionist rhetoric in late eighteenth-century Britain, particularly in the debates in the House of Commons. Wood has also analyzed the pornographic elements of British antislavery illustrations, particularly those involving the whipping of naked slaves in texts such as John Stedman's 1796 *Narrative of a Five Years' Expedition against the Revolted Negroes of Surinam* and his c. 1810 *Curious Adventures of Captain Stedman* (234–39).

16. The sexual titillation of antislavery accounts of flogging and rape of slave women was not the only way that abolitionism may have broadened its appeal; a sense of common oppression shared by slaves and women could also have strengthened its appeal among female readers. Ferguson argues throughout her book *Subject to Others* that British antislavery women identified with the oppression of slave women to some extent and encouraged their female readers to do likewise.

17. See Looby, "'Innocent Homosexuality': The Fiedler Thesis in Retrospect" (542–44), for a discussion of the sexual abuse of male slaves.

18. Wallis briefly discusses the pornographic elements of Agassiz's daguerreotypes of slaves and of "scientific" interest in the "Hottentot Venus" in "Black Bodies, White Science" (54).

19. For Douglass's account of this incident, see his article "Colorphobia in New York!" originally published in *The North Star* on 25 May 1849 and reprinted in Foner, *The Life and Writings of Frederick Douglass* (1: 384–87).

20. Dennison writes that this song is "one of the most amazing products of the period, in that the total effect is one of true affection for the black female, an attitude held by such a microscopically few people that the failure of the song was assured. The literature of the minstrel stage fails to yield another example such as this, and the song itself is rare in sheet music collections today" (126–27).

21. Dennison points out that the "white gall" of the original version of "Long Tail Blue" was changed to a "brown gal" in an 1840 version, while other versions simply omitted reference to a white woman (76).

22. Toll claims that the first black minstrel troupes first appeared in 1855 (195, 198), but Frederick Douglass's 1849 article "Gavitt's Original Ethiopian Serenaders" describes an earlier troupe that may have been black. This emphasis on the "genuineness" of African-American min-

strel performers was present in Ireland as well (Riach 234). See Riach, "Blacks and Blackface on the Irish Stage, 1830–60," for information about blackface minstrelsy in Ireland during the mid-nineteenth century.

23. Toll writes that black troupes of the 1860s were run by African Americans, but whites began to manage black minstrel troupes during the early 1870s (199).

24. The editor of *Dwight's Journal of Music* was not the only white American commentator to comment on minstrelsy's counterfeit nature. John Boyle O'Reilly, editor of the Boston Irish-Catholic newspaper *The Pilot*, commented in his 1871 essay "The Stage Irishman":

> The people who make up the "Negro Minstrel Troupes" are not colored men, nor are they even white men who have carefully studied the black man's character with a view to giving a fair copy. The troupes are mostly composed of young fellows who have learned the mysteries of dancing in clogs, the frequenters of the lowest "saloons" in our large cities, who blacken their faces and dress themselves ridiculously as a proper preparation for dancing "the celebrated plantation dance." The performers on the "bones" and the banjo, have learned all their quips and tricks and smart sayings, not in South Carolina, but in the Bowery. Their whole accomplishment, or ability, or whatever it may be called, consists in saying the funny things from the newspapers in an exaggerated attempt at "nigger English."

I thank Lauren Onkey for bringing this passage to my attention.

25. Another article in *Dwight's Journal*, originally printed in the *Philadelphia Bulletin*, points out the counterfeit nature of blackface performance more simply. The author observes of "Ethiopian Melodies" that "aside from the affectation of dialect, there is nothing Ethiopian about them. The airs are known to be the production of a pure Caucasian head. . . . These 'Negro Melodies' are white melodies, strictly national songs of our country and people" ("New Theory" 101).

CHAPTER TWO

1. The Emancipation Act of 1833 did not abolish slavery in British India and Ceylon, where it was abolished in the 1843 and 1845 respectively (Temperley 108–09).

2. James Somerset was an American slave who was brought to England by his master Charles Stewart. While there he escaped and was captured, and Stewart threatened to bring him back to Jamaica (Fryer 121). For an extended description of the Somerset case, see Gerzina, *Black London* (116–33); Fryer, *Staying Power* (120–26); and Walvin, *The Black Presence* (95–114) and *Black and White* (117–29).

3. For instance, *Chambers's Journal of Popular Literature, Science, and Art* incorrectly claimed in 1891 that Mansfield had ruled that "as soon as a slave sets foot on the soil of the British Islands he becomes free" (JJC). One earlier text that understood Mansfield's ruling was Thomas Pringle's "Supplement to the History of Mary Prince" (1831), which concludes: "It would well become the character of the present Government to introduce a Bill into the Legislature making perpetual

that freedom which the slave has acquired by his passage here, and thus to declare, in the most ample sense of the words (what indeed we had long fondly believed to be the fact, though it now appears that we have been mistaken) THAT NO SLAVE CAN EXIST WITHIN THE SHORES OF GREAT BRITAIN" (*History* 237–38).

4. See Chapter 1 of Blackett, *Building an Antislavery Wall*; Lorimer, *Colour, Class and the Victorians* (45–56); and Chapter 6 of Quarles, *Black Abolitionists*, for extended descriptions of how African American abolitionists were received by white Britons.

5. In his travel narrative *The American Fugitive in Europe* (1855; previously published in England as *Three Years in Europe* in 1852), Brown makes several comparisons between lack of race prejudice in Britain and American racial bigotry in describing his experiences in Britain during the late 1840s and early 1850s (*Travels* 98, 200–01, 220–23). Douglass also attacks American prejudice by comparing it to British enlightenment in a letter to Garrison dated 1 Jan. 1846, written in Belfast, and included in *My Bondage and My Freedom* (372–75).

6. Jacobs's letter of 13 Apr. 1863 to Martin appears in the *Freed-man's Aid Society*, 26 May 1863 (RH).

7. Several historians have discussed the nationalist elements of British abolitionism. Hall points out the nationalism of England's abolitionist self-image: "In 1833 the dominant definition of Englishness included the gratifying element of liberator of enslaved Africans" ("Missionary Stories" 242). Bratton also writes that "by the time of the brewing and outbreak of the American Civil War in the 1860s it was firmly established in the [English] popular mind that England was the land of the free, and that the revolted American colonists proved their inferiority by their refusal to recognize black men as brothers" (132). Wood also points out England's "triumphalist narrative" as the enlightened advocate of abolitionism (7, 24), and Fisch discusses England's claim of moral superiority over the United States regarding slavery (28–32, 47–51, 63–64). Fisch argues that English reviewers of slave narratives constructed them "as a transatlantic product, meant to highlight English national identity" (67), and that "Englishness was . . . a fragile and contested identity. And American slavery was one ground on which an emerging mid-Victorian English identity could be contested, re-worked, and ultimately re-forged" (68).

8. *The Daily Telegraph*, 8 Oct. 1875 (RH). Two other MPs, Matthew W. Ridley and Andrew Lush, also celebrated Britain's antislavery tradition while criticizing the Fugitive Slave Circular in their speeches to Parliament in February 1876. See the 9 Feb. 1876 issue of *The Times* for an account of Ridley's speech and the 4 Feb. 1876 issue of the *Daily News* for a report on Lush's speech (RH).

9. One of the most comprehensive studies of the relationships between British and American abolitionists is Fladeland, *Men and Brothers: Anglo-American Antislavery Cooperation*. Also see Taylor, *British and American Abolitionists*, for a collection of correspondence between abolitionists from both nations.

10. The end of Richard Hildreth's novel *Archy Moore, The White Slave; or, Memoirs of a Fugitive* makes a similar statement about Britain as a sanctuary for slaves, but also extends it to victims of European tyranny: "When we touched the British shore we felt safe. Thank God, there is a land that impartially shelters fugitives alike from European and from American tyranny—Hungarian exiles and American slaves!" (403)

11. Lee argues that Emerson expressed antislavery sentiments in his writings throughout his life but did not commit himself to the abolitionist movement because he feared that it would distract him from his philosophical pursuits, and he criticized abolitionists as fanatics well into the 1840s. Lee later mentions, however, that Emerson became actively involved in the movement after the passage of the 1850 Fugitive Slave Act (*Slavery, Philosophy* 166, 169).

12. Another American abolitionist who rejected the notion that Britain was a land of liberty simply because it had abolished chattel slavery was Nathaniel P. Rogers. In his article "British Abolitionism," he claims that "the character of British abolitionism . . . has been misunderstood among us, . . . and greatly overrated" (98), and he argues that all British citizens are subjects of the queen and the Church (101–02, 104). Rogers also criticizes British abolitionists for excluding the American abolitionist Lucretia Mott from a meeting because of her gender, and he denounces Britain's Emancipation Act because it instituted the system of apprenticeship and taxed British workers in order to compensate slaveholders for the economic costs of emancipation (107–09). Some British abolitionists also thought Britain was as culpable as the United States regarding slavery. See Taylor, "Negro Slavery" (36–38).

13. For an extended analysis of the lives of Anglo-Africans in the eighteenth and early nineteenth centuries, see Gerzina, *Black London*.

14. Fisch points out that most English reviews of this narrative ignored or downplayed England's failure to protect John Glasgow, a free black Briton whose enslavement by Americans is recorded in Brown's book (65–67).

15. Letter to Miss [Caroline?] Weston, 8 May 1851 (BPL). In a letter to Reverend Samuel May dated 17 July 1860, however, William Craft blames the proslavery sentiment in Britain on white American visitors (BPL). See Blackett, *Building* (158–60), for a description of African Americans' encounters with racism in Britain.

16. In the poem "Britannia's Sweet Tooth," the magazine *Punch,* which was often skeptical of abolitionism despite being antislavery, ridiculed the hypocrisy of Britons who prided themselves on their moral correctness regarding slavery but consumed slave-produced sugar.

17. See Clarkson, *Thoughts on the Necessity of Improving the Condition of the Slaves in the British Colonies,* and Martineau, "Demerara," for examples of abolitionist arguments that wage labor was more profitable than slave labor.

18. Hall makes a similar argument about British antislavery's implicit imperialist agenda in her essay "Missionary Stories" (243).

19. One literary illustration of the links between Britain's project of civilizing nonwhite Others, its profit motives, and its ethnocentrism is Martineau's 1845 novella *Dawn Island,* in which white visitors to the island persuade the natives to end the practice of human sacrifice. The novel ends with the words of the white captain, which combine missionary and economic purposes with romantic racialism: "Every thing is honoured, be it what it may, . . . which is an instrument for introducing the principles and incitements of civilization among a puerile people. . . . It warmed my heart and filled my head to see how these children of nature were clearly destined to be carried on some way towards becoming men and Christians by my bringing Commerce to their shores" (93–94).

20. Rice performed at the Surrey Theatre and the Adelphi Theatre in London in 1836–37, 1838–40, and 1842–43 (Lhamon, *Jump Jim Crow* 63–65).

21. Reynolds states that a minstrel troupe performed for Queen Victoria at Balmoral Castle in 1868 and that she attended a performance of Haverly's Mastodon Minstrels at Her Majesty's Theatre in Haymarket, London, in 1880 (191, 20).

For more information about blackface street busking in nineteenth-century England, see Rehin, "Blackface Street Minstrels in Victorian London and Its Resorts."

22. Minstrel troupes that tried to emulate the Ethiopian Serenaders include the Lantum Ethiopian Serenaders, the New Orleans Ethiopian Serenaders, the Female American Serenaders, the Ethiopian Harmonists, and later, the African Opera Troupe. For *Punch's* reactions to the blackface craze in England, see "Music in Ebony," "The Serenading Mania," "Glut of Ethiopians," "Ethiopian Fashions," "What Is Ethiopia?" "Britannia and the Blacks," and "Washing the Metropolis of All Its Blacks."

23. In November 1843, after Rice's last British tour and the success of the Virginia Minstrels, the *Era* also predicted the end of blackface mimicry ("The Theatres" 6). *Punch* seemed to change its attitude toward minstrel songs by 1856, when it printed the article "The American Ballads," which praised the blackface song "Keemo, Kimo" (which it attributed to Stowe) and observed its great popularity in England (151).

24. For instance, see "A Nigger Professor of Cramanology."

25. See Wood, *Blind Memory,* for a more extended analysis of the racism of illustrations for *Uncle Tom's Cabin* by Cruikshank and other illustrators (173–80, 193–201).

26. Lott offers the 1836 pantomime *Cowardy, Cowardy, Custard; or Harlequin Jim Crow and the Magic Mustard Pot* as an example of British theatre's articulation of Rice's "Jim Crow" to its earlier stage harlequin tradition (22), though Jim Crow is not mentioned in the libretto. In another pantomime, *Harlequin and George Barnwell; or, The London 'Prentice* (1836) Jim Crow sings a song in a cameo appearance.

27. Other versions of the Inkle and Yarico story date as far back as Richard Steele's 1711 version in the *Spectator*. See Felsenstein, *English Trader, Indian Maid* for the various versions of the Inkle and Yarico tradition.

28. For information about "Negro" characters and songs in English drama before 1800, see Nathan (3–19), Green (385–87), and Gerzina (7–11).

29. Pickering makes a similar point about British audiences preferring British blackface performers ("imitation niggers") over "authentic" African-American minstrel performers ("White Skin" 80). See Fryer (441–44); Brody (*Impossible* 74–86); Lorimer (86–91); and Blackett (*Divided Hearts* 43–47) for more information about minstrelsy in Britain.

30. Recent books that take such a transatlantic approach toward blackface minstrelsy include Lhamon, *Jump Jim Crow;* Sarah Meer, *Uncle Tom Mania;* and Brody, *Impossible Purities* (74–86). Also see Pickering, "White Skin, Black Masks"; Rehin, "Harlequin Jim Crow"; Bratton, "English Ethiopians"; and Blair, "Blackface Minstrels in Cross-Cultural Perspective."

31. For more information on the rise of British racism that began around mid-century, see Hall, "The Economy of Intellectual Prestige" (182, 193–94); Chapter 3 ("Jamaica, 1865: The

Turning Point") of Bolt, *Victorian Attitudes to Race;* Chapters 6 ("Mid-Victorian Gentlemen, 'Nig-ger Philanthropy,' and the Growth of Racialism") and 7 ("Scientific Racism and Mid-Victorian Racial Attitudes") of Lorimer, *Colour, Class, and the Victorians;* Chapter 7 ("The Rise of English Racism") of Fryer, *Staying Power;* and Chapter 10 ("Black Caricature: The Roots of Racialism") of Walvin, *Black and White.*

32. Other scholars who discuss the Irish, English, and Scottish folk elements of blackface minstrelsy include Rogin (*Blackface* 56–58); Roediger (*Wages* 117–18); Cockrell (199 n. 43); Wittke (199–200); and Nathan (161, 166, 182, 194, 207).

CHAPTER THREE

1. Lott comments upon the sexual connotations of Kemble's dismissal of northern minstrelsy by pointing out "the list of adjectives with the inevitable sexual parry 'faint, feeble, impotent—in a word, pale Northern reproductions of that ineffable black conception'" (116).

2. Actually, Jim Crow does refer to himself as "James" in William Leman Rede's 1836 play *Flight to America* (Lhamon, *Jump* 65, 241), in which Rice performed at London's Royal Adelphi Theatre. The *Knickerbocker* in 1840 also jocularly referred to Jim Crow as JAMES CROW, Esquire!" (qtd. in Lott 142).

3. Allmendinger has analyzed Kemble's use of slavery as a metaphor for acting, a profession that was forced upon her, and reads the Jim Crow passage through the lens of this metaphor, suggesting that slavery entails acting (507, 511).

4. Carens claims that Dickens based Mrs. Jellyby on the English reformer Mrs. Caroline Chis-holm, who established the Family Colonization Loan Society (123), while Pope-Hennessy notes that several of Dickens's contemporaries saw Mrs. Jellyby as a parody of Harriet Martineau (302).

In its 4 March 1865 issue, *Punch* used the phrase "telescopic philanthropy" as a caption to an illustration that featured a woman representing Brittania looking at slaves in the distance through a telescope while she stood next to three poor children, apparently white but with skin darkened by dirt. One child, labeled a "Little London Arab" below the caption, implores her, "Please 'm, ain't we black enough to be cared for?"

5. Another Victorian novel that has attracted considerable scholarly attention for its treat-ment of race and slavery is Charlotte Brontë's *Jane Eyre.* For example, Lee analyzes the parallels between Jane's tale and Douglass's 1845 narrative in "The (Slave) Narrative of *Jane Eyre,*" while Thomas and Meyer examine Brontë's depiction of Rochester's West Indian wife Bertha Mason as both a racial Other and a dissipated colonial. Because this chapter focuses on Victorian texts that use blackface tropes in commenting on black people, slavery, and abolitionism, I have decided not to analyze Brontë's novel, in which such tropes are absent.

6. I am borrowing Gubar's neologism from her book *Racechanges: White Skin, Black Face in American Culture,* in which she uses the word to refer to the "traversing of race boundaries, racial imitation or impersonation, cross-racial mimicry or mutability, white posing as black or black passing as white, pan-racial mutuality" (5).

7. See Sutherland, "Thackeray as Victorian Racialist" for a brief analysis of the author's anti-

Semitism, racism, and anti-abolitionism. Walvin notes that many Jewish merchants migrated to the West Indies (*Making* 93), but Thackeray seems less interested in portraying the Jewish presence in the West Indies than in reinforcing the stereotype of the greedy Jew.

8. For an insightful analysis of Thackeray's depiction of the mulatta West Indian Rhoda Swartz and her role as a foil to Amelia Sedley and Becky Sharp, see Brody, *Impossible Purities* (27–45).

9. See Dabydeen, *Hogarth's Blacks*, for an excellent analysis of Hogarth's representations of black people.

10. The novel takes place during the Regency period, shortly after Saartjie ("Sarah") Baartman was exhibited as the "Hottentot Venus" in London in 1810.

11. Bolt claims that a later event—the 1865 Morant Bay uprising in Jamaica—was a critical moment in the rise of anti-black racism in Britain (75–76).

12. John Stuart Mill's rejoinder to Carlyle's essay, "The Negro Question," was published the following January in *Fraser's Magazine*. Mill's essay was more of a defense of philanthropists and an attack on Carlyle's notions of work as a good in itself than a defense of black people in general. Regarding Carlyle's ridicule of abolitionism as the "Universal Abolition of Pain Association," Mill claims that there is a "deficiency . . . of philanthropy" and asks, "Can any worthier object of endeavour be pointed out than that of diminishing pain? Is the labour which ends in growing spices noble, and not that which lessens the mass of suffering?" (94).

Predictably, William Wells Brown's comments on Carlyle and his statement on West Indian freed people are critical; he writes that Carlyle likes to display his intelligence, puts forth unpopular or new arguments for the sake of their unpopularity and novelty, and contradicts himself (*Travels* 167). Further, he writes of Carlyle: "His heart is with the poor; yet the blacks of the West Indies should be taught that if they will not raise sugar and cotton by their own free will, 'Quashy should have the whip applied to him.' He frowns upon the reformatory speakers upon the boards of Exeter Hall; yet he is the prince of reformers" (167).

CHAPTER FOUR

1. I am borrowing this neologism from Lhamon, *Jump Jim Crow* (15).

2. One of the most interesting recent scholarly approaches to the American Renaissance, which challenges traditional conceptions of the period, is Powell, *Ruthless Democracy: A Multicultural Interpretation of the American Renaissance*. Powell examines the competing forms of nationalism (expansionist and nativist) in mid-nineteenth-century history and literature, featuring the works of Stowe, William Wells Brown, and John Rollin Ridge, as well as Hawthorne, Thoreau, and Melville in his study. Like Powell, I am studying the canonical authors of the American Renaissance in new contexts, but while Powell is interested in exploring the contradiction between America's democratic rhetoric and its racial exclusiveness, I am interested in comparing minstrelsy's nationalism with that of the American Renaissance canon and of the discourse surrounding slave narratives.

3. See, for example, Kennedy and Weissberg, ed., *Romancing the Shadow: Poe and Race*; Klammer, *Whitman, Slavery, and the Emergence of* Leaves of Grass; Lee, *Slavery, Philosophy, and*

American Literature, 1830–1860; Pease, *Visionary Compacts: American Renaissance Writings in Cultural Context;* Reynolds, *Beneath the American Renaissance: The Subversive Imagination in the Age of Emerson and Melville;* and Sundquist, "Slavery, Revolution, and the American Renaissance."

4. Other examples of recent scholarship that examine minstrelsy in connection with mid-nineteenth-century American literature include Anthony, "Class, Culture, and the Trouble with White Skin in Hawthorne's *The House of the Seven Gables*"; Okker and Williams, "'Reassuring Sounds': Minstrelsy and *The Hidden Hand*"; and Stafford, "Edgar Allan Poe's 'The Gold-Bug,' the Trickster, and the 'Long-Tail'd Blue.'" Anthony examines how Jim Crow gingerbread cookies function as a link and commodity exchange between the white upper class and lower class in Hawthorne's novel, arguing that Hawthorne figures class difference in racial terms. Okker and Williams analyze Southworth's use of minstrelsy to define white womanhood in *The Hidden Hand,* while Stafford traces Poe's black buffoon character Jupiter to the comical character "Long Tail'd Blue" of early minstrelsy. While these works offer valuable insights into how minstrelsy relates to issues of race, gender, class, and commodification, they do not focus on the issues of masculinity and anti-European nationalism in minstrelsy and literature that I analyze here.

5. Another literary nationalist, Walt Whitman, declares in the Preface to the 1855 edition of *Leaves of Grass:* "Of all nations the United States with veins full of poetical stuff most need poets and will doubtless have the greatest and use them the greatest" (8). Sixteen years later, in his essay "Democratic Vistas," Whitman again issues a call for an original national literature: "I demand races of orbic bards, with unconditional uncompromising sway. Come forth, sweet democratic despots of the west!" (974).

6. I am not implying that Emerson generally supported Manifest Destiny; in fact, he equated it with the expansion of slavery and opposed the Mexican War and the annexation of Texas (Gougeon 65–66, 67, 70). ·

7. For an extended analysis of "Oh! Susanna" and other songs by Stephen Foster, see Emerson, *Doo-Dah! Stephen Foster and the Rise of American Popular Culture.*

8. Similar anti-British sentiments appeared in the following lines from a version of "Jim Crow" that, according to Lhamon, was published by Leonard Deming in Boston between 1837 and 1840 (*Jump* 424 n. 33):

> I went across to Charlestown, and on to Bunker Hill,
> Which once de British tried to climb, but found it diffikil. . . .
> Near it [the Navy Yard] lay de ship ob war, among dem de Constitution,
> Which our brave heroes sail'd in, and put England in confusion.
> De finest fun dat ever happened, was in de city ob New York,
> When dey told de British soger it was time to walk and talk. . . .
> So dey [the British soldiers] gaddered up dare fixeds, and 'gan to march away,
> And sailed for land ob Johnny Bull, about de brake ob day.
> When dey got back to England dey didn't fear de debbil,
> Buy [*sic*] dey radder be excused, dan fight wid Yankee rebel. (qtd. in *Jump* 134–35)

9. See Chapter 4 of Toll, *Blacking Up*, for an analysis of minstrelsy's pro-Union stance during the Civil War.

10. For example, T. Allston Brown's 1864 article "Negro Minstrelsy" (HTC) links minstrelsy with George McClellan and Unionists in opposition to "radicals" (i.e., abolitionists).

11. Dennison notes that the ridicule of black soldiers in "Abraham's Daughter" is made primarily through the cover illustration of the sheet music. He adds, "An examination of the text shows little of the attitude of the composer on the question of the black soldier. Indeed, that the troops in this instance *are* black is discovered primarily through the cover illustration, and only secondarily through such textual references as 'Zou-Zou,' or Zouave, the term applied to volunteers of several regiments patterned after French infantry corps recruited in Algeria from the Zwawa tribe" (211).

12. Another minstrel song that supports the Union is Tom Russell's "That's What the Niggers Then Will Do" (1863), a non-dialect song that (despite its title) sympathetically depicts black soldiers fighting for the Union (SSMC).

13. Paul Morphy was an American chess player from New Orleans who traveled to England in 1858 at the age of twenty-one and defeated most of England's top chess players.

14. See Chapter 16 ("British Abolitionists and the American Civil War") of Fladeland, *Men and Brothers;* Taylor, *British and American Abolitionists* (454–540 passim); Temperley, *British Antislavery* (248–57); and Blackett, *Divided Hearts,* for information about British attitudes and relationships toward the Union and the Confederacy during the Civil War.

15. For at least one Scottish reader, it was not Hawthorne's *Mosses* but Stowe's *Uncle Tom's Cabin* that put America on the literary map, as he stated in a meeting during Stowe's 1853 British tour:

> We have long been accustomed to despise American literature—I mean as compared with our own. I have heard eminent *litterateurs* say, "Pshaw! the Americans have no national literature." It was thought that they lived entirely on plunder—the plunder of poor slaves, and of poor British authors. [Loud cheers.] Their own works, when they came among us, were treated either with contempt or with patronizing wonder—yes, the "Sketch Book" was a very good book to be an American's. To parody two lines of Pope, we
> "Admired such wisdom in a Yankee shape,
> And showed an Irving as they show an ape."
> [Loud cheers.] . . . Let us hear no more of the poverty of American brains, or the barrenness of American literature. Had it produced only Uncle Tom's Cabin, it had evaded contempt just as certainly as Don Quixote, had there been no other product of the Spanish mind, would have rendered it forever illustrious. (qtd. in Stowe, *Sunny Memories* xxxvii–xxxviii)

16. Melville's frustration with the idolization of Shakespeare conveniently glosses over the fact that Shakespeare's dramas were popular in nineteenth-century America, and not only among the cultural elite (Levine, *Highbrow* 4). Despite Melville's nationalism in "Hawthorne and His Mosses," he supported the English actor William Charles Macready during his feud with his

American rival Edwin Forrest that led to the Astor Place riot of May 1849, and he signed a petition to encourage Macready to keep his engagement at the Astor Place Opera House despite a near-riot by a pro-Forrest, nationalist mob (Berthold 429, 434). The feud was sparked when both actors were performing in productions of Shakespeare's *Macbeth* in New York City simultaneously, and the ensuing violence was the bloodiest theatre riot in American history.

17. In the same review, Melville also writes:

> Let America then prize and cherish her writers; yea, let her glorify them. They are not so many in number, as to exhaust her good-will. And while she has good kith and kin of her own, to take to her bosom, let her not lavish her embraces upon the household of an alien. For believe it or not England, after all, is, in many things, an alien to us. . . . But even were there no Hawthorne, no Emerson, no Whittier, no Irving, no Bryant, no Dana, no Cooper, no Willis . . . were there none of these, and others of like calibre among us, nevertheless, let America first praise mediocrity even, in her own children, before she praises . . . the best excellence in the children of any other land. Let her own authors, I say, have the priority of appreciation. (247)

18. Another example of literary nationalism that privileges American originality over English literary notions of excellence appears in a *Putnam's Monthly* article about *Uncle Tom's Cabin:* "Apart from all considerations of the subject, or motive, of Uncle Tom's Cabin, the great success of the book shows what may be accomplished by American authors who exercise their genius upon American subjects. Imitations of foreign and classical literature, though equal to the originals, will not command success. The American author or artist who is ambitious of success must confine himself to the illustration of American subjects" ("Uncle Tomitudes" 101–02).

19. Appiah coined the phrase "Naipaul fallacy" to describe the practice of any African author who "asks the reader to understand Africa by embedding it in European culture" (146).

20. See Gilmore, *The Genuine Article* (10), for a discussion of how professional writing was associated with femininity in mid-nineteenth-century American culture. With this in mind, Melville's emphasis on masculinity in this essay relates as much to authorship as it does to nationalism. For an extended analysis of masculinity and nineteenth-century American literature, see Leverenz, *Manhood and the American Renaissance.*

21. Interestingly, *Punch* made a similar comment about English music: "At this moment there is no song of English origin which is commanding the sympathies of the public so strongly as certain imported melodies. The American poets have supplied us with some lyrics which now entrance the British public. At a dozen theatres, every night, one or other of these efforts of the Trans-Atlantic muse is thrilling the audiences, and eliciting the most enormous shouts of applause" ("American" 151). One of the three songs mentioned in this article that enraptured English audiences is the blackface song "Keemo Kimo."

22. See Chapter 3 ("Opera for the Masses: Burlesques of English and Italian Opera") in Mahar, *Behind the Burnt Cork Mask.*

23. Several nineteenth-century and twentieth-century critics and historians have commented on minstrelsy's distinctively American character. For example, see Hutton, "The Negro on the Stage" (133); the preface to *Carncross & Dixey's Minstrel Melodies* (qtd. in Dennison 241); Moody, "Negro Minstrelsy" (321); and Wittke, *Tambo and Bones* (5). Paraphrasing a comment made by jazz critic Henry Osgood in 1926, Michael Rogin writes, "Not Negro spirituals but minstrel songs made up the authentic American national music" (*Blackface* 44).

24. This fact is mentioned in the article "Who Writes Our Songs?" in the *New York Evening Post* and reprinted in *Dwight's Journal of Music*. Foster's date of birth also coincided with the deaths of John Adams and Thomas Jefferson.

25. The anti-English element of much blackface minstrelsy was due not only to minstrelsy's nationalism and anti-bourgeois stance (Americans often associated Englishness with the upper class), but also in part to the presence of Irish-American minstrel performers, who resented English domination over Ireland or who were anti-abolitionist and therefore anti-British because of the activism of high-profile British abolitionists. For discussion of the involvement of Irish Americans in blackface minstrelsy, see Lott (95–96, 148–49), Toll (175–80), and Rogin (*Blackface* 56–58).

26. Mahar mentions this song in a group of minstrel songs whose structure resembled that of many African American songs, which suggests the likelihood that it originated in African American musical culture (*Behind* 230).

27. As Mahar has noted, "The minstrels parodied the Anglo-American tradition because, as postcolonialist and sometimes nativist entertainers, they imitated the styles they enjoyed but also resisted dependence on English material. The African American materials were respected for their uniqueness as well, but the recognition of the musical creativity was controlled by a generally racist attitude toward the people whose music promised so much" (*Behind* 266).

28. See the final third of Lott's chapter, "'Genuine Negro Fun': Racial Pleasure and Class Formation in the 1840s," in *Love and Theft* for an extended analysis of masculinity in minstrel shows. Lott also points out elements of homoeroticism in minstrel songs and shows (53–54, 120–22).

29. See Nathan (52–56) for an extended comparison between Southwest humor characters and minstrel characters.

30. Such was not always the case. Hollis contends that between 1823 and the advent of Garrisonian abolitionism in the 1840s, British workers were indifferent to, when not antagonistic toward, abolitionism (295). See Hollis (295–97, 309) and Gallagher (7–10) for more discussion of hostility toward abolitionism among British laborers and critics of industrial capitalism during the early nineteenth century.

31. One of the most important studies of the relationship between British abolitionists and labor is Fladeland, *Abolitionists and Working-Class Problems in the Age of Industrialization*. Fladeland also traces British abolitionism's relationship to Chartism in her essay, "'Our Cause being One and the Same': Abolitionists and Chartism."

32. See Collins's letter to Maria Weston Chapman, 23 Aug. 1843 (BPL) for his account of this conflict.

33. Roediger points out that "wage slavery" was used less than "white slavery" during the 1840s (*Wages* 72), but because the latter phrase has come to mean prostitution, I use "wage

slavery" to avoid confusion. For an extended discussion of the uses of wage slavery rhetoric, see Chapter 4 ("White Slaves, Wage Slaves, and Free White Labor") of Roediger, *The Wages of Whiteness*. Other sources analyzing the comparisons between chattel slavery and wage slavery include Foner, "Abolitionism and the Labor Movement in Antebellum America"; Gallagher, *The Industrial Reform of English Fiction* (3–33); Lorimer, *Colour, Class, and the Victorians* (92–100); and Hollis, "Anti-Slavery and British Working-Class Radicalism in the Years of Reform." Gallagher writes that this comparison was originally used in proslavery arguments and that it was later used by critics of capitalism as well (4).

34. For example, see Fitzhugh, *Sociology for the South* (162–63, 250–52). Anti-abolitionist British authors such as Anthony Trollope also used such rhetoric; see *The West Indies and the Spanish Main* (66, 68 66–69).

35. This play is reproduced in Hirsch's dissertation, "Uncle Tom's Companions: The Literary and Popular Reaction to *Uncle Tom's Cabin*" (425–41). Also see Meer, *Uncle Tom Mania*, for analyses of proslavery minstrel shows that criticized or parodied *Uncle Tom's Cabin* (62–67).

36. See Berthold, "Class Acts" (429–44), for another discussion of nationalism, class conflict, and the Astor Place riot.

37. Pete Williams was the black owner of a Five Points tavern that was associated with interracial dancing. Douglass had recently caused a stir by walking arm-in-arm down Broadway with the white Griffiths sisters (Berthold 434).

38. See Roediger, Chapter 6 ("White Skins, Black Masks: Minstrelsy and White Working Class Formation before the Civil War") of *The Wages of Whiteness*; Lhamon, *Raising Cain* and the introduction to *Jump Jim Crow*; and Lott, *Love and Theft*, for analyses of early minstrelsy's working-class and artisan orientation.

39. Perhaps the most well-known British slave narratives are Equiano, *The Interesting Narrative of the Life of Olaudah Equiano, Written by Himself* (1789) and *The History of Mary Prince, a West Indian Slave* (1831).

40. See Andrews, "The 1850s: The First Afro-American Literary Renaissance," for an analysis of early African American literature in light of the American Renaissance.

41. Similarly, in his 1853 novella *The Heroic Slave*, Douglass depicts his protagonist Madison Washington as "a man who loved liberty as well as Patrick Henry,—who deserved it as much as Thomas Jefferson,—and who fought for it with a valor as high, an arm as strong, and against odds as great, as he who led all the armies of the American colonies through the great war for freedom and independence" (25).

42. For an analysis of the Franklinesque qualities of Douglass's *Narrative*, see Seelye, "The Clay Foot of the Climber," which posits Douglass as Franklin's black shadow (125). Although Washington's *Up from Slavery* emphasizes the American work ethic and rags-to-riches myth as much as any slave narrative, I have chosen not to analyze it here because it was published in 1901, much later than the period with which I am concerned.

43. Andrews also argues that the narratives of Brown, Henry Bibb, and James W. C. Pennington do not conform to the heroic image that Douglass drew of himself in his narrative (*To Tell* 143–44).

CHAPTER FIVE

1. For other analyses of minstrel elements in "Benito Cereno," see Lhamon (*Raising* 82–90) and Sundquist (*To Wake* 152–54). Lhamon writes that Melville's use of minstrelsy "upset[s] these conventions . . . without ever 'transcending' minstrelsy. . . . Melville tried to fulfill, not contradict, blackface lore" (84), in that Babo's subversion parallels the class subversion of early minstrelsy. Unlike Lhamon, my interpretation of Babo does not focus on this element of early minstrelsy, since it had faded by the time Melville wrote and published "Benito Cereno." My analysis overlaps more with that of Sundquist, who examines Babo's performance of Delano's racial stereotypes, which were typical of white antislavery liberals as well as proslavery whites, though my reading differs from Sundquist's by focusing on Delano's simplicity and his projection of that trait onto Babo and Africans generally. Sundquist observes:

> Delano's offensive stereotypes allow us to see that the trope of African American docility and gaiety was generated as much by sympathetic liberalism as by the harsh regime of slavery. Minstrelsy—in effect, the complete show of the tale's action staged for Delano—is a product, as it were, of his mind, of his willingness to accept Babo's Sambo-like performance. Melville in this way nearly collapses the distance between proslavery and antislavery, South and North, so as to display the combined stagecraft that preserved slavery. Paternalistic benevolence is coextensive with minstrelsy, on the plantation or on the stage. (*To Wake* 153)

While Delano does not seem deeply opposed to slavery—he even offers to buy Babo from Cereno—neither does he express support for it, and in one instance he reflects on slavery's encouragement of violence.

2. According to the Oxford English Dictionary, "In 1663 the Royal Mint was authorized to coin gold pieces of the value of 20s. 'in the name and for the use of the Company of Royal Adventurers of England trading with Africa.'" Thus, the two meanings of the word "guinea" grew out of the commodification of western Africa and of its people as slaves.

3. The image of a black man offering his open mouth as a target for pitching pennies later appears in Nevin, "Stephen C. Foster and Negro Minstrelsy," in describing Cuff, the porter whose clothes Rice borrowed in one of his first stage performances as Jim Crow (609). Lott has also noted the parallel between this scene in Melville's novel and the passage in Nevin's article (61).

4. See Lott (61–62) and Lhamon (*Raising* 122) for discussions of minstrel elements and references in *The Confidence-Man*. Lott focuses on the commodification and counterfeit of "blackness" in the Black Guinea scene, which he sees as characteristic of minstrelsy. Lhamon focuses more generally on the confidence man as Cain, whom Lhamon reads as a trickster figure akin to the blackface characters of minstrelsy.

5. In writing about the connection between this passage from *Blake* and Foster's "Old Folks at Home," Emerson writes that "the lyrics, too transparently and unironically imitative to be a parody, are almost Foster's, too" (*Doo-Dah!* 121).

6. Engle points out that because many Philadelphia firemen during this time were Irish, Stevens's disguise denotes both class and ethnicity (160).

7. In "Fathering and Blackface in *Uncle Tom's Cabin*," Zwarg writes of this portrait, "Stowe unites with her characters Chloe and Tom by transforming the racist conventions of blackface into a political satire serving a still more complex feminist poetics" (279).

8. Sánchez-Eppler writes that in the story's conclusion, "The only solution to racial prejudice that Child's story can offer is rubbing off blackness; though she does not say this, it is impossible to imagine what one could produce by such a purging except whiteness. . . . the freedom it [Mary's weeping] offers depends upon the black being washed white. The problem of antislavery fiction is that the very effort to depict goodness in black involves the obliteration of blackness" (102). Though Sánchez-Eppler is correct that the conclusion offers no other solution to racism, I do not think that it proposes any solution at all to the problem of race prejudice; rather, it simply emphasizes the problem and its absurdity.

9. In his Preface to *Negro Minstrel Melodies*, William James Henderson gives credence to Higginson's earlier claim of authenticity in representing the slave songs in the following anecdote:

The manner in which the negro sometimes produced his song was discovered by Col. Thomas Wentworth Higginson to his own delight. He asked a negro boatman in the southern islands how songs came to be, and the man replied: "Some good sperituals are start jess out o' curiosity. I benn raise a sing myself once. Once we boys went for tote some rice, and de nigger-driver he keep a callin' on us; and' [sic] I say, 'O de ole nigger-driver!' Den annuder said, 'Fust ting my mammy told me was, notin' so bad as nigger-drivers.' Den I made a sing, just puttin' a word and den annuder word."

Then, to illustrate his description, he began to sing and the other men after listening a moment joined in the chorus as if it were an old friend, though they had evidently never heard it before. Thus Colonel Higginson saw how a negro song originated and took root. But the process should have sufficed to satisfy that the negro was merely reproducing in a crude and disfigured form some phrases, possibly not all from the same melody, which he had picked up while hearing the band at the military post in the evening or his mistress at her piano in the morning. (iv)

As with Fuller's and Kemble's comments on African Americans singing, Henderson's account of Higginson's encounter with the Negro boatman emphasizes the imitative nature of black singing.

10. Stowe's biographers do not mention her attitudes toward minstrelsy, but she condemned theatre in general in her letter to publisher Asa Hutchinson, who had requested permission to dramatize the play:

Any attempt on the part of Christians to identify themselves with them [plays] will be productive of danger to the individual character, and to the general cause. If the barrier which now keeps young people of Christian families from theatrical entertainments is once broken down by the introduction of respectable and moral plays, they will then be open to all the temptations of those who are not such, as there will be, as the world now is, five bad plays to one good. (qtd. in Wagenknecht 132)

11. Meer makes a similar point about the blackface humor elements of a later speech by Sam (33).

12. The *New York Daily Times* did not recognize these minstrel elements in Stowe's novel, and in fact praised it for rejecting blackface characters and dialect: "The slang of 'Ethiopian Serenaders' for once gives place to thoughts and language racy of the soil, and we need not say how refreshing it is to be separated for a season from the conventional Sambo of the modern stage" (qtd. in Hedrick 211).

13. Meer's analysis of Stowe's use of blackface comedy in her characterization of Topsy focuses largely on how her interactions with Ophelia resemble the endman-interlocutor dialogues of minstrelsy (37–40). Like these dialogues, Meer argues, the Ophelia/Topsy encounters are ambiguous in that readers were sometimes encouraged to laugh at the "interlocutor" Ophelia and at other times at the "endman" Topsy.

14. Conversely, the fact that Stowe's melodramatic depictions of separated slave families resembled those portrayed in minstrelsy points to its incorporation of sentimental abolitionism. In other words, minstrelsy was not only absorbed by abolitionism, but also exploited some of the same emotions and images found in antislavery rhetoric and literature.

AFTERWORD

1. For instance, Ben Vereen blacked up in his performance of Bert Williams at the 1981 Inauguration Ball for Ronald Reagan, and Ted Danson appeared in blackface and told racist jokes at a Friar's Club dinner in 1993 as a joke for his friend Whoopi Goldberg. Both were heavily criticized for their actions, though Goldberg defended Danson and claimed to have written some of the jokes told by him (Garrett 31, 42 n. 6). More recently, a controversy erupted in October 2009 on the Australian television show *Hey Hey It's Saturday,* in which five white men in blackface and afro wigs, joined by a sixth white man in whiteface sporting a similar wig, performed a song and dance routine as "The Jackson Jive." Harry Connick, Jr., one of the celebrity judges on the show, strongly objected to the performance, leading the show's host to apologize to him on the air.

2. Spike Lee, for instance, remarks: "Gangsta rap videos, a lot of the TV shows on UPN and WB—a lot of us are still acting like buffoons and coons" (Crowdus and Georgkas 9), and in the director's commentary on the DVD version of *Bamboozled,* he comments, "Gangsta rap is a twenty-first century version of minstrel shows." See Lee's interview in *Cineaste* with Crowdus and Georgkas, Stanley Crouch's interview with Jung in *All About Jazz,* and Caryl Phillips's comments in Foot's review of his novel *Dancing in the Dark* in the *Camden New Journal.*

BIBLIOGRAPHY

Archival Sources

Anti-Slavery Manuscripts. Rare Books and Manuscripts Division. Boston Public Library. Boston, Mass.

Billy Rose Theatre Collection. New York Library for the Performing Arts. New York, N.Y.

Harvard Theatre Collection. Houghton Library. Harvard University. Cambridge, Mass.

John Johnson Collection of Printed Ephemera. Bodleian Library. University of Oxford. Oxford, U.K.

Nicholas M. Williams Memorial Ethnological Collection. John J. Burns Library. Boston College. Boston, Mass.

Papers of the Anti-Slavery Society. Bodleian Library of Commonwealth and African Studies at Rhodes House. University of Oxford. Oxford, U.K.

Slavery and Abolition Collection, 1700–1890. Schomburg Center for Research in Black Culture. New York, N.Y.

Starr Sheet Music Collection. Lilly Library. Indiana University. Bloomington, Ind.

Printed Primary Sources

"Abolitionism Dramatized." *New York Daily Tribune.* 8 Aug. 1853: 1.

Adams, Nehemiah. *A South-Side View of Slavery; or, Three Months at the South, in 1854.* Boston: Marvin and Mussey, 1854.

"The American Ballads." *Punch, or the London Charivari* 31 (18 Oct. 1856): 151.

"American Opera." *Dwight's Journal of Music* 6.18 (3 Feb. 1855): 140–41.

"Barefaced Recognition of White Slavery." *Punch, or the London Charivari* 13 (Jul.–Dec. 1847): 130.

Behn, Aphra. *Oroonoko, or, The Royal Slave.* 1688. New York: Norton, 1973.

"The Benefit of Mr. Pell, The Bones of the Ethiopian Serenaders." *The Era* 9.457 (27 June 1847): 12.

Bibb, Henry. *Narrative of the Life and Adventures of Henry Bibb, an American Slave, Written by Himself.* 1849. *I Was Born a Slave: An Anthology of Classic Slave Narratives.* Vol. 2. Ed. Yuval Taylor. Chicago: Lawrence Hill, 1999. 4–101.

Bickerstaff, Isaac. *The Padlock: A Farce.* 1768. *Sharpe's British Theatre.* London: John Sharpe, 1805. 1–27.

"The Black Opera." *New York Daily Tribune*. 30 June 1855: 6.

Bones, His Gags and Stump Speeches: Nigger and Dutch Stories and Dialogues, "Broken China" Dialect Pieces, and Other Conundrums. New York: Wehman, 1879.

Brent, Linda [Harriet A. Jacobs]. *Incidents in the Life of a Slave Girl*. 1861. San Diego: Harvest-Harcourt Brace, 1973.

"Britannia and the Blacks." *Punch, or the London Charivari* 12 (8 May 1847): 176.

"Britannia's Sweet Tooth." *Punch, or the London Charivari* 18 (Jan.–Jun. 1850): 130.

Brontë, Charlotte. *Jane Eyre: An Authoritative Text, Contexts, Criticism*. 1847. 3rd ed. Ed. Richard J. Dunn. New York: Norton, 2001.

Brown, John. *Slave Life in Georgia: A Narrative of the Life, Sufferings, and Escape of John Brown, A Fugitive Slave, Now in England*. 1855. *I Was Born a Slave: An Anthology of Classic Slave Narratives*. Vol. 2. Ed. Yuval Taylor. Chicago: Lawrence Hill, 1999. 322–411.

Brown, William Wells. *The Black Man, His Antecedents, His Genius, and His Achievements*. 1863. New York: Arno-New York Times, 1969.

———. *Clotel; or, The President's Daughter: A Narrative of Slave Life in the United States*. 1853. Ed. Robert S. Levine. Boston: Bedford-St. Martin's, 2000.

———. *The Escape: or, a Leap for Freedom. The Roots of African American Drama: An Anthology of Early Plays, 1858–1938*. Ed. Leo Hamalian and James V. Hatch. Detroit: Wayne State UP, 1991. 42–95.

———. "Fugitive Slaves in England." *The Liberator*. 25 July 1851. 118.

———. *My Southern Home*. 1880. *From Fugitive Slave to Free Man: The Autobiographies of William Wells Brown*. Ed. William L. Andrews. New York: Mentor-Penguin, 1993.

———. *The Travels of William Wells Brown: Including Narrative of William Wells Brown, A Fugitive Slave, and The American Fugitive in Europe. Sketches of Places and People Abroad*. Ed. Paul Jefferson. New York: Markus Wiener, 1991.

Carlyle, Thomas. "Occasional Discourse on the Nigger Question." 1849. *Carlyle's Works*. Vol. 18. Boston: Dana Estes, n.d. 293–326.

Child, David L. *The Despotism of Freedom; or the Tyranny and Cruelty of American Republican Slave-Masters*. Boston: Boston Young Men's Anti-Slavery Association, 1833.

Child, Lydia Maria. *An Appeal in Favor of That Class of Americans Called Africans*. Boston: Allen and Ticknor, 1833.

———. "The Black Saxons." 1841. *A Lydia Maria Child Reader*. Ed. Carolyn L. Karcher. Durham, NC: Duke UP, 1997. 182–91.

———. "Mary French and Susan Easton." *Juvenile Miscellany* 3.6 (May 1834): 186–202.

———. *A Romance of the Republic*. 1867. Miami: Mnemosyne, 1969.

Christy, E. Byron, and William E. Christy. *Christy's New Songster and Black Joker*. New York: Dick & Fitzgerald, 1863.

Clarkson, Thomas. *Thoughts on the Necessity of Improving the Condition of the Slaves in the British Colonies, with a View to Their Ultimate Emancipation; and on the Practicability, the Safety, and the Advantages of the Latter Measure.* 2nd ed. London: Society for the Mitigation and Gradual Abolition of Slavery throughout the British Dominions, 1823.

Collins, Julia C. *The Curse of Caste; or The Slave Bride: A Rediscovered African American Novel.* 1865. Ed. William L. Andrews and Mitch Kachun. New York: Oxford UP, 2006.

"A Complaint on Behalf of Native Composers." *Dwight's Journal of Music* 5.12 (24 June 1854): 94–95.

Cowper, William. *The Poems of William Cowper.* Ed. John D. Baird and Charles Ryskamp. 3 vols. Oxford, U.K.: Clarendon-Oxford UP, 1980.

Craft, William, and Ellen Craft. *Running a Thousand Miles for Freedom.* 1860. Athens: U of Georgia P, 1999.

Crafts, Hannah. *The Bondwoman's Narrative.* Ed. Henry Louis Gates, Jr. New York: Warner, 2002.

de Crèvecoeur, J. Hector St. John. *Letters from an American Farmer.* 1782. Mineola, N.Y.: Dover, 2005.

Delany, Martin R. *Blake; or the Huts of America.* 1861–62. Boston: Beacon, 1970.

de Tocqueville, Alexis. *Democracy in America.* 1835, 1840. Ed. Isaac Kramnick. Trans. Gerald E. Bevan. London: Penguin, 2003.

Dickens, Charles. *American Notes.* 1842. Greenwich, Conn.: Fawcett, 1961.

———. *Bleak House.* 1853. New York: Bantam, 1983.

———. *Martin Chuzzlewit.* 1843–44. Ed. James Kinsley. Oxford, U.K.: Clarendon-Oxford UP, 1986.

———. *The Posthumous Papers of the Pickwick Club.* 1836–37. Ed. Margaret Cardwell. Oxford, U.K.: Clarendon-Oxford UP, 1982.

"Disturbances in the City." *Morning Courier and New-York Enquirer.* 10 July 1834: 2.

Douglass, Frederick. *The Heroic Slave.* 1853. *Three Classic African-American Novels.* Ed. William L. Andrews. New York: Mentor-Penguin, 1990. 23–69.

———. *My Bondage and My Freedom.* 1855. *Frederick Douglass Autobiographies.* Ed. Henry Louis Gates, Jr. New York: Library of America, 1994. 103–452.

———. *Narrative of the Life of Frederick Douglass, an American Slave. Written by Himself.* 1845. *Frederick Douglass Autobiographies.* Ed. Henry Louis Gates, Jr. New York: Library of America, 1994. 1–102.

Emerson, Ralph Waldo. "An Address Delivered in the Court-House in Concord, Massachusetts, on 1st August, 1844, on the Anniversary of the Emancipation of the Negroes in the British West Indies." Boston: James Munroe, 1844.

———. "The American Scholar." 1837. *The Portable Emerson*. Ed. Carl Bode and Malcolm Cowley. New ed. New York: Penguin, 1981. 51–71.

———. "The Poet." 1844. *The Portable Emerson*. Ed. Carl Bode and Malcolm Cowley. New ed. New York: Penguin, 1981. 241–65.

———. "Self-Reliance." 1841. *The Portable Emerson*. Ed. Carl Bode and Malcolm Cowley. New ed. New York: Penguin, 1981. 138–64.

Equiano, Olaudah. *The Interesting Narrative of the Life of Olaudah Equiano, Written by Himself*. 1789. Ed. Robert J. Allison. Boston: Bedford, 1995.

"Ethiopian Fashions." *Punch, or the London Charivari* 12 (3 Apr. 1847): 138.

"First Impressions of New-York." *Knickerbocker Magazine* 43.2 (Feb. 1854): 111–14.

"First Performance of Signor Arditi's Opera, 'La Spia.'" *Dwight's Journal of Music* 8.26 (29 Mar. 1856): 203.

Fitzhugh, George. *Sociology for the South, or the Failure of Free Society*. 1854. New York: Burt Franklin, 1965.

Follen, Eliza Lee. "The Melancholy Boy." *The Liberty Bell* 5 (1844): 91–95.

Foster, S. C. "Old Folks at Home." Boston: Ditson, 1851. *The Lester S. Levy Collection of Sheet Music*. Johns Hopkins University. 10 Aug. 2008 levysheetmusic.mse.jhu/index.html.

Franklin, Benjamin. *The Autobiography of Benjamin Franklin*. 1791. Boston: Bedford-St. Martin's, 1993.

Fuller, S. Margaret. "American Literature: Its Position in the Present Time, and Prospects for the Future." *Papers on Literature and Art Part II*. London: Wiley & Putnam, 1846. 122–59.

———. "Entertainments of the Past Winter." *The Dial* 3.1 (July 1842): 46–72.

[Gilbert, Olive.] *Narrative of Sojourner Truth*. 1850. New York: Penguin, 1998.

Gladstone, John. "Facts, Relating to Slavery in the West-Indies and America, Contained in a Letter Addressed to the Right Hon. Sir Robert Peel, Bart." 2nd ed. London: Balwin and Cradock, 1830.

"Glut of Ethiopians." *Punch, or the London Charivari* 12 (20 Mar. 1847): 122.

Hawthorne, Nathaniel. *The House of the Seven Gables: Authoritative Text, Contexts, Criticism*. 1851. Ed. Robert S. Levine. New York: Norton, 2006.

Headley, Joel Tyler. *The Great Riots of New York, 1712 to 1873*. 1873. Miami: Mnemosyne, 1969.

Henderson, W. J. Preface. Harry Thacker Burleigh, ed. *Negro Minstrel Melodies: A Collection of Twenty-Five Songs with Piano Accompaniment, by S. C. Foster and Others*. New York: G. Schirmer, 1910.

Higginson, Thomas Wentworth. *Army Life in a Black Regiment*. 1869. Boston: Beacon, 1962.

Hildreth, Richard. *Archy Moore, The White Slave; or, Memoirs of a Fugitive.* 1856. New York: Negro Universities Press, 1969.

———. *Despotism in America: An Inquiry into the Nature, Results, and Legal Basis of the Slave-Holding System in the United States.* Boston: Jewett, 1854.

The History of Mary Prince, a West Indian Slave. 1831. *The Classic Slave Narratives.* Ed. Henry Louis Gates, Jr. New York: Mentor-New American Library, 1987. 183–238.

Hone, Philip. *The Diary of Philip Hone, 1828–1851.* Ed. Allan Nevins. New York: Dodd, Mead, 1936.

Hume, David. "Of National Characters." *Essays: Moral, Political, and Literary.* Ed. Eugene F. Miller. Revised ed. Indianapolis: Liberty Fund, 1987. 202–20.

"The Hutchinson Family.—Hunkerism." *The North Star.* 27 Oct. 1848: 2.

Hutton, Laurence. "The Negro on the Stage." *Harper's New Monthly Magazine* 79.469 (June 1889): 131–45.

Kemble, Frances Anne. *Journal of a Residence on a Georgian Plantation in 1838–1839.* New York: Harper, 1863.

Kennard, James K., Jr. "Who Are Our National Poets?" *Knickerbocker Magazine* 26.4 (Oct. 1845): 331–41.

"The Last of the Ethiopians." *Punch, or the London Charivari* 12 (19 June 1847): 249.

Lauter, Paul, et al., ed. *The Heath Anthology of American Literature.* 3rd ed. Vol. 1. Boston: Houghton Mifflin, 1998.

"A Letter from A. W. T. on Oratorio Practice, American Voices, &c." *Dwight's Journal of Music* 1.22 (4 Sept. 1852): 170.

"Letter from a Teacher at the South." *Dwight's Journal of Music* 2.21 (26 Feb. 1853): 164.

"Logic for the Legrees." *Punch, or the London Charivari* 24 (5 Feb. 1853): 52.

"London Music Halls." *The Era* 28.1458 (2 Sept. 1866): 12.

Martineau, Harriet. *Dawn Island: A Tale.* Manchester: J. Gadsby, 1845.

———. "Demerara: A Tale." 1833. *Illustrations of Political Economy.* 3rd ed. Vol. 2. London: Charles Fox, 1834. 1–143.

———. *The Hour and the Man; A Historical Romance.* 1841. New York: AMS, 1974.

———. *The Martyr Age of the United States.* 1839. New York: Arno, 1969.

———. *Society in America.* 1837. Vol. 2. New York: AMS, 1966.

Maryland Historical Society. "African Slave Trade in Jamaica, and Comparative Treatment of Slaves." Baltimore: Toy, 1854.

Matthews, Brander. "The Rise and Fall of Negro-Minstrelsy." *Scribner's Magazine* 57 (1915): 754–59.

Mattison, Hiram. *Louisa Picquet, the Octoroon: or Inside Views of Southern Domestic Life.* New York: H. Mattison, 1861. Documenting the American South. 2004. University

Library, University of North Carolina at Chapel Hill. 28 June 2004 docsouth.unc. edu/neh/picquet/picquet.html.

[Mayhew, Henry.] *London Labour and the London Poor; A Cyclopaedia of the Conditions and Earnings of Those That* Will *Work, Those That* Cannot *Work, and Those That* Will Not *Work. Extra Volume. Those That Will Not Work.* 2nd ed. London: Griffin, Bohn, 1862.

Melville, Herman. "Benito Cereno." 1855. *Billy Budd, Sailor and Other Stories.* New York: Penguin, 1986. 159–258.

———. *The Confidence-Man: His Masquerade.* 1857. New York: Norton, 1971.

———. "Hawthorne and His Mosses." 1850. *The Writings of Herman Melville.* Vol. 9. Ed. Harrison Hayford, et al. Evanston: Northwestern UP-Newberry, 1987. 239–53.

"Metropolitan Theatres." *The Theatrical Journal* 4.160 (7 Jan. 1843): 3.

Mill, John Stuart. "The Negro Question." 1850. *Collected Works.* Vol. 21. Toronto: U of Toronto P, 1963. 87–95.

"Music for the People." *Dwight's Journal of Music* 3.12 (25 June 1853): 94–95.

"Music in Ebony." *Punch, or the London Charivari* 11 (19 Dec. 1846): 263.

Narrative of the Life of Henry Box Brown, Written by Himself. 1851. Ed. Richard Newman. New York: Oxford UP, 2002.

[Nathanson, Y. S.] "Negro Minstrelsy—Ancient and Modern." *Putnam's Monthly Magazine* 5.25 (Jan. 1855): 72–79.

"National Music." *Dwight's Journal of Music* 6.18 (3 Feb. 1855): 139–40.

"Native Musical Talent." *Dwight's Journal of Music* 5.8 (27 May 1854): 61–62.

"Negro Minstrelsy." *Dwight's Journal of Music* 1.16 (24 July 1852): 124.

"Negro Minstrelsy in London." *Dwight's Journal of Music* 15.9 (28 May 1859): 67–68.

Nevin, Robert P. "Stephen C. Foster and Negro Minstrelsy." *Atlantic Monthly* 20.121 (Nov. 1867): 608–16.

"New Theory of Negro Minstrelsy." *Dwight's Journal of Music* 7.13 (30 June 1855): 101–2.

"Nigger Peculiarities." *Punch, or the London Charivari* 1 (July–Dec. 1841): 184.

"A Nigger Professor of Cramanology." *Punch, or the London Charivari* 2 (Jan.–June 1842): 49.

"Obituary, Not Eulogistic." *Dwight's Journal of Music* 13.15 (10 July 1858): 118.

Olmsted, Frederick Law. *The Cotton Kingdom: A Traveller's Observations on Cotton and Slavery in the American Slave States. Based upon Three Former Volumes of Journeys and Investigations.* 2 vols. New York: Mason, 1861.

Owen, Robert Dale. *The Wrong of Slavery, the Right of Emancipation, and the Future of the African Race in the United States.* Philadelphia: Lippincott, 1864.

Parker, Theodore. "The Position and Duties of the American Scholar." 1849. *Theodore Parker: American Transcendentalist.* Ed. Robert E. Collins. Metuchen, N.J.: Scarecrow, 1973. 103–38.

Parker, William. *The Freedman's Story*. 1866. *I Was Born a Slave: An Anthology of Classic Slave Narratives*. Vol. 2. Ed. Yuval Taylor. Chicago: Lawrence Hill, 1999. 745–87.

Peabody, Ephraim. "Narratives of Fugitive Slaves." 1849. *The Slave's Narrative*. Ed. Charles T. Davis and Henry Louis Gates, Jr. Oxford, U.K.: Oxford UP, 1985. 19–28.

Poe, Edgar Allan. "The Gold-Bug." *Edgar Allan Poe: Complete Tales & Poems*. Edison, NJ: Castle, 2001. 75–98.

"Popular Songs." *Dwight's Journal of Music* 11.131 (27 June 1857): 99–100.

"Punch's Political Dictionary." *Punch, or the London Charivari* 10 (20 June 1846): 277.

Ray, Gordon N., ed. *The Letters and Private Papers of William Makepeace Thackeray*. Vol. 3 Cambridge, Mass.: Harvard UP, 1946.

Reynolds, Harry. *Minstrel Memories: The Story of Burnt Cork Minstrelsy in Great Britain from 1836 to 1927*. London: Alston Rivers, 1928.

Riis, Thomas, ed. *Nineteenth-Century American Musical Theater*. Vol. 5. *Uncle Tom's Cabin*. George L. Aiken and George C. Howard. 1852. New York: Garland, 1994.

Rogers, N. P. "British Abolitionism." *The Liberty Bell* 3 (1842): 97–111.

Roper, Moses. *A Narrative of the Adventures and Escape of Moses Roper, from American Slavery*. 1838. *I Was Born a Slave: An Anthology of Classic Slave Narratives*. Vol. 1. Ed. Yuval Taylor. Chicago: Lawrence Hill, 1999. 489–521.

"The Serenading Mania." *Punch, or the London Charivari* 12 (27 Feb. 1847): 94.

"Sisters and Slavery." *Punch, or the London Charivari* 24 (22 Jan. 1853): 37.

"Slave Traffic in England." *Punch, or the London Charivari* 17 (Jul.–Dec. 1849): 140.

"Songs of the Blacks." *Dwight's Journal of Music* 10.7 (15 Nov. 1856): 51–52.

Soran, Charles. "Aunt Harriet Becha Stowe." Baltimore: McCaffrey, 1853. *The Lester S. Levy Collection of Sheet Music*. Johns Hopkins University. 10 Aug. 2008 levysheetmusic.mse.jhu/index.html.

Southworth, E. D. E. N. *The Hidden Hand; or, Capitola the Madcap*. 1859. Ed. Joanne Dobson. New Brunswick, N.J.: Rutgers UP, 1988.

"The Stage Irishman." *The Pilot*. 30 Sept. 1871: 4.

"State of the Slave-Market." *Punch, or the London Charivari* 12 (12 Apr. 1847): 164.

Stowe, Harriet Beecher. *Dred: A Tale of the Great Dismal Swamp*. 1856. Ed. Robert S. Levine. Chapel Hill: U of North Carolina P, 2006.

———. *Sunny Memories of Foreign Lands*. Vol. 1. Boston: Phillips, Sampson, 1854.

———. *Uncle Tom's Cabin: Authoritative Text, Backgrounds and Contexts, Criticism*. 1852. Ed. Elizabeth Ammons. New York: Norton, 1994.

Strong, George Templeton. *Diary of George Templeton Strong*. Vol. 3. Ed. Allan Nevins and Milton Halsey Thomas. New York: Macmillan, 1952.

"A Talk with Mrs. Tyler." *Punch, or the London Charivari* 24 (26 Feb. 1853): 89.

Tappan, Lewis. *The Life of Arthur Tappan*. New York: Hurd and Houghton, 1870.

Taylor, Clare, ed. *British and American Abolitionists: An Episode in Transatlantic Understanding.* Edinburgh, U.K.: Edinburgh UP, 1974.

Taylor, R. "Negro Slavery; or, A View of Some of the More Prominent Features of That State of Society, as It Exists in the United States of America and in the Colonies of the West Indies, Especially in Jamaica." London: Hatchard, 1823.

Thackeray, William Makepeace. *The Adventures of Philip on His Way through the World, Showing Who Robbed Him, Who Helped Him, and Who Passed Him By.* 1862. New York: Harper, 1899.

———. *Vanity Fair: A Novel Without a Hero.* 1848. New York: Modern Library, 1950.

"The Theatres." *The Era* 5.248 (25 June 1843): 5.

"The Theatres." *The Era* 6.269 (19 Nov. 1843): 6.

"The Theatres." *The Spectator* 459 (15 Apr. 1837): 349.

Trollope, Anthony. *The West Indies and the Spanish Main.* 1860. 4th ed. London: Dawsons, 1968.

Trollope, Frances. *Domestic Manners of the Americans.* 1832. Barre, Mass.: Imprint Society, 1969.

"Uncle Tomitudes." *Putnam's Monthly* 1.1 (Jan. 1853): 97–102.

"Washing the Metropolis of All Its Blacks." *Punch, or the London Charivari* 17 (Jul.–Dec. 1849): 231.

Washington, Booker T. *Up from Slavery.* 1901. New York: Penguin, 1986.

Webb, Frank J. *The Garies and Their Friends.* 1857. Ed. Robert Reid-Pharr. Baltimore: Johns Hopkins UP, 1997.

Wedderburn, Robert. *The Horrors of Slavery and Other Writings.* New York: Markus Wiener, 1991.

Weld, Theodore Dwight. *American Slavery as It Is: Testimony of a Thousand Witnesses.* 1839. New York: Arno, 1968.

"What Is Ethiopia?" *Punch, or the London Charivari* 12 (24 Apr. 1847): 167.

Whitely, Henry. *Three Months in Jamaica in 1832: Comprising a Residence of Seven Weeks on a Sugar Plantation.* London: Hatchard, 1833.

Whitman, Walt. *Complete Poetry and Collected Prose.* Ed. Justin Kaplan. New York: Library of America, 1982.

Whittier, John Greenleaf. "The Freed Islands." *The Poetical Works of Whittier.* Ed. Hyatt H. Waggoner. Boston: Houghton Mifflin, 1975. 298.

———. "To Englishmen." *The Poetical Works of Whittier.* Ed. Hyatt H. Waggoner. Boston: Houghton Mifflin, 1975. 336.

Wilson, Harriet E. *Our Nig; or, Sketches from the Life of a Free Black, in a Two-Story White House, North.* 1859. New York: Vintage-Random, 1983.

"Who Writes Our Songs?" *Dwight's Journal of Music* 15.7 (14 May 1859): 51–52.

"Yeomen for Sale!" *Punch, or the London Charivari* 5 (Jul.–Dec. 1843): 15, 17.

Secondary Sources

Allmendinger, Blake. "Acting and Slavery: Representations of Work in the Writings of Fanny Kemble." *Mississippi Quarterly: The Journal of Southern Culture* 41.4 (1988): 507–13.

American Anti-Slavery Group. 2009. 23 Apr. 2009 www.iabolish.org.

Anderson, Lisa M. "From Blackface to 'Genuine Negroes': Nineteenth-Century Minstrelsy and the Icon of the 'Negro.'" *Theatre Research International* 21.1 (1996): 17–23.

Andrews, William L. "The 1850s: The First Afro-American Literary Renaissance." *Literary Romanticism in America*. Ed. William L. Andrews. Baton Rouge: Louisiana State UP, 1981. 38–60.

———. *To Tell a Free Story: The First Century of Afro-American Autobiography, 1760–1865.* Urbana: U of Illinois P, 1986.

Anthony, David. "Class, Culture, and the Trouble with White Skin in Hawthorne's *The House of the Seven Gables*." *Yale Journal of Criticism* 12.2 (1999): 249–68.

"Anti-Slavery: Today's Fight for Tomorrow's Freedom." *Anti-Slavery International*. 2009. 23 Apr. 2009 www.antislavery.org.

Appiah, Anthony. "Strictures on Structures: The Prospects for a Structuralist Poetics of African Fiction." *Black Literature and Literary Theory*. Ed. Henry Louis Gates, Jr. New York: Methuen, 1984. 127–50.

Austen, Ralph A. "From the Atlantic to the Indian Ocean: European Abolition, the African Slave Trade, and Asian Economic Structures." *The Abolition of the Atlantic Slave Trade: Origins and Effects in Europe, Africa, and the Americas*. Ed. David Eltis and James Walvin. Madison: U of Wisconsin P, 1981. 117–39.

Bamboozled. Dir. Spike Lee. 2000. DVD. New Line Home Entertainment, 2001.

Banks, Marva. "*Uncle Tom's Cabin* and Antebellum Black Response." *Readers in History: Nineteenth-Century American Literature and the Contexts of Response*. Ed. James L. Machor. Baltimore: Johns Hopkins UP, 1993. 209–27.

Bay, Mia. *The White Image in the Black Mind: African-American Ideas about White People, 1830–1925*. New York: Oxford UP, 2000.

Bean, Annemarie, and James V. Hatch, ed. *Inside the Minstrel Mask: Readings in Nineteenth-Century Blackface Minstrelsy*. Hanover, N.H.: UP of New England, 1996.

Bell, Michael Davitt. "Melville and 'Romance': Literary Nationalism and Fictional Form." *American Transcendental Quarterly* 24 (1974): 56–62.

Berthold, Dennis. "Class Acts: The Astor Place Riots and Melville's 'The Two Temples.'" *American Literature* 71.3 (1999): 429–61.

Blackett, R. J. M. *Building an Antislavery Wall: Black Americans in the Atlantic Abolitionist Movement, 1830–1860*. Ithaca, N.Y.: Cornell UP, 1983.

———. *Divided Hearts: Britain and the American Civil War*. Baton Rouge: Louisiana State UP, 2001.

Blair, John. "Blackface Minstrels in Cross-Cultural Perspective." *American Studies International* 28.2 (1990): 52–65.

Bolt, Christine. *Victorian Attitudes to Race.* London: Routledge & Kegan Paul, 1971.

Bourne, Stephen. *Black in the British Frame: The Black Experience in British Film and Television.* London: Continuum, 2001.

Boylan, Anne M. "Benevolence and Antislavery Activity among African American Women in New York and Boston, 1820–1840." *The Abolitionist Sisterhood: Women's Political Culture in Antebellum America.* Ed. Jean Fagan Yellin and John C. Van Horne. Ithaca, N.Y.: Cornell UP, 1994. 119–37.

Bratton, J. S. "English Ethiopians: British Audiences and Black-Face Acts, 1835–1865." *The Yearbook of English Studies* 11 (1981): 127–42.

Broadbent, R. J. *Annals of the Liverpool Stage from the Earliest Period to the Present Time, Together with Some Account of the Theatres and Music Halls in Bootle and Birkenhead.* Liverpool: Edward Howell, 1908.

Brody, Jennifer DeVere. *Impossible Purities: Blackness, Femininity, and Victorian Culture.* Durham, N.C.: Duke UP, 1998.

———. "Memory's Movements: Minstrelsy, Miscegenation, and American Race Studies." *American Literary History* 11.4 (1999): 736–45.

Butler, Judith. *Gender Trouble: Feminism and the Subversion of Identity.* New York: Routledge, 1990.

Cameron, Kenneth Walter. "An Ungathered Emerson Address before the Rowdies at the Anti-Slavery Society in Boston (Jan. 24, 1861)." *American Transcendental Quarterly* 36 (1977): 39–42.

Carens, Timothy L. "The Civilizing Mission at Home: Empire, Gender, and National Reform in *Bleak House.*" *Dickens Studies Annual: Essays on Victorian Fiction* 26 (1998): 121–45.

Cockrell, Dale. *Demons of Disorder: Early Blackface Minstrels and Their World.* Cambridge, U.K.: Cambridge UP, 1997.

Coleman, Deirdre. "Conspicuous Consumption: White Abolitionism and English Women's Protest Writing in the 1790s." *English Literary History* 61 (1994): 341–62.

Coles, Robert. *Black Writers Abroad: A Study of Black American Writers in Europe and Africa.* New York: Garland, 1999.

Crowdus, Gary, and Dan Georgakas. "Thinking About the Power of Images: An Interview with Spike Lee." *Cineaste:* 26.2 (2001): 4–9.

Dabydeen, David. *Hogarth's Blacks: Images of Blacks in Eighteenth-Century English Art.* Manchester, U.K.: Manchester UP, 1987.

Davis, Angela Y. *Women, Race, and Class.* New York: Random House, 1981.

Davis, Charles T., and Henry Louis Gates, Jr., ed. Introduction. *The Slave's Narrative.* New York: Oxford UP, 1985. xi–xxxiv.

Davis, Susan G. *Parades and Power: Street Theatre in Nineteenth-Century Philadelphia.* Philadelphia: Temple UP, 1986.

Dayan, Joan. "Romance and Race." *The Columbia History of the American Novel.* Ed. Emory Elliott. New York: Columbia UP, 1991. 89–109.

Dennison, Sam. *Scandalize My Name: Black Imagery in American Popular Music.* New York: Garland, 1982.

Drescher, Seymour. *Capitalism and Antislavery: British Mobilization in Comparative Perspective.* New York: Oxford UP, 1987.

Duchartre, Pierre-Louis. *The Italian Comedy: The Improvisation, Scenarios, Lives, Attributes, Portraits, and Masks of the Illustrious Characters of the Commedia dell'Arte.* Trans. Randolph T. Weaver. New York: Dover, 1966.

Ellison, Ralph. "Twentieth-Century Fiction and the Black Mask of Humanity." 1953. *Shadow and Act.* New York: Random House, 1964. 24–44.

Emerson, Ken. *Doo-Dah! Stephen Foster and the Rise of American Popular Culture.* New York: Da Capo, 1998.

Emery, Allan Moore. "'Benito Cereno' and Manifest Destiny." *Nineteenth-Century Fiction* 39.1 (1984): 48–68.

Engle, Anna. "Depictions of the Irish in Frank Webb's *The Garies and Their Friends* and Frances E. W. Harper's *Trial and Triumph.*" *MELUS* 26.1 (2001): 151–71.

Fabi, M. Giulia. "Representing Slavery in Nineteenth-Century Britain: The Anxiety of Non/Fictional Authorship in Charles Dickens' *American Notes* (1842) and William Brown's *Clotel* (1853)." *Images of America: Through the European Looking-Glass.* Ed. William L. Chew. Brussels: VUB UP, 1997. 125–40.

———. "The 'Unguarded Expressions of the Feelings of the Negroes': Gender, Slave Resistance, and William Wells Brown's Revisions of *Clotel.*" *African American Review* 27.4 (1993): 639–54.

Farrison, William Edward. *William Wells Brown: Author and Reformer.* Chicago: U of Chicago P, 1969.

Faulk, Barry J. *Music Hall and Modernity: The Late-Victorian Discovery of Popular Culture.* Athens: Ohio UP, 2004.

Favor, J. Martin. *Authentic Blackness: The Folk in the New Negro Renaissance.* Durham, N.C.: Duke UP, 1999.

Favret, Mary A. "Flogging: The Anti-Slavery Movement Writes Pornography." *Essays and Studies* 51 (1998): 19–43.

Felsenstein, Frank. *English Trader, Indian Maid: Representing Gender, Race, and Slavery in the New World: An Inkle and Yarico Reader.* Baltimore: Johns Hopkins UP, 1999.

Ferguson, Moira. *Subject to Others: British Women Writers and Colonial Slavery, 1670–1834.* New York: Routledge, 1992.

Fielding, K. J., and Anne Smith. "*Hard Times* and the Factory Controversy: Dickens vs. Harriet Martineau." *Nineteenth-Century Fiction* 24.4 (1970): 404–27.

Finson, Jon W. *The Voices that Are Gone: Themes in Nineteenth-Century American Popular Song.* New York: Oxford UP, 1997.

Fisch, Audrey A. *American Slaves in Victorian England: Abolitionist Politics in Popular Literature and Culture.* Cambridge, U.K.: Cambridge UP, 2000.

Fladeland, Betty. *Abolitionists and Working-Class Problems in the Age of Industrialization.* Baton Rouge: Louisiana State UP, 1984.

———. *Men and Brothers: Anglo-American Antislavery Cooperation.* Urbana: U of Illinois P, 1972.

———. "'Our Cause Being One and the Same': Abolitionists and Chartism." *Slavery and British Society, 1776–1846.* Ed. James Walvin. Baton Rouge: Louisiana State UP, 1982. 69–99.

Foner, Eric. "Abolitionism and the Labor Movement in Antebellum America." *Anti-Slavery, Religion, and Reform: Essays in Memory of Roger Anstey.* Ed. Christine Bolt and Seymour Drescher. Folkestone, U.K.: Dawson, 1980. 254–71.

Foner, Philip S. *Frederick Douglass.* New York: Citadel P, 1964.

———, ed. *The Life and Writings of Frederick Douglass.* 5 vols. New York: International Publishers, 1950.

Foreman, P. Gabrielle. "Sentimental Abolition in Douglass's Decade: Revision, Erotic Conversion, and the Politics of Witnessing in *The Heroic Slave* and *My Bondage and My Freedom.*" *Sentimental Men: Masculinity and the Politics of Affect in American Culture.* Ed. Mary Chapman and Glenn Hendler. Berkeley: U of California P, 1999. 149–62.

Foot, Tom. "Phillips Claims Rappers Are Modern Minstrels." *New Journal Enterprises* 9 Sept. 2005. 13 July 2006 www.camdennewjournal.co.uk/090805/r090805_02.htm.

Fredrickson, George M. *The Black Image in the White Mind: The Debate on Afro-American Character and Destiny, 1817–1914.* New York: Harper & Row, 1971.

Free the Slaves. 2007. 3 July 2008 www.freetheslaves.net/NETCOMMUNITY/Page. aspx?pid=183.

Freeman, Rhoda Goldman. *The Free Negro in New York City in the Era before the Civil War.* New York: Garland, 1994.

Friedman, Lawrence J. *Gregarious Saints: Self and Community in American Abolitionism, 1830–1870.* Cambridge, U.K.: Cambridge UP, 1982.

Fryer, Peter. *Staying Power: Black People in Britain since 1504.* Atlantic Highlands, N.J.: Humanities P, 1984.

Gallagher, Catherine. *The Industrial Reformation of English Fiction: Social Discourse and Narrative Form, 1832–1867.* Chicago: U of Chicago P, 1985.

Gardner, Jared. *Master Plots: Race and the Founding of an American Literature, 1787–1845.* Baltimore: Johns Hopkins UP, 1998.

Garfield, Deborah M., and Rafia Zafar, ed. *Harriet Jacobs and* Incidents in the Life of a Slave Girl: *New Critical Essays.* Cambridge, U.K.: Cambridge UP, 1996.

Garrett, Shawn-Marie. "Return of the Repressed." *Theater* 32.2 (2002): 27–43.

Gates, Henry Louis, Jr. *Figures in Black: Words, Signs, and the "Racial" Self.* New York: Oxford UP, 1987.

——, and Hollis Robbins, ed. *In Search of Hannah Crafts: Critical Essays on* The Bondwoman's Narrative." New York: Basic Civitas, 2004.

Gerteis, Louis. "St. Louis Theatre in the Age of the Original Jim Crow." *Gateway Heritage* 15.4 (1995): 32–41.

Gerzina, Gretchen. *Black London: Life before Emancipation.* New Brunswick, N.J.: Rutgers UP, 1995.

Gilje, Paul A. *The Road to Mobocracy: Popular Disorder in New York City, 1763–1834.* Chapel Hill: U of North Carolina P, 1987.

Gilmore, Paul. *The Genuine Article: Race, Mass Culture, and American Literary Manhood.* Durham, N.C.: Duke UP, 2001.

Gilroy, Paul. *The Black Atlantic: Modernity and Double Consciousness.* Cambridge, Mass.: Harvard UP, 1993.

Goodman, Paul. *Of One Blood: Abolitionism and the Origins of Racial Equality.* Berkeley: U of California P, 1998.

Gougeon, Len. "The Anti-Slavery Background of Emerson's 'Ode Inscribed to W. H. Channing.'" *Studies in the American Renaissance.* Ed. Joel Myerson. Charlottesville: UP of Virginia, 1985. 63–77.

Green, Alan W. C. "'Jim Crow,' 'Zip Coon': The Northern Origins of Negro Minstrelsy." *Massachusetts Review* 11 (1970): 385–97.

Gubar, Susan. *Racechanges: White Skin, Black Face in American Culture.* New York: Oxford UP, 1997.

Hall, Catherine. "The Economy of Intellectual Prestige: Thomas Carlyle, John Stuart Mill, and the Case of Governor Eyre." *Cultural Critique* 12 (1989): 167–96.

——. "Missionary Stories: Gender and Ethnicity in England in the 1830s and 1840s." *Cultural Studies.* Ed. Lawrence Grossberg, Cary Nelson, and Paula A. Treichler. New York: Routledge, 1992. 240–70.

Hansen, Debra Gold. "The Boston Female Anti-Slavery Society and the Limits of Gender Politics." *The Abolitionist Sisterhood: Women's Political Culture in Antebellum America.* Ed. Jean Fagan Yellin and John C. Van Horne. Ithaca, N.Y.: Cornell UP, 1994. 45–65.

Haywood, Charles. "Negro Minstrelsy and Shakespearean Burlesque." *Folklore and*

Society: Essays in Honor of Benjamin A. Botkin. Ed. Jackson Bruce. Hatboro, Pa.: Folklore Associates, 1966. 77–92.

Hedrick, Joan D. *Harriet Beecher Stowe: A Life.* New York: Oxford UP, 1994.

Heglar, Charles J. "Rhoda Swartz in *Vanity Fair*: A Doll Without Admirers." *College Language Association Journal* 37.3 (1994): 336–47.

Hirsch, Stephen A. "Uncle Tom's Companions: The Literary and Popular Reaction to *Uncle Tom's Cabin*." Ph.D. diss. SUNY–Albany, 1975. Ann Arbor: UMI, 1976.

Holland, Frederic May. *Frederick Douglass: The Colored Orator.* 1895. Revised ed. New York: Haskell House, 1969.

Hollis, Patricia. "Anti-Slavery and British Working-Class Radicalism in the Years of Reform." *Anti-Slavery, Religion, and Reform: Essays in Memory of Roger Anstey.* Ed. Christine Bolt and Seymour Drescher. Folkestone, U.K.: Dawson, 1980. 294–315.

Honour, Hugh. *The Image of the Black in Western Art from the American Revolution to World War I.* Vol. 4:1. Cambridge, Mass.: Harvard UP, 1989.

Horsley-Meacham, Gloria. "Bull of the Nile: Symbol, History, and Racial Myth in 'Benito Cereno.'" *New England Quarterly* 64.2 (1991): 225–42.

Johnson, Charles, Patricia Smith, and the WGBH Series Research Team. *Africans in America: America's Journey through Slavery.* New York: Harcourt Brace, 1998.

Jones, Gavin. "Dusky Comments of Silence: Language, Race, and Herman Melville's 'Benito Cereno.'" *Studies in Short Fiction* 32.1 (1995): 39–50.

Jordan, Winthrop D. *White over Black: American Attitudes toward the Negro, 1550–1812.* Chapel Hill: U of North Carolina P, 1968.

Jung, Fred. "A Fireside Chat with Stanley Crouch." *All About Jazz* 22 Feb. 2005. 4 July 2006 www.allaboutjazz.com/php/article.php?id=16623.

Kennedy, J. Gerald, and Liliane Weissberg, ed. *Romancing the Shadow: Poe and Race.* Oxford, U.K.: Oxford UP, 2001.

Kerber, Linda K. "Abolitionists and Amalgamators: The New York City Race Riots of 1834." *New York State Historical Association* 48 (1967): 28–39.

Klammer, Martin. *Whitman, Slavery, and the Emergence of* Leaves of Grass. University Park: Pennsylvania State UP, 1995.

Knoper, Randall. *Acting Naturally: Mark Twain in the Culture of Performance.* Berkeley: U of California P, 1995.

Lapsansky, Phillip. "Graphic Discord: Abolitionist and Antiabolitionist Images." *The Abolitionist Sisterhood: Women's Political Culture in Antebellum America.* Ed. Jean Fagan Yellin and John C. Van Horne. Ithaca, N.Y.: Cornell UP, 1994. 201–30.

Lee, Julia Sun-Joo. "The (Slave) Narrative of *Jane Eyre*." *Victorian Literature and Culture* 36 (2008): 317–29.

Lee, Maurice S. *Slavery, Philosophy, and American Literature, 1830–1860.* Cambridge, U.K.: Cambridge UP, 2005.

Leonard, William Torbert. *Masquerade in Black*. Metuchen, N.J.: Scarecrow P, 1986.

Leverenz, David. *Manhood and the American Renaissance*. Ithaca, N.Y.: Cornell UP, 1989.

Levine, Lawrence W. *Black Culture and Black Consciousness: Afro-American Folk Thought from Slavery to Freedom*. New York: Oxford UP, 1978.

———. *Highbrow/Lowbrow: The Emergence of Cultural Hierarchy in America*. Cambridge, Mass.: Harvard UP, 1988.

Levine, Robert S. "'Whiskey, Blacking, and All': Temperance and Race in William Wells Brown's *Clotel*." *The Serpent in the Cup: Temperance in American Literature*. Ed. David S. Reynolds and Debra J. Rosenthal. Amherst: U of Massachusetts P, 1997. 93–114.

Lhamon, W. T., Jr. *Jump Jim Crow: Lost Plays, Lyrics, and Street Prose of the First Atlantic Popular Culture*. Cambridge, Mass.: Harvard UP, 2003.

———. *Raising Cain: Blackface Performance from Jim Crow to Hip Hop*. Cambridge, Mass.: Harvard UP, 1998.

Looby, Christopher. "'As Thoroughly Black as the Most Faithful Philanthropist Could Desire': Erotics of Race in Higginson's *Army Life in a Black Regiment*." *Race and the Subject of Masculinities*. Ed. Harry Stecopoulos and Michael Uebel. Durham, N.C.: Duke UP, 1997. 71–115.

———. "'Innocent Homosexuality': The Fiedler Thesis in Retrospect." *Adventures of Huckleberry Finn: A Case Study in Critical Controversy*. By Mark Twain. 1885. Ed. Gerald Graff and James Phelan. Boston: Bedford/St. Martin's, 1995. 535–50.

Lorimer, Douglas A. *Colour, Class, and the Victorians: English Attitudes to the Negro in the Mid-Nineteenth Century*. Leicester, U.K.: Leicester UP, 1978.

Lott, Eric. *Love and Theft: Blackface Minstrelsy and the American Working Class*. New York: Oxford UP, 1993.

Lovell, Thomas B. "By Dint of Labor and Economy: Harriet Jacobs, Harriet Wilson, and the Salutary View of Wage Labor." *Arizona Quarterly* 52.3 (1996): 1–32.

Mahar, William J. "'Backside Albany' and Early Blackface Minstrelsy: A Contextual Study of America's First Blackface Song." *American Music* 6.1 (1988): 1–27.

———. *Behind the Burnt Cork Mask: Early Blackface Minstrelsy and Antebellum American Popular Culture*. Urbana: U of Illinois P, 1999.

Martin, S. I. *Britain's Slave Trade*. London: Channel 4-Macmillan, 1999.

Martin, Waldo E., Jr. *The Mind of Frederick Douglass*. Chapel Hill: U of North Carolina P, 1984.

Mayer, David. *Harlequin in His Element: The English Pantomime, 1806–1836*. Cambridge, Mass.: Harvard UP, 1969.

McBride, Dwight A. *Impossible Witnesses: Truth, Abolitionism, and Slave Testimony*. New York: New York UP, 2001.

McFeely, William S. *Frederick Douglass*. New York: Norton, 1991.

McKivigan, John R. "The Frederick Douglass–Gerrit Smith Friendship and Political Abolitionism in the 1850s." *Frederick Douglass: New Literary and Historical Essays.* Ed. Eric J. Sundquist. Cambridge, U.K.: Cambridge UP, 1990. 205–32.

Meer, Sarah. *Uncle Tom Mania: Slavery, Minstrelsy, and Transatlantic Culture in the 1850s.* Athens: U of Georgia P, 2005.

Meyer, Susan. *Imperialism at Home: Race and Victorian Women's Fiction.* Ithaca, N.Y.: Cornell UP, 1996.

Mitchell, Loften. *Black Drama: The Story of the American Negro in the Theatre.* New York: Hawthorn, 1967.

Moody, Richard. "Negro Minstrelsy." *Quarterly Journal of Speech* 30 (1944): 321–28.

Morrison, Toni. *Playing in the Dark: Whiteness and the Literary Imagination.* New York: Vintage, 1992.

Moses, Wilson J. "Writing Freely? Frederick Douglass and the Constraints of Racialized Writing." *Frederick Douglass: New Literary and Historical Essays.* Ed. Eric J. Sundquist. Cambridge, U.K.: Cambridge UP, 1990. 66–83.

Mott, Frank Luther. *A History of American Magazines, 1741–1850.* Vol. 2. New York: Appleton, 1930.

Musgrave, Marian E. "Patterns of Violence and Non-Violence in Pro-Slavery and Anti-Slavery Fiction." *College Language Association Journal* 16 (1973): 426–37.

Nathan, Hans. *Dan Emmett and the Rise of Early Negro Minstrelsy.* Norman: U of Oklahoma P, 1962.

Newman, Richard. Introduction. *Narrative of the Life of Henry Box Brown, Written by Himself.* New York: Oxford UP, 2002. xi–xxxii.

Nicoll, Allardyce. *The World of Harlequin: A Critical Study of the Commedia dell'Arte.* Cambridge, U.K.: Cambridge UP, 1963.

Norton, Sandy Morey. "The Ex-Collector of Boggley-Wollah: Colonialism in the Empire of *Vanity Fair.*" *Narrative* 1.2 (1993): 124–37.

OED Online. 6 July 2005. dictionary.oed.com.proxy.bsu.edu/entrance.dtl.

Okker, Patricia, and Jeffrey R. Williams. "'Reassuring Sounds': Minstrelsy and *The Hidden Hand.*" *American Transcendental Quarterly* 12.2 (1998): 133–44.

Oldfield, J. R. *Popular Politics and British Anti-Slavery: The Mobilisation of Public Opinion against the Slave Trade, 1787–1807.* Manchester, U.K.: Manchester UP, 1995.

Pease, Donald E. *Visionary Compacts: American Renaissance Writings in Cultural Context.* Madison: U of Wisconsin P, 1987.

Pease, William H., and Jane Pease. *Black Utopia: Negro Communal Experiments in America.* Madison: U of Wisconsin P, 1972.

———. "Boston Garrisonians and the Problem of Frederick Douglass." *Canadian Journal of History* 2.2 (1967): 29–48.

Phillips, Elizabeth C. "'His Right of Attendance': The Image of the Black Man in the Works of Poe and Two of His Contemporaries." *No Fairer Land: Studies in Southern Literature Before 1900.* Troy, N.Y.: Whitson, 1986. 172–84.

Pickering, Michael. "The Blackface Clown." *Black Victorians/Black Victoriana.* Ed. Gretchen Holbrook Gerzina. New Brunswick, N.J.: Rutgers UP, 2003. 159–74.

———. "Mock Blacks and Racial Mockery: The 'Nigger' Minstrel and British Imperialism." *Acts of Supremacy: The British Empire and the Stage, 1790–1930.* Ed. J. S. Bratton. Manchester, U.K.: Manchester UP, 1991. 179–236.

———. "White Skin, Black Masks: 'Nigger' Minstrelsy in Victorian England." *Music Hall: Performance and Style.* Ed. J. S. Bratton. Milton Keynes, U.K.: Open UP, 1986. 70–91.

Pope-Hennessy, Una. *Charles Dickens.* New York: Howell, Soskin, 1946.

Porter, Dale H. *The Abolition of the Slave Trade in England, 1784–1807.* Hamden, Conn.: Archon, 1970.

Powell, Timothy B. *Ruthless Democracy: A Multicultural Interpretation of the American Renaissance.* Princeton, N.J.: Princeton UP, 2000.

Quarles, Benjamin. *Black Abolitionists.* New York: Oxford UP, 1969.

———. "The Breach Between Douglass and Garrison." *Journal of Negro History* 23.2 (1938): 144–54.

Radano, Ronald Michael, and Philip V. Bohlman, ed. *Music and the Racial Imagination.* Chicago: U of Chicago P, 2000.

Rehin, George F. "Blackface Street Minstrels in Victorian London and its Resorts: Popular Culture and Its Racial Connotations As Revealed in Polite Opinion." *Journal of Popular Culture* 15.1 (1981): 19–38.

———. "The Darker Image: American Negro Minstrelsy through the Historian's Lens." *American Studies* 9.3 (1975): 365–73.

———. "Harlequin Jim Crow: Continuity and Convergence in Blackface Clowning." *Journal of Popular Culture* 9.3 (1975): 682–701.

Reynolds, David S. *Beneath the American Renaissance: The Subversive Imagination in the Age of Emerson and Melville.* New York: Knopf, 1988.

Reynolds, Larry J. *European Revolutions and the American Literary Renaissance.* New Haven, Conn.: Yale UP, 1988.

Rhodes, Jane. *Mary Ann Shadd Cary: The Black Press and Protest in the Nineteenth Century.* Bloomington: Indiana UP, 1998.

Riach, Douglas C. "Blacks and Blackface on the Irish Stage, 1830–60." *Journal of American Studies* 7.3 (1973): 231–41.

Rice, Alan J. *Radical Narratives of the Black Atlantic.* London: Continuum, 2003.

———, and Martin Crawford, ed. *Liberating Sojourn: Frederick Douglass and Transatlantic Reform.* Athens: U of Georgia P, 1999.

Rice, C. Duncan. "Literary Sources and the Revolution in British Attitudes to Slavery." *Anti-Slavery, Religion, and Reform: Essays in Memory of Roger Anstey*. Ed. Christine Bolt and Seymour Drescher. Folkestone, U.K.: Dawson, 1980. 319–34.

———. "The Missionary Context of the British Anti-Slavery Movement." *Slavery and British Society, 1776–1846*. Ed. James Walvin. Baton Rouge: Louisiana State UP, 1982. 150–63.

Richards, Jason. "Melville's (Inter)national Burlesque: Whiteface, Blackface, and 'Benito Cereno.'" *American Transcendental Quarterly* 21.1 (2007): 73–94.

Riss, Arthur. "Racial Essentialism and Family Values in *Uncle Tom's Cabin*." *American Quarterly* 46.4 (1994): 513–44.

Rodgers, Nini. *Ireland, Slavery, and Anti-Slavery, 1612–1865*. Basingstoke, U.K.: Palgrave Macmillan, 2007.

Roediger, David R. *The Wages of Whiteness: Race and the Making of the American Working Class*. London: Verso, 1991.

———. *Working toward Whiteness: How America's Immigrants Became White: The Strange Journey from Ellis Island to the Suburbs*. New York: Basic, 2005.

Rogin, Michael. *Blackface, White Noise: Jewish Immigrants in the Hollywood Melting Pot*. Berkeley: U of California P, 1996.

———. *Subversive Genealogy: The Politics and Art of Herman Melville*. New York: Knopf, 1983.

Rourke, Constance. *American Humor: A Study of the National Character*. New York: Harcourt Brace, 1931.

Runcie, John. "'Hunting the Nigs' in Philadelphia: The Race Riot of August 1834." *Pennsylvania History* 39.2 (1972): 187–218.

Rust, Marion. "The Subaltern as Imperialist: Speaking of Olaudah Equiano." *Passing and the Fictions of Identity*. Ed. Elaine K. Ginsberg. Durham, N.C.: Duke UP, 1996. 21–36.

Ryan, Susan M. "Misgivings: Melville, Race, and the Ambiguities of Benevolence." *American Literary History* 12.4 (2000): 685–712.

Sacks, Howard L., and Judith Rose Sacks. *Way Up North in Dixie: A Black Family's Claim to the Confederate Anthem*. Washington, D.C.: Smithsonian Institution, 1993.

Saillant, John. "The Black Body Erotic and the Republican Body Politic, 1790–1820." *Sentimental Men: Masculinity and the Politics of Affect in American Culture*. Ed. Mary Chapman and Glenn Hendler. Berkeley: U of California P, 1999. 89–111.

Samuels, Shirley. "The Identity of Slavery." *The Culture of Sentiment: Race, Gender, and Sentimentality in Nineteenth-Century America*. Ed. Shirley Samuels. New York: Oxford UP, 1992. 157–71.

Sánchez-Eppler, Karen. "Bodily Bonds: The Intersecting Rhetorics of Feminism and Abolitionism." *The Culture of Sentiment: Race, Gender, and Sentimentality in Nineteenth-Century America*. Ed. Shirley Samuels. New York: Oxford UP, 1992. 92–114.

Saxton, Alexander. *The Rise and Fall of the White Republic: Class Politics and Mass Culture in Nineteenth-Century America*. London: Verso, 1990.

Seelye, John. "The Clay Foot of the Climber: Richard M. Nixon in Perspective." *Literary Romanticism in America*. Ed. William L. Andrews. Baton Rouge: Louisiana State UP, 1981. 109–34.

Shalom, Jack. "The Ira Aldridge Troupe: Early Blackface Minstrelsy in Philadelphia." *African American Review* 28.4 (1994): 653–57.

Shyllon, F. O. *Black Slaves in Britain*. London: Oxford UP, 1974.

Sotiropoulos, Karen. *Staging Race: Black Performers in Turn-of-the-Century America*. Cambridge, Mass.: Harvard UP, 2006.

Stafford, Norman. "Edgar Allan Poe's 'The Gold-Bug,' the Trickster, and the 'Long-Tail'd Blue.'" *Thalia: Studies in Literary Humor* 18.1–2 (1998): 72–83.

Stepto, Robert B. *From Behind the Veil: A Study of Afro-American Narrative*. Urbana: U of Illinois P, 1979.

Stern, Julia. "Spanish Masquerade and the Drama of Racial Identity in Uncle Tom's Cabin." *Passing and the Fictions of Identity*. Ed. Elaine K. Ginsberg. Durham, N.C.: Duke UP, 1996. 103–30.

Strausbaugh, John. *Black Like You: Blackface, Whiteface, Insult, and Imitation in American Popular Culture*. New York: Jeremy P. Tarcher–Penguin, 2006.

Sundquist, Eric J. "Slavery, Revolution, and the American Renaissance." *The American Renaissance Reconsidered*. Ed. Walter Benn Michaels and Donald E. Pease. Baltimore: Johns Hopkins UP, 1985. 1–33.

———. *To Wake the Nations: Race in the Making of American Literature*. Cambridge, Mass.: Harvard UP, 1993.

Sutherland, John. "Thackeray as Victorian Racialist." *Essays in Criticism* 20.4 (1970): 441–45.

Swerdlow, Amy. "Abolition's Conservative Sisters: The Ladies New York City Anti-Slavery Societies, 1834–1840." *The Abolitionist Sisterhood: Women's Political Culture in Antebellum America*. Ed. Jean Fagan Yellin and John C. Van Horne. Ithaca, N.Y.: Cornell UP, 1994. 31–44.

Temperley, Howard. *British Antislavery, 1833–1870*. London: Longman, 1972.

Thomas, Helen. *Romanticism and Slave Narratives: Transatlantic Testimonies*. Cambridge, U.K.: Cambridge UP, 2000.

Thomas, Sue. "The Tropical Extravagance of Bertha Mason." *Victorian Literature and Culture* 27.1 (1999): 1–17.

Tillery, Tyrone. "The Inevitability of the Douglass-Garrison Conflict." *Phylon* 37 (1976): 137–49.

Toll, Robert C. *Blacking Up: The Minstrel Show in Nineteenth-Century America*. New York: Oxford UP, 1974.

Toner, Jennifer Dilalla. "The 'Remarkable Effect' of 'Silly Words': Dialect and Signature in 'The Gold-Bug.'" *Arizona Quarterly* 49.1 (1993): 1–20.

von Sneidern, Maja-Lisa. "*Wuthering Heights* and the Liverpool Slave Trade." *English Literary History* 62 (1995): 171–96.

Wagenknecht, Edward. *Harriet Beecher Stowe: The Known and the Unknown*. New York: Oxford UP, 1965.

Wallis, Brian. "Black Bodies, White Science: Louis Agassiz's Slave Daguerreotypes." *American Art* 9.2 (1995): 39–61.

Walvin, James. *Black and White: The Negro and English Society, 1555–1945*. London: Allen Lane-Penguin, 1973.

———. *The Black Presence: A Documentary History of the Negro in England, 1555–1860*. London: Orbach & Chambers, 1971.

———. *Making the Black Atlantic: Britain and the African Diaspora*. London: Cassell, 2000.

Ward, Andrew. *Dark Midnight When I Rise: The Story of the Jubilee Singers Who Introduced the World to the Music of Black America*. New York: Farrar, Straus, and Giroux, 2000.

Watson, Reginald. "Images of Blackness in the Works of Charlotte and Emily Brontë." *College Language Association Journal* 44.4 (2001): 451–70.

Weinauer, Ellen W. "'A Most Respectable Looking Gentleman': Passing, Possession, and Transgression in *Running a Thousand Miles for Freedom*." *Passing and the Fictions of Identity*. Ed. Elaine K. Ginsberg. Durham, N.C.: Duke UP, 1997. 37–56.

West, Shearer, ed. *The Victorians and Race*. Aldershot, U.K.: Ashgate, 1996.

Williams, Carolyn. "The Female Antislavery Movement: Fighting Against Racial Prejudice and Promoting Women's Rights in Antebellum America." *The Abolitionist Sisterhood: Women's Political Culture in Antebellum America*. Ed. Jean Fagan Yellin and John C. Van Horne. Ithaca, N.Y.: Cornell UP, 1994. 159–78.

Winks, Robin W. "The Making of a Fugitive Slave Narrative: Josiah Henson and Uncle Tom—A Case Study." *The Slave's Narrative*. Ed. Charles T. Davis and Henry Louis Gates, Jr. Oxford: Oxford UP, 1985. 112–46.

Wittke, Carl. *Tambo and Bones: A History of the American Minstrel Stage*. Durham, N.C.: Duke UP, 1930.

Wood, Marcus. *Blind Memory: Visual Representations of Slavery in England and America, 1780–1865*. New York: Routledge, 2000.

Yellin, Jean Fagan. *Harriet Jacobs: A Life*. New York: Basic Civitas, 2004.

———. *Women and Sisters: The Antislavery Feminists in American Culture*. New Haven, Conn.: Yale UP, 1989.

Zwarg, Christina. "Fathering and Blackface in *Uncle Tom's Cabin*." *Novel* 22.3 (1989): 274–87.

INDEX

abolition of slave trade: in United Kingdom, 42, 94; in United States, 42

abolition of slavery: in British India and Ceylon, 68, 172n1; in British West Indian colonies, 1, 41, 42, 43, 49, 50, 56, 57, 66, 67, 80, 89, 97; in United States, 11, 46, 48, 65, 97, 98, 99

abolitionist literature, 37, 67, 132; authentication of descriptions of slavery in, 35, 68–69; depictions of sexual abuse of black people in, 26–31, 171nn15–17; racial indeterminacy in, 151–53, 155–61, 165; racism in, 161–65; use of blackface tropes in, 139, 140–41, 146–47, 151–53, 155–65; use of minstrel songs in, 140, 146, 147–51

abolitionist meetings. *See* antislavery meetings

abolitionist movement: African Americans in, 11, 15–16, 34–36, 40, 53, 166, 168, 174n15; and British colonialism, 9, 54, 58–59, 99, 174nn18–19; and early feminism, 8; as transatlantic movement, 1, 7, 53, 137, 166, 173n9; associated with miscegenation, 32–34, 41, 90, 94; claims of authenticity in, 11, 24, 35–36, 40, 68–69; conflict within, 4; critiques of American hypocrisy in, 9, 135; decline of, 5, 43–44, 47, 60, 61, 64–70, 81, 86, 89, 96, 98–99; fascination with black bodies in, 3, 11, 25, 26–27, 31, 32, 35, 40–41, 43, 54–55; hostility toward in northern U.S., 3, 126–28, 154; in United Kingdom, 1, 5, 8, 41–60, 61–62, 64–69,

78, 79, 80–81, 93, 94, 98–99, 126, 128, 137, 169n2, 171n15, 174n12, 181nn30–31; in United States, 7, 10–12, 15–27, 31–36, 40–41, 47, 49–51, 53, 56, 59, 126–32, 135, 137, 169n2, 174n12; indifference toward capitalist exploitation of poor in, 7–8, 65, 85–88, 127–32; middle-class support for, 7, 127, 131–32; opposition to slave rebellion in, 17, 18; racism in, 10–12, 15–16, 17, 54–56, 64, 65, 70, 75, 98, 99, 168, 183n1; relationship to blackface minstrelsy, 1–2, 4, 7, 10, 19–25, 31, 32, 35, 40–41, 42–44, 54–55, 60, 61–62, 64–65, 66–70, 75, 78–79, 80–83, 85, 89, 93, 98–99, 116, 126, 140, 146–47, 149–51, 166–67, 170n9, 185n14; representations of African Americans in, 1, 6, 10, 34–35, 40–41, 54–56, 61, 62, 67–69, 78, 80, 81, 85, 126, 166–67; women in, 8, 32; working-class attitudes toward (*see* working class: attitudes toward abolitionist movement). *See also* antislavery meetings; antislavery songs

Adelphi Theatre (London), 62, 68, 175n20, 176n2

African Americans: abolitionist representations of (*see* abolitionist movement: representations of African Americans in); as blackface minstrel performers (*see* blackface minstrelsy: African American performers in); attitudes toward United Kingdom, 44–47, 53–55, 173n5; in abolitionist movement (*see* abolitionist movement: African Americans in); in United

African Americans (*continued*)
Kingdom, 7, 42–43, 44–47, 53–56, 61, 70, 173n5, 174n15; literary representations of, 80–85, 86, 90–92, 102–3, 141–45, 147, 151–53, 156–65; racism against (*see under* racism); representations of in blackface minstrelsy (*see* blackface minstrelsy: representations of African Americans in)

African Opera Troupe, 175n22

Anne of Denmark (queen consort of England and Ireland), 71

Agassiz, Louis, 31, 171n18

Aiken, George, 10, 21, 23

Amazing Grace (film), 167

American Anti-Slavery Group, 168

American Anti-Slavery Society, 1

American and Foreign Anti-Slavery Society, 4

American Renaissance, 101, 132, 136, 137, 138, 141; and blackface minstrelsy, 5–6, 101, 114–15, 138, 177n2, 178n4; and literary nationalism, 6, 115–16, 137, 138; and slave narratives, 5–6, 101, 132, 137–38, 177n2

American Revolutionary War, 44, 45–46, 56, 75, 103; and African American slaves, 44; in minstrel songs, 109, 110

American Serenaders, 169n4

American War of Independence. *See* American Revolutionary War

Amistad (film), 167

Amistad mutiny, 170n8

Anglo-American relations, 2, 6, 7, 42–44, 47–48, 49–51, 53, 166–67, 173n7

anti-abolitionist riots, 128, 130–31

Anti-Slavery International, 168

antislavery literature. *See* abolitionist literature

antislavery meetings, 11, 25, 26; conventional nature of, 23–24, 34–35, 40; performance of ex-slaves in, 3, 23–26, 34–36

antislavery movement. *See* abolitionist movement

Anti-Slavery Society (of United Kingdom), 42

antislavery songs: "A Song for Freedom," 148; "Get off the Track," 148; "The North Star," 148

apprenticeship system in British West Indian colonies, 1, 41, 42, 57–58, 61, 174n12

Astor Place Riot, 131, 180n16

Baartman, Saartjie ("Hottentot Venus"), 171n18, 177n10

Barnum, P. T., 39, 61

Behn, Aphra: *Oroonoko,* 71

Bibb, Henry, 27–28, 182n43

Bickerstaffe, Isaac: *The Padlock,* 71

Black and White Minstrel Show, The, 73

Black Atlantic (theory), 6

blackface: and busking in Britain, 61, 74, 175n21; early traditions in England, 5, 7, 9, 43–44, 60, 71–72, 73–77, 78, 99, 115, 123–24; used by London beggars, 67. *See also* blackface minstrelsy

Blackface Atlantic, 6, 9, 72, 73, 168

blackface minstrelsy: African American musical elements in, 78, 181nn26–27; African American performers in, 37–40, 72–73, 118, 168, 171n22, 172n23, 175n29; African musical elements in, 78, 83–84, 123; American nationalism in, 5, 8–9, 62, 72, 100–102, 103, 104, 106–11, 114, 116, 119, 126, 130, 131, 132, 137, 177n2, 181n25; American origins of, 1, 71–72, 123–24; and U.S. Civil War, 109–11, 179n12; and the American Renaissance (*see* American Renaissance: and blackface minstrelsy); and U.S. territorial expansion, 104–7; anti-abolitionist sentiment in, 3, 4, 5, 7, 8, 12, 33, 80, 101, 109, 110, 126, 130, 131, 179n10; anti-British sentiment in, 5, 8–9, 100–101, 107–8, 109–11, 119, 126, 130, 131, 138, 178n8, 181n25; anti-European sentiment in, 100–102,

105; antislavery sentiment in, 3, 4–5, 7,
11, 12–15, 18, 19, 21–23, 43, 60, 61–62,
64, 66, 67–69, 75, 89, 102, 139, 140,
146–47, 148, 151, 165, 169n4, 185n14; as
American national culture, 8, 19, 62, 71,
78, 100–102, 113, 114–24, 137, 138, 140,
181n23; as street performance, 61, 74,
175n21; as transatlantic phenomenon,
1, 2, 7, 60–63, 71–72, 73–74, 166;
black dialect in, 4, 35, 96, 115, 117, 125,
164–65; British theatrical influences
in, 77; burlesque of European music in,
113, 115, 116; changes in, 4, 13, 60, 61,
63–64, 80; commercialization of, 146;
commodification of blackness in, 118–19,
145, 152; conventional nature of, 11, 23,
35, 37, 40, 73, 146, 152; cross-dressing in,
33; dance styles in, 4, 77–78, 116, 117–18;
"dandy" characters in, 16–17, 96, 153;
differences between American and British versions, 7, 62–64, 66, 73–75, 169n2;
endmen in, 7, 35, 131, 142, 161, 162,
185n13; European musical elements in,
78, 83–84; fascination with black bodies
in, 11, 25, 31–34, 40–41, 82, 102; female
characters in, 32, 33, 95, 125; humor in,
20, 22, 35, 60, 62, 64, 77, 161–65, 185n11,
185n13; ideological ambivalence in, 4,
25, 33, 61, 80, 98, 147, 165, 167; in United
Kingdom, 5, 7, 9, 41, 43, 60–81, 98–99,
115, 169n4, 172n23; in United States, 7,
9, 10–23, 25–26, 31–41, 72, 100–111, 113,
114–26, 129–30, 131; instrumentation
of, 78, 124; interlocutors in, 7, 35, 131,
161, 185n13; Irish-Americans performers
in, 78, 181n25; Jim Crow in, 1, 2, 9, 19,
35, 60, 61–62, 72, 73, 75, 81–82, 100,
106, 114, 124, 125–26, 140, 160, 161, 168;
male audience of, 7, 21, 25–26, 63, 102,
125; masculinity in, 6, 8, 101, 102, 103,
104, 107–8, 114, 124–26; miscegenation

represented in, 33–34, 90; misogyny in,
8, 32, 125; middle-class audience of, 4, 13,
61, 64; proslavery sentiment in, 3, 18, 20,
60, 61, 64, 80, 99, 102, 140, 146–47, 148,
151, 165; racial authenticity in, 11, 35–37,
38–40, 68–69, 73, 81–83, 90–91, 115–16,
117–19, 124, 141, 144, 145, 160; racial
counterfeit in, 36–37, 38–40, 73, 81, 82,
83, 90–91, 92, 93, 104, 116–19, 120, 123,
142, 144–46, 152–53, 158, 172nn24–25,
175n29; racial performance in, 25, 35–40,
104, 141, 146, 152, 157; racism in, 3, 4–5,
11, 16–18, 20, 23, 35, 37, 41, 43–44, 60,
61, 64–65, 69, 70, 74, 80, 91, 95–99,
131, 140–41, 144, 146–47, 148, 153, 163,
165; recent appropriations of in popular
culture, 167, 185nn1–2; relationship to
abolitionism (see abolitionist movement:
relationship to blackface minstrelsy);
representations of African American
people and culture in, 1, 3, 6, 7, 10, 17–18,
31–32, 33–34, 35–41, 60, 61, 62, 64–65,
67, 68–70, 72–73, 74, 75–76, 80–82, 85,
101, 102, 103, 104, 113, 115–20, 122, 123,
124, 126, 131, 141, 144, 146, 158, 160–65,
166–67; respectability of, 63–64; ridicule
of bourgeoisie in, 5, 7, 8, 60, 101–2, 126,
131–32, 138, 181n25; sentimentality in,
13–15, 18, 20, 62, 64, 69, 85, 151, 185n14;
sexual content of, 31–32, 33–34, 76,
102; slave revolts represented in, 17–18;
structure of, 35, 37, 68; stump speeches
in, 35, 105, 108–9, 147, 161; trickster
figures in, 7, 18, 19, 60, 142, 162; "wage
slavery" mentioned in, 7, 101–2, 130;
working-class associations in, 4, 7, 13,
43, 63–64, 100, 101–2, 119, 125–26, 130,
131; working-class audience of, 7, 8, 21,
25–26, 60, 61, 63, 102, 126, 130, 131–32;
Unionist sentiment in, 109, 110, 179n12;
Zip Coon in, 16–17, 35, 83, 95, 96, 100,

blackface minstrelsy (*continued*)
114, 124, 147, 153. *See also* blackface;
minstrel songs
Bowery Theatre (New York City), 1, 19, 131
Bratton, J. S., 6, 66, 75
British and Foreign Anti-Slavery Society, 4, 42
British Broadcasting Corporation, 73
Brontë, Charlotte: *Jane Eyre*, 176n5
Brown, Henry "Box," 135; literary use of
minstrel songs by, 147–48, 149–50, 151;
mentioned 25, 55, 170n12
Brown, John (ex-slave): *Slave Life in Georgia*,
55, 174n14
Brown, T. Allston, 20, 170n9
Brown, William Wells, 47; attitude toward
Thomas Carlyle, 177n12; in United
Kingdom, 54; literary use of blackface
elements by, 147, 151–52; literary use
of minstrel songs by, 147–48, 151; men-
tioned, 19, 25, 136, 137, 140, 150, 182n43
—works: *American Fugitive, The*, 54; *Anti-
Slavery Harp, The*, 148; *Black Man, The*,
30; *Clotel*, 20, 147, 148–49, 151–52;
Escape; or, A Leap for Freedom, The, 147,
148; "Fugitive Slaves in England," 53–54;
*Narrative of William Wells Brown, a Fugi-
tive Slave*, 45–46
Browne, Lucy, 56–57
Bryant, Dan, 78
Bryant's Minstrels, 109

California Gold Rush, 15, 104, 106
Callender, Charles, 37
Campbell, Matt, 78
Carlyle, Thomas, 99, 177n12; "Occasional
Discourse on the Nigger Question," 5, 79,
80–81, 96–97, 98
Canada: as refuge for African American
slaves, 45, 47, 49
Cassell, John, 42, 69
Chapman, Maria Weston, 16, 56, 170nn5–6,
181n32

Chartist movement, 128, 181n31
Chatham Street Chapel (New York City),
19, 21
Child, Lydia Maria: "Black Saxons," 158–60;
"Mary French and Susan Easton,"
157–58; mentioned, 140
Christy, E. P., 119, 123
Christy, George, 78
Christy's Minstrels, 15, 106, 109, 162, 164
civil rights movement, 168
Civil War (U.S.). *See* U.S. Civil War
Clarke, Lewis, 24
Clarkson, Thomas, 53, 56; *Thoughts on the
Necessity of Improving the Condition of the
Slaves in the British Colonies*, 174n17
Clown (character in pantomime), 123
clowns, 76, 77
Coleman, George: *Inkle and Yarico*, 71, 175n27
Collins, John, 23–24, 59, 128–29, 169n5, 181n
commedia dell'arte, 71, 76, 123
Confederate States of America, 46, 53, 81, 98,
109, 111
Congo Minstrels, 119
Connick, Harry, Jr., 185n1
Conway, Howard J., 23
*Cowardy, Cowardy, Custard; or Harlequin Jim
Crow and the Magic Mustard Pot*, 175n26
Cowper, William: and support for British
colonialism, 58–59; "Task, The" 45, 58
Craft, Ellen, 55
Crafts, Hannah: *The Bondwoman's Narrative*,
155–56
Crèvecoeur, J. Hector St. John de: *Letters from
an American Farmer*, 133
Crockett Almanacks, 114, 125
Crouch, Stanley, 185n2
Cruikshank, George, 69, 175n25

Danson, Ted, 185n1
Delany, Martin, 20; *Blake*, 150–51, 183n5;
literary use of minstrel songs by, 147–48,
150–51

Dickens, Charles, 85, 176n4; attitudes toward abolitionism, 85–89, 98, 98; attitudes toward industrial capitalism, 87; attitudes toward slavery, 85–86, 87–88, 92, 98; attitudes toward United States, 85–86; description of William Henry Lane ("Juba"), 90–91; mentioned, 79

—works: *American Notes*, 85, 86, 87, 90–92, 96, 98; *Bleak House*, 5, 80, 85, 86–90; *Hard Times*, 86; *Martin Chuzzlewit*, 85–86; *Posthumous Papers of the Pickwick Club, The*, 85, 86

Douglass, Anna Murray, 137

Douglass, Frederick, 19–20, 34–35, 47; attitudes toward blackface minstrelsy, 19–20, 38–39, 65, 147; British perceptions of, 47; in United Kingdom, 45, 54, 65; relationship with Gerrit Smith, 4, 11; relationship with William Lloyd Garrison, 4, 16, 137, 169n5; perception of British racial attitudes, 45, 54, 65, 173n5; perception of European racial attitudes, 54; personal appearance of, 31; white abolitionist perceptions of, 11, 16; with Julia and Eliza Griffiths, 32, 182n37; mentioned, 70, 101, 129, 138, 173n5

—newspapers and works: *Frederick Douglass's Paper*, 53; *Heroic Slave, The*, 45, 182n41; *Life and Times of Frederick Douglass*, 136; *My Bondage and My Freedom*, 11, 23–24, 136, 137, 173n5; *Narrative of Frederick Douglas, The*, 12, 29–30, 83, 135, 136–37, 176n5, 182n42; *North Star*, 4, 38

Dunmore's proclamation, 44

Ellison, Ralph, 102, 141

Emancipation Act of 1833, 1, 9, 42, 44, 47, 56, 59, 60, 67, 172n1, 174n12; and compensation of planters, 43, 57–58, 174n12

Emerson, Billy, 78

Emerson, Ralph Waldo, 103–4; attitude toward Mexican War, 178n6; attitude toward slavery, 49–50, 174n11; mentioned, 100, 101, 102, 105, 109, 111, 112, 113, 114, 115, 120, 132, 136, 138, 140

—works: address commemorating tenth anniversary of emancipation in British West Indies, 49–50; "American Scholar" address, 103, 109; "Poet, The" 103–4, 109; "Self-Reliance," 103, 137

Emmett, Dan, 78

Equiano, Olaudah: *Interesting Narrative of Olaudah Equiano*, 58, 182n39; and British colonialism, 58; mentioned, 19

Ethiopian Harmonists, 175n22

Ethiopian Serenaders, 10, 14, 19, 60, 61, 62, 63, 64, 70, 119, 175n22

Eyre, Edward John (Governor of Jamaica), 98

Female American Serenaders, 175n22

Fink, Mike, 113, 125–26

Fisk Jubilee Singers, 20, 46, 61, 170n10

Fitzhugh, George, 129

Forrest, Edwin, 131, 180n16

Forster, William Edward, 48

Foster, Stephen C., 10, 78, 106, 115, 148, 149–51, 183n5

Franklin, Benjamin, 136, 182n42

free labor: compared to slave labor, 57, 174n17

Free the Slaves, 168

Fugitive Slave Act, 174n11

Fugitive Slave Circular, 48, 173n8

Fuller, Sarah Margaret: "American Literature," 132–33; "Entertainments of the Past Winter," 117–18; mentioned, 101, 102, 111, 138, 140, 184n9

Garrison, William Lloyd, 12, 16, 135; and *The Liberator*, 1, 53; relationship with Frederick Douglass (*see* Douglass, Frederick: relationship with William Lloyd Garrison); mentioned, 4, 59, 70, 128, 130, 173n5

Gavitt's Original Ethiopian Serenaders, 38

Georgia Minstrel Troupe, 72–73

Gilroy, Paul, 6
Goldberg, Whoopi, 185n1
Greeley, Horace, 116
Griffiths, Eliza, 32, 182n37
Griffiths, Julia, 32, 182n37

Hague, Sam, 37, 72–73
Harlequin, 71, 76–77, 123, 124, 175n26
*Harlequin and George Barnwell; or, The London
    'Prentice,* 175n26
Haverly, J. H., 37
Haverly's Mastodon Minstrels, 175n21
Hawkins, Micah, 107
Hawthorne, Nathaniel, 112–13; *House of the
    Seven Gables,* 178n4; *Mosses from an Old
    Manse,* 112, 179n15
Henderson, William James, 122–23, 184n9
Hendrix, Jimi, 167
Henry, Patrick, 135, 182n41
Hey Hey It's Saturday, 185n1
Higginson, Thomas Wentworth, 184n9; *Army
    Life in a Black Regiment,* 160–61, 163–65;
    mentioned, 140, 141
"highbrow" culture, 138
Hildreth, Richard: *Archy Moore, The White
    Slave,* 173n10
hip hop, 167, 185n2
History of Mary Prince, a West Indian Slave:
    171n15, 182n39
Hone, Philip, 62
"Hottentot Venus." *See* Baartman, Saartjie
Howard, George, 10, 23

indentured servants (in West Indies), 57
industrial capitalism: and abolitionism, 8, 9,
    87–88, 127–29; critique of in blackface
    minstrelsy, 101–2
Irish people, 68, 184n6; attitudes toward
    abolitionism, 128, 181n25; involvement
    in blackface minstrelsy, 78, 181n25;
    relationship to African Americans, 128;
    theatrical depictions of, 77–78

Jacobs, Harriet (Linda Brent), 46, 135; *Inci-
    dents in the Life of a Slave Girl,* 30–31, 46;
    mentioned, 27, 137, 138, 173n6
Jews, 93, 176n7; in Thackeray's *Vanity Fair,*
    93, 176n7
Jonson, Ben: *Masque of Blacknesse,* 71

Kelley, Abby, 16
Kemble, Frances Anne, 176n1, 176n3, 184n9;
    *Journal of a Residence on a Georgian Plan-
    tation,* 80, 81–85, 96, 163; mentioned, 79,
    90, 91, 98, 163, 184n9
Kennard, James K., Jr., 100, 120–21, 123

Lane, William Henry ("Juba"), 39–40, 118;
    described in Dickens's *American Notes,*
    90–91
Lee, Spike, 185n2
Liberator, The. See Garrison, William Lloyd:
    and *The Liberator*
literary nationalism, 100, 111–15, 120, 132–35,
    137–38, 140, 180n18; and masculinity,
    113–14, 180n20
London Freedman's Aid Society, 46
Long, Edward: *History of Jamaica,* 97–98
"lowbrow" culture, 138

Macready, William Charles, 62, 131, 179n16
Manifest Destiny, 104, 108, 113; in minstrel
    songs, 104–7
Mansfield, 1st Earl of (William Murray) 44, 45
Martineau, Harriet, 176n4; *Dawn Island,*
    174n19; "Demerara," 174n17; *Martyr Age of
    the United States,* 59; *Society in America,* 33
Massachusetts Anti-Slavery Society, 23
Mathews, Charles, 60–61, 63, 71, 100, 123,
    169n3
Mattison, Hiram: *Louisa Picquet,* 26–27
May, Samuel J., Jr., 16, 170n7, 174n15
Meer, Sarah, 5, 185n13
Melville, Herman, 141–42, 179n16; attitudes
    toward slavery, 146; literary nationalism

of, 112–14, 140, 179n16; literary use of blackface minstrelsy elements by, 140, 141–46; mentioned, 100, 102, 103, 111, 116, 120, 132, 134, 138

—works: "Benito Cereno," 140, 141, 142–44, 152, 183n1; *The Confidence-Man*, 140, 141, 144–46; "Hawthorne and His Mosses," 112–14, 134, 179–80nn16–17

Mexican War, 104, 113; mentioned in minstrel songs, 106–7

Mill, John Stuart: "The Negro Question," 177n12

minstrel shows. *See* blackface minstrelsy

minstrel songs: "Abraham's Daughter" (*see* minstrel songs: "Raw Recruits, or Abraham's Daughter"); "Astonishing Nose," 31; "Aunt Harriet Becha Stowe," 130; "Backside Albany," 107; "Blue-Tail'd Fly," 4; "Brack Eyed Susianna," 106; "Canaan," 109; "Coal Black Rose," 31; "Colored Fancy Ball, The" 17; "Dan Tucker" (*see* minstrel songs: "Old Dan Tucker"); "Dandy Jim," 148; "Dandy Jim from Caroline," 17; "Dearest Lilla," 4, 14; "Den I was Gone," 106; "Folks That Put on Airs," 111; "Gombo Chaff," 126; "Hush-a-Bye-Baby," 15; "Jim Brown," 17, 31; "Jim Crow," 1, 118, 125–26, 178n8; "Jim Crow Polka," 106–7; "Jim Crow's Trip to France," 62; "Juney at the Gate," 14; "Kate of Carolina," 106; "Keemo Kimo," 175n23, 180n21; "Long Tail Blue," 17, 33; "Lubly Fan," 4, 31, 32; "Miss Lucy Neale," 14; "My Old Aunt Sally," 19; "Negro's Departure or Dinah Broom, The" 14; "Now Hold Your Horses, Will You!" 31; "Oh! I'se So Wicked," 10, 21; "Oh! Susanna," 106, 148, 151; "Old Dan Tucker," 148; "Old Folks at Home," 4, 10, 12, 21, 150–51, 183n5; "Old Uncle Ned" (*see* minstrel songs: "Uncle Ned"); "Our Union None Can Sever," 109; "Raw Recruits, or Abraham's Daughter," 109–10, 164, 179n11; "Revolutionary Echoes," 107–8; "She's Black, But That's No Matter," 33; "So Early in de Morning," 169n4; "That's What the Niggers Then Will Do," 179n12; "Uncle Gabriel the Negro General," 17–18, 119, 181n26; "Uncle Ned," 12, 148, 149–50; "Uncle Sam," 109; "Uncle Sam's Cooks," 109; "Zip Coon," 16–17

miscegenation, 32–33, 151–52. *See also* blackface minstrelsy: miscegenation represented in

missionary movement, 75, 87, 174n19

Morant Bay Rebellion of 1865 (Jamaica), 98, 177n11

Morrison, Toni, 102–3, 122; and theory of "American Africanism," 102, 141–42, 143

mummer's plays, 71, 74, 77, 123

Nathanson, Y. S., 118–19

National Theatre (New York City), 21

nationalism: American, 2, 7, 8, 9, 49, 100–101, 103–35, 137, 138, 166–67, 178n5; and American expansionism, 105–7; and American working class, 8, 101, 104, 130–31; and masculinity, 101, 103, 104, 107–8, 114, 130–31; British, 2, 7, 8, 9, 42–43, 47, 48, 50–51, 59, 166–67, 173n7; in American abolitionism, 8, 9, 49, 50–53; in blackface minstrelsy (*see* blackface minstrelsy: American nationalism in); in British abolitionism, 8, 42–44, 47–48, 50–52, 59, 60, 62, 67, 173n7, 173n8. *See also* literary nationalism.

Nevin, Robert P., 124, 183n3

New Orleans Ethiopian Serenaders, 175n22

Nightingale Serenaders, 106

O'Connell, Daniel, 85–86

"one drop" rule, 90

O'Reilly, John Boyle, 172n24

pantomime, 71, 73, 76, 77, 123, 175n26

Parker, Theodore: "Mercantile Classes" 111–12; "Position and Duties of the American Scholar" 112, 133–34; mentioned, 9, 101, 102, 114, 137, 138

Peabody, Ephraim: "Narratives of the Fugitive Slaves," 134; mentioned, 9, 133, 134, 137

Peel, Matt, 78

Phillips, Caryl, 185n2

Phillips, Wendell, 130

Pickering, Michael, 76–77

Porter, Maggie, 46–47

Powell, Timothy B., 178n2

Powers, Hiram: "The Greek Slave" (sculpture), 31

Presley, Elvis, 167

Pringle, Thomas, 172n3

proslavery literature, 37

Prosser, Gabriel, 17

Punch, or the London Charivari, 48–49, 180n21; attitudes toward abolitionism, 174n17, 176n4; attitudes toward America, 48–49, 69; attitudes toward black people, 69; attitudes toward blackface minstrelsy, 63, 175nn22–23; attitudes toward slavery, 174n17

Quincy, Edmund, 16, 170n7

"racechange," 89, 90, 155, 176n6

racial classification, 151–52, 153, 154, 155, 156, 157–58, 159–61

racism: in abolitionist movement (*see* abolitionist movement: racism in); in blackface minstrelsy (*see* blackface minstrelsy: racism in); in Europe, 54; in France, 65; in United Kingdom, 2, 5, 9, 42–44, 54–56, 60, 61, 64–66, 69, 70–71, 74–77, 78–79, 81, 98–99, 174n15, 177n11; in United States, 12, 41, 44, 55, 99, 122, 126–27, 129, 136, 173n5. *See also* aboli-

tionist literature: racism in; romantic racialism; scientific racism

rap music. *See* hip hop

Rede, William Leman: *Flight to America,* 62, 176n2

Rehin, George, 7, 74–75, 76

Remond, Charles Lenox, 16, 129

Remond, Sarah Parker, 65, 147

Revolutionary War. *See* American Revolutionary War

Reynolds, Harry, 63, 123–24

Rice, Thomas Dartmouth, 117, 118, 123–24; as Jim Crow, 1, 2, 19, 21, 60, 61–62, 63, 64, 71, 91, 103, 115, 124, 175n26, 176n2, 183n3; as Uncle Tom, 1, 2, 19, 21–22; English ancestry of, 78; in England, 1, 41, 43–44, 60, 61–62, 63, 64, 70, 71, 73, 75, 81, 103, 115, 166, 175n20, 175n23, 175n26; in *Flight to America,* 62, 176n2; *Life of Jim Crow,* 19; mentioned, 120, 145, 169n3

Rochester Ladies' Anti-Slavery Society, 19

rock and roll, 167

Rogers, Nathaniel P., 59, 174n12

Rolling Stones, The, 167

romantic racialism, 10, 11, 70, 85, 121, 169n1, 174n19; in abolitionist movement, 10–11, 83, 85, 98, 99; in "Benito Cereno," 142–43, 144; in blackface minstrelsy, 83, 85; in *Uncle Tom's Cabin,* 11–12

Roper, Moses, 27, 30, 45, 152

Sable Harmonists, 72

Sanford, Sam, 36

Sanford's Minstrels, 170n9

scientific racism, 37, 54, 64–65

self-reliance, 102; and Benjamin Franklin, 136; and Frederick Douglass, 136–37

Shakespeare, William, 112–13, 116; *Macbeth,* 180n16

Sharp, Granville, 53, 56

Sharpley's Minstrels, 106

Sierra Leone colony, 56

slave narratives, 19, 35, 139, 182n39; and the American Renaissance (*see* American Renaissance: and slave narratives); as American national literature, 9, 19, 102, 132–33, 137, 138; authentication of, 35, 135; blackface tropes used in (*see* abolitionist literature: use of blackface tropes in); depictions of sexual abuse in, 27–31; depictions of United Kingdom in, 45–46

slave trade: in Africa, 89; in United Kingdom, 42, 44, 49, 57, 58, 94; in United States, 42. *See also* abolition of slave trade

slavery, 2, 3, 4, 8, 9, 23, 28, 32–33, 58, 61, 81, 93–94, 97, 101, 152, 158, 168; in Britain, 44, 59; in British East Indian colonies, 172n1; in British West Indian colonies, 1, 42, 44, 48, 57, 59, 61; in United States, 42–43, 45–49, 51–52, 53, 59, 66, 105, 128–29, 135; represented in blackface minstrelsy (*see* blackface minstrelsy: antislavery sentiment in; blackface minstrelsy: proslavery sentiment in). *See also* abolition of slavery; abolitionist literature; abolitionist movement; antislavery meetings; slave narratives

Smith, Gerrit, 4, 11

Somerset case, 44, 45, 172n2; Lord Mansfield's ruling in, 44; misinterpretation of Lord Mansfield's ruling in, 44, 45, 172n3

Southworth, E. D. E. N.: *The Hidden Hand*, 178n4

Stedman, John: *Curious Adventures of Captain Stedman*, 171n15; *Narrative of a Five Years' Expedition Against the Revolted Negroes of Surinam*, 171n15

Stowe, Harriet Beecher: attitudes toward theater, 161, 184n10; *Dred*, 162; *Key to "Uncle Tom's Cabin,"* 35; racial attitudes of, 11–12, 141, 163; mentioned, 101, 138, 140, 175n23, 179n15. See also *Uncle Tom's Cabin*

Surrey Theatre (London), 60, 62; and Thomas Rice, 60, 175n20; and working-class audiences, 60

Sweeney, Joel Walker, 78

Tappan, Lewis, 130

temperance: relationship to abolitionism, 128; relationship to American working class, 128

Thackeray, William Makepeace: anti-Semitism of, 93, 176–n7; attitudes toward abolitionism, 92–95, 96, 98; attitudes toward blackface minstrelsy, 92–93; racial attitudes of, 92–96; mentioned, 79, 99

—works: *Adventures of Philip, The*, 80, 94–95, 96, 98; *Vanity Fair*, 80, 93–94, 95, 98

Thirteenth Amendment to U.S. Constitution, 1, 20, 98

Thompson, George, 130, 170n7

transatlantic culture, 2, 7, 9, 72, 168

Trollope, Anthony: *West Indies and the Spanish Main, The*, 81, 97–98, 182n34; mentioned, 79, 97, 99

Trollope, Frances: *Domestic Manners of the Americans*, 48, 86

Turner, Nat, 17, 170n8

Uncle Tom's Alamanack or Abolitionist Memento, 42, 47

Uncle Tom's Cabin, 11–12, 13, 49, 67, 84, 85, 92, 138, 156–57, 160, 161–63, 165, 179n15, 180n18; blackface tropes in, 156–57, 161–63, 184n7, 185nn11–13; comparison of wage labor and chattel slavery in, 130; George Harris in, 156–57; illustrations in, 69, 175n25; racism in, 22–23, 163; relationship to blackface minstrelsy, 5, 20, 21–23, 69, 129–30, 161–63, 170n8, 185n14; sentimentality in, 23; stage productions of, 1, 10, 21–22, 69, 130, 162; Topsy in, 10, 21, 162–63, 185n13; Uncle

Uncle Tom's Cabin, (continued)

Tom in, 10, 21. *See also* romantic racial-ism: in *Uncle Tom's Cabin*

United Kingdom: abolitionist movement in (*see* abolitionist movement: in United Kingdom); African Americans in (*see* African Americans: in United Kingdom); and U.S. Civil War, 9, 46, 51, 98; and Confederate States of America, 46, 53, 81, 98, 109, 111; as refuge for African Americans, 44–47, 53–54, 173n5; black population of, 5, 41, 59, 67, 73, 74, 75, 80, 91, 174n13; blackface minstrelsy in (*see* blackface minstrelsy: in United Kingdom); blackface performance before 1836 in, 60–61, 63, 81 (*see also* blackface: early traditions in England); colonial possessions of, 43, 57, 58–59, 66, 76; crit-icism of American slavery in, 8, 9, 42, 44, 46, 47–49, 50–53, 65–66, 69, 173n7; dis-dain toward American culture in, 62, 67; economic changes in, 43, 57; nationalism in (*see* nationalism: in British abolition-ism); oppression of industrial workers in, 128–29; racism in (*see* racism: in United Kingdom); relationship to United States (*see* Anglo-American relations); relation-ship between abolitionism and blackface minstrelsy in (*see* abolitionist movement: relationship to blackface minstrelsy)

U.S. Civil War, 9, 44, 46, 51, 81, 98, 105, 109, 111, 160; mentioned in blackface minstrelsy (*see* blackface minstrelsy: and U.S. Civil War)

Vassa, Gustavas. *See* Equiano, Olaudah

Vereen, Ben, 185n1

Victoria (Queen), 46–47, 61, 175n21

Virginia Minstrels, 60, 63, 68, 166, 169n3, 175n23

Virginia Serenaders, 14, 36

"wage slavery," 181n33; in anti-abolitionist rhetoric, 7–8, 87–88, 128–30; in black-face minstrelsy, 101–2, 130; in critiques of industrial capitalism, 88, 129–30

War of 1812: mentioned in minstrel songs, 107, 109–10

Washington, Booker T.: *Up From Slavery,* 136, 182n42

Webb, Frank J.: *Garies and Their Friends,* 153–55, 157; mentioned, 140, 156

Webb, Richard D., 170n5, 170n7

Wedgwood, Josiah, 169n3

Wedgwood anti-slavery medallion, 12, 60, 169n3

Weld, Theodore: *American Slavery As It Is,* 35; mentioned, 82

"white slavery." *See* "wage slavery"

Whitely, Henry: *Three Months in Jamaica in 1832,* 171n15

Whitman, Walt: "Democratic Vistas," 178n5; *Leaves of Grass,* 178n5

Whittier, John Greenleaf: attitude toward slavery, 50–52, 53; attitude toward United Kingdom, 50–53; "Free Islands," 50–51, 52, 53; "To Englishmen," 51–53; mentioned, 59

Wilberforce, William, 53

Williams, Bert, 185n1

Wilson, Harriet E.: *Our Nig,* 151–52

working class: and blackface minstrelsy (*see* blackface minstrelsy: working-class associations in; blackface minstrelsy, working-class audience of); attitudes toward abolitionist movement, 7–8, 126–32, 181n30; attitudes toward slavery, 126, 129, 130, 131; in United Kingdom, 126, 166, 181n30; in United States, 7–8, 126–32, 166; relationship to nationalism (*see* nationalism: and American working class)